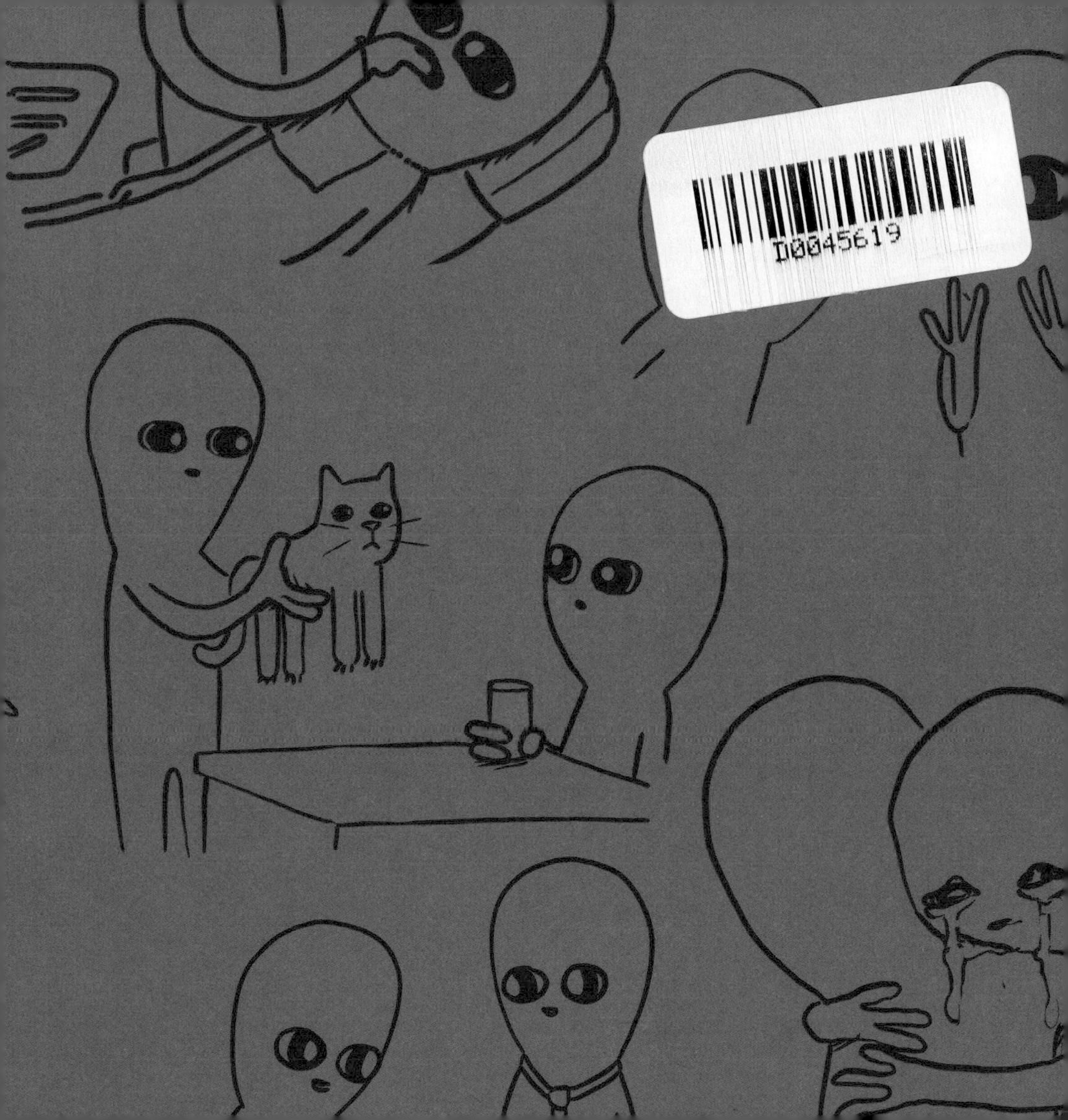

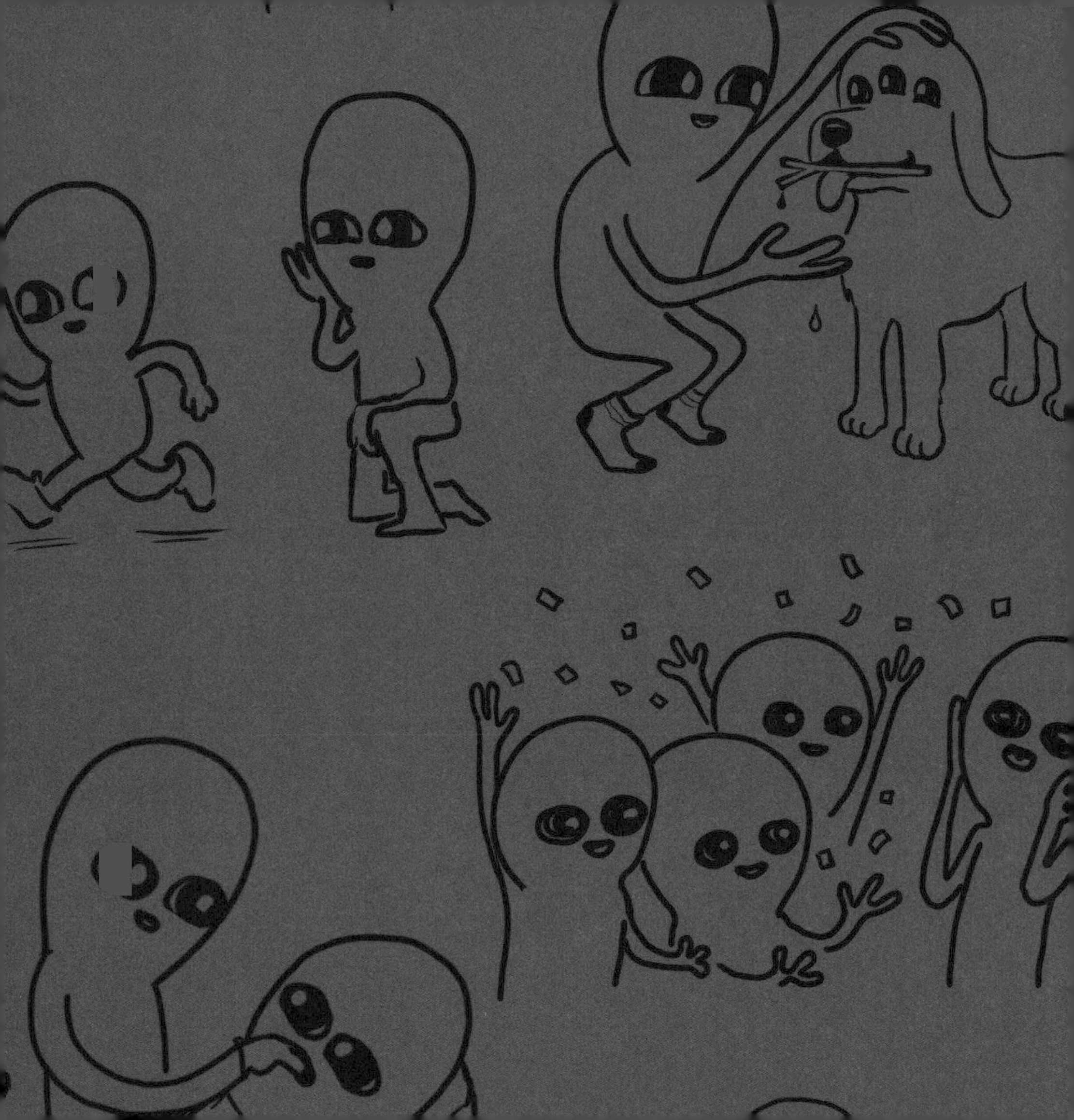

WELCOME TO STRANGE PLANET

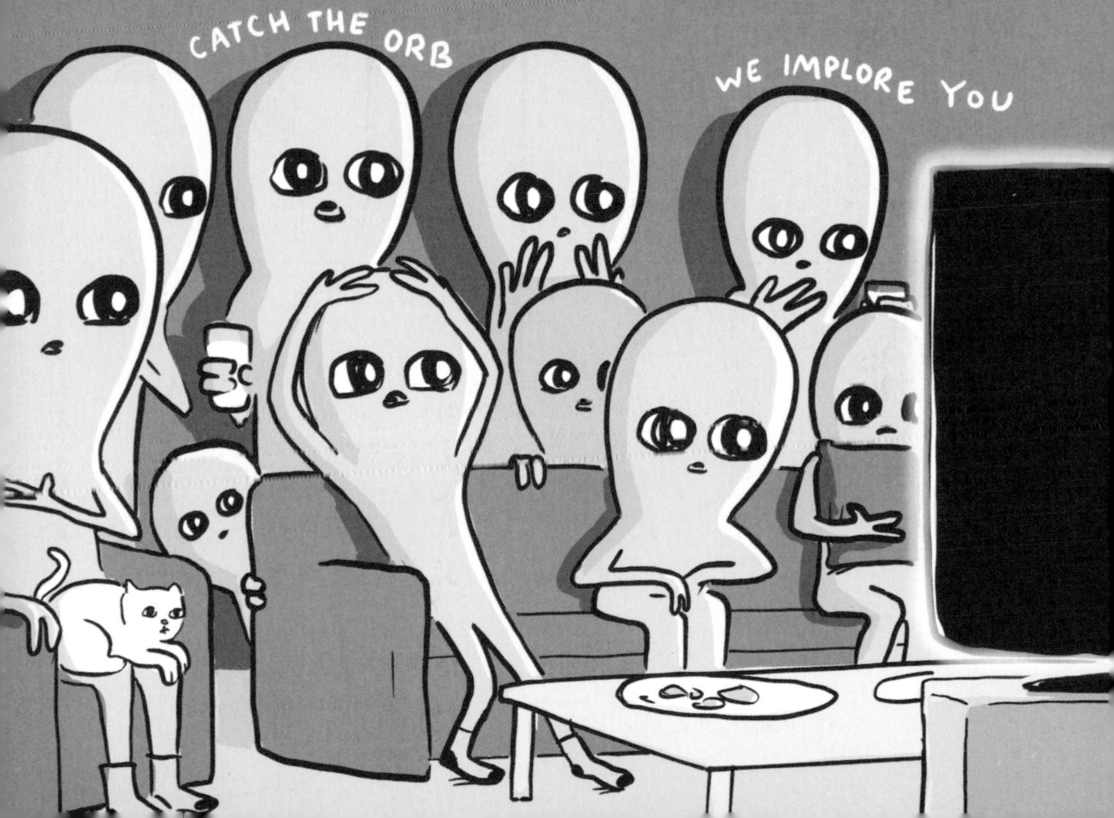
CATCH THE ORB
WE IMPLORE YOU

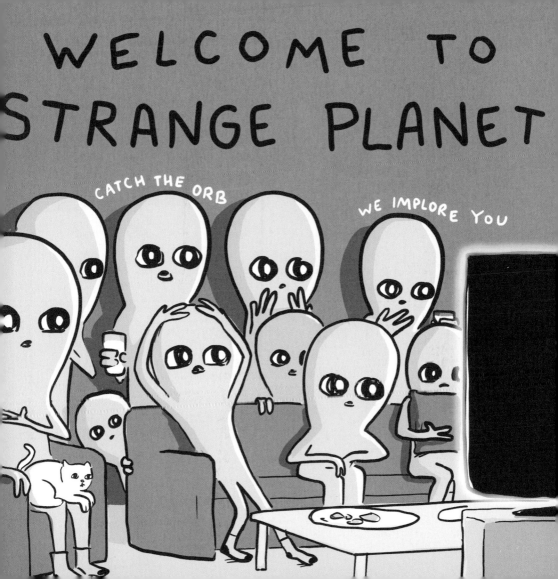

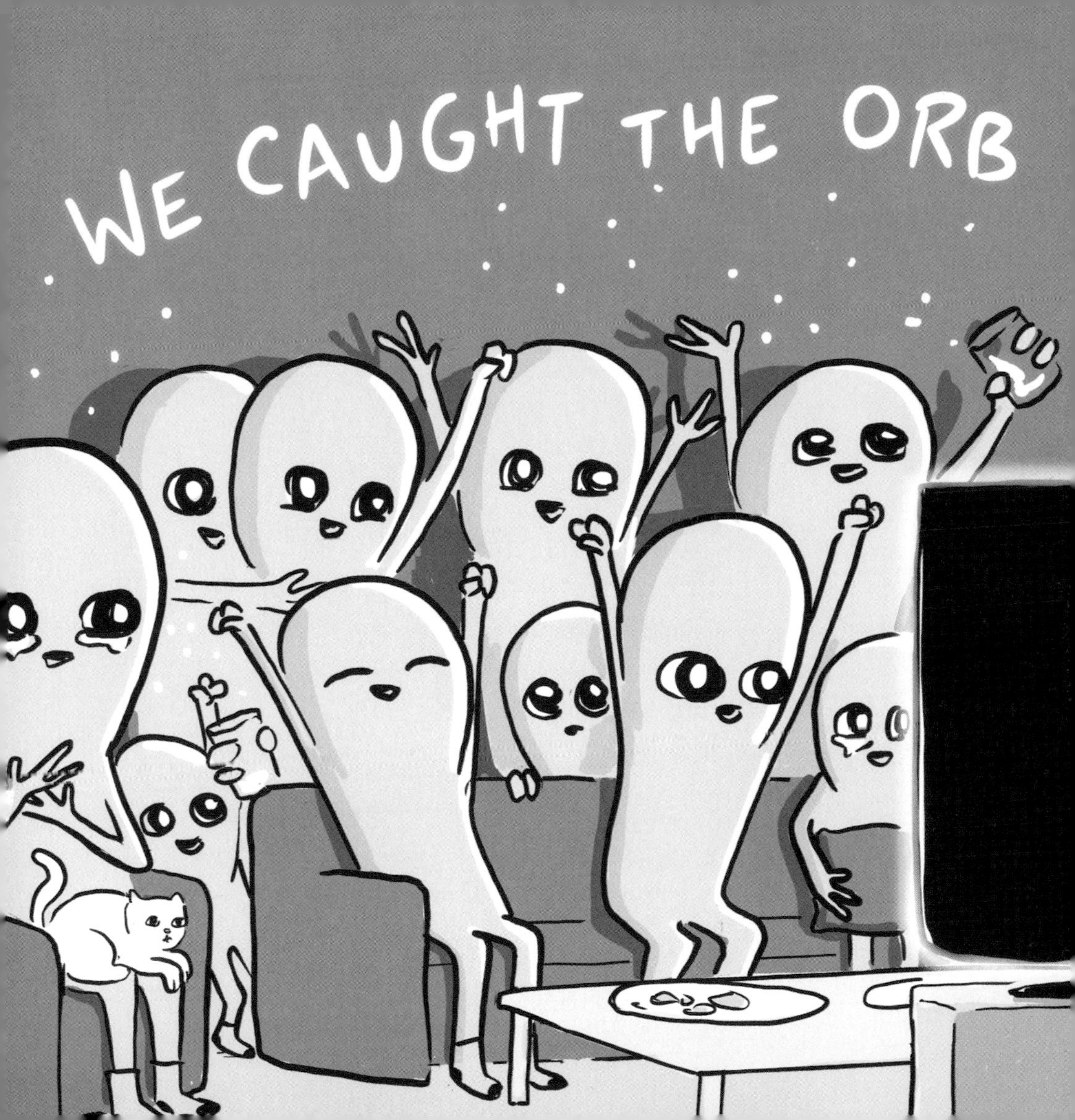
WE CAUGHT THE ORB

NATHAN W PYLE

STRANGE PLANET

MORROW
GIFT

FOR INFORMATION, ADDRESS HARPERCOLLINS PUBLISHERS, 195 BROADWAY, NEW YORK, NY 10007.

HARPERCOLLINS BOOKS MAY BE PURCHASED FOR EDUCATIONAL, BUSINESS, OR SALES PROMOTIONAL USE. FOR INFORMATION, PLEASE EMAIL THE SPECIAL MARKETS DEPARTMENT AT SPSALES@HARPERCOLLINS.COM.

FIRST EDITION

LIBRARY OF CONGRESS CATALOGING-IN-PUBLICATION DATA HAS BEEN APPLIED FOR.

ISBN 978-0-06-297070-1

19 20 21 22 23 LSC 10 9 8 7 6 5 4 3 2

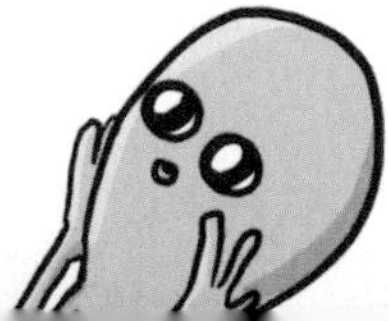

TO TAYLOR:

YOU REMOVE THE AIR
FROM MY LUNGS

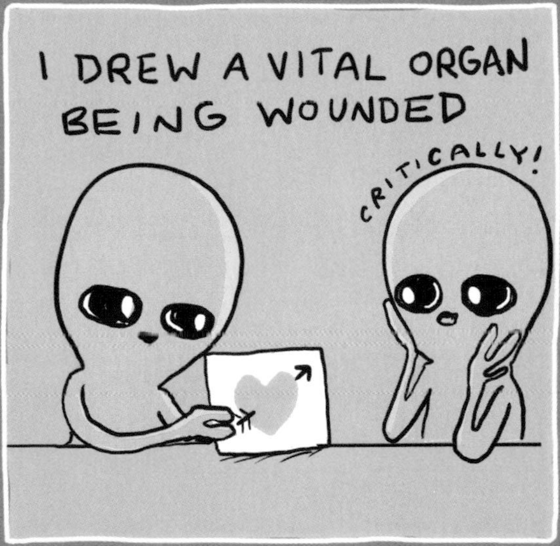
I DREW A VITAL ORGAN BEING WOUNDED
CRITICALLY!

IMAGINE PLEASANT NONSENSE

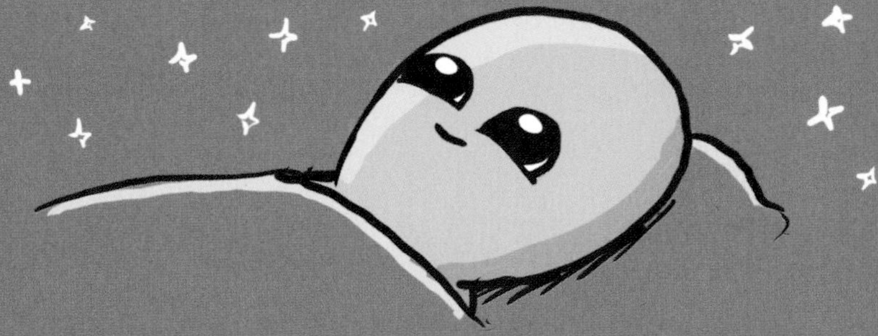

YOUNG BEINGS

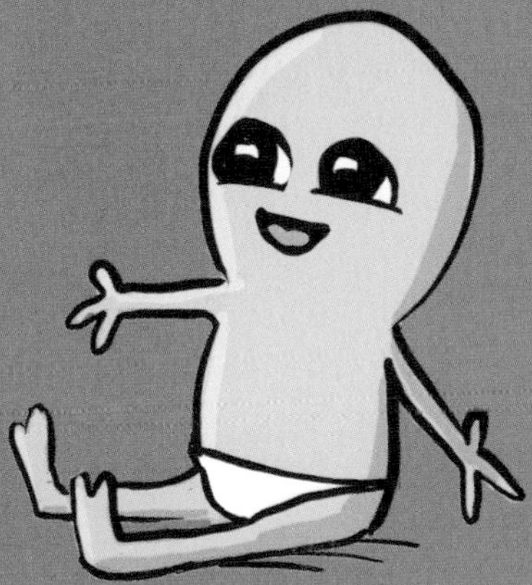

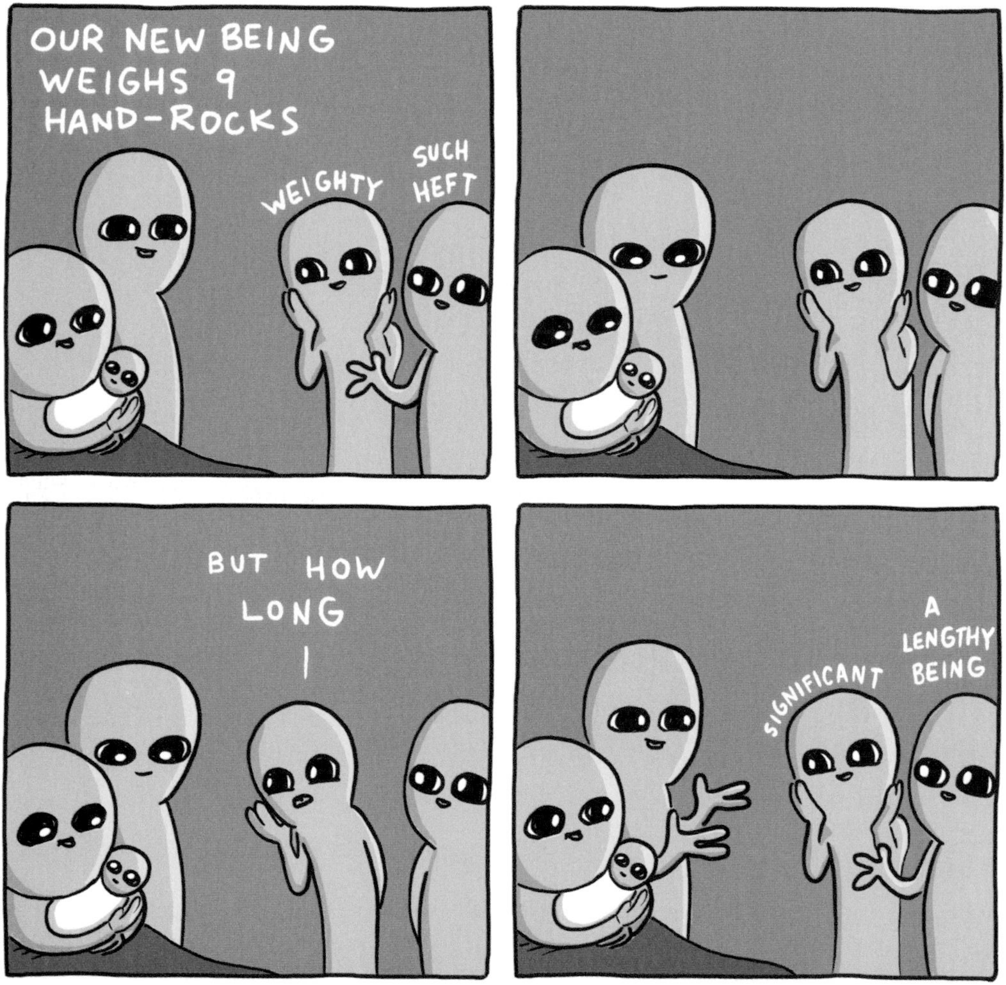
OUR NEW BEING WEIGHS 9 HAND-ROCKS
WEIGHTY
SUCH HEFT
BUT HOW LONG
SIGNIFICANT
A LENGTHY BEING

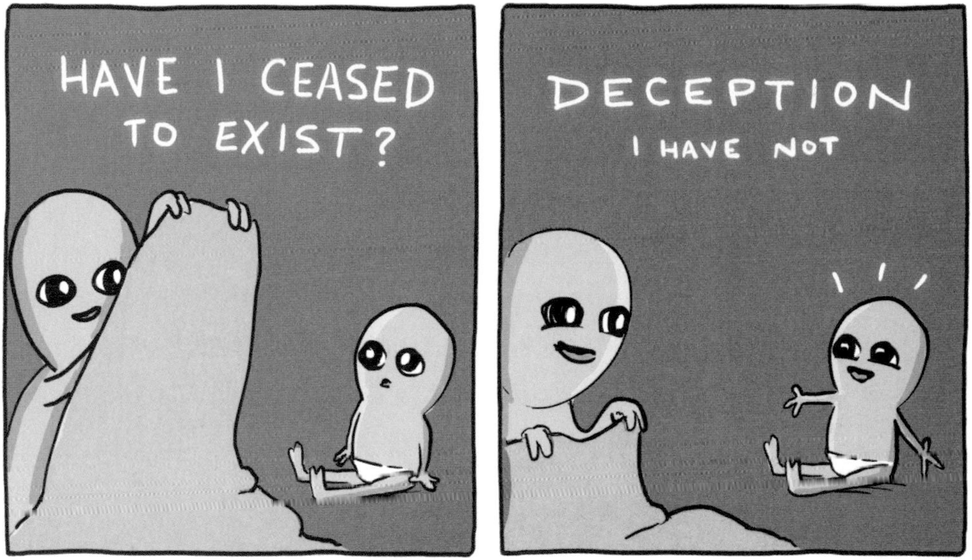
HAVE I CEASED TO EXIST?
DECEPTION
I HAVE NOT

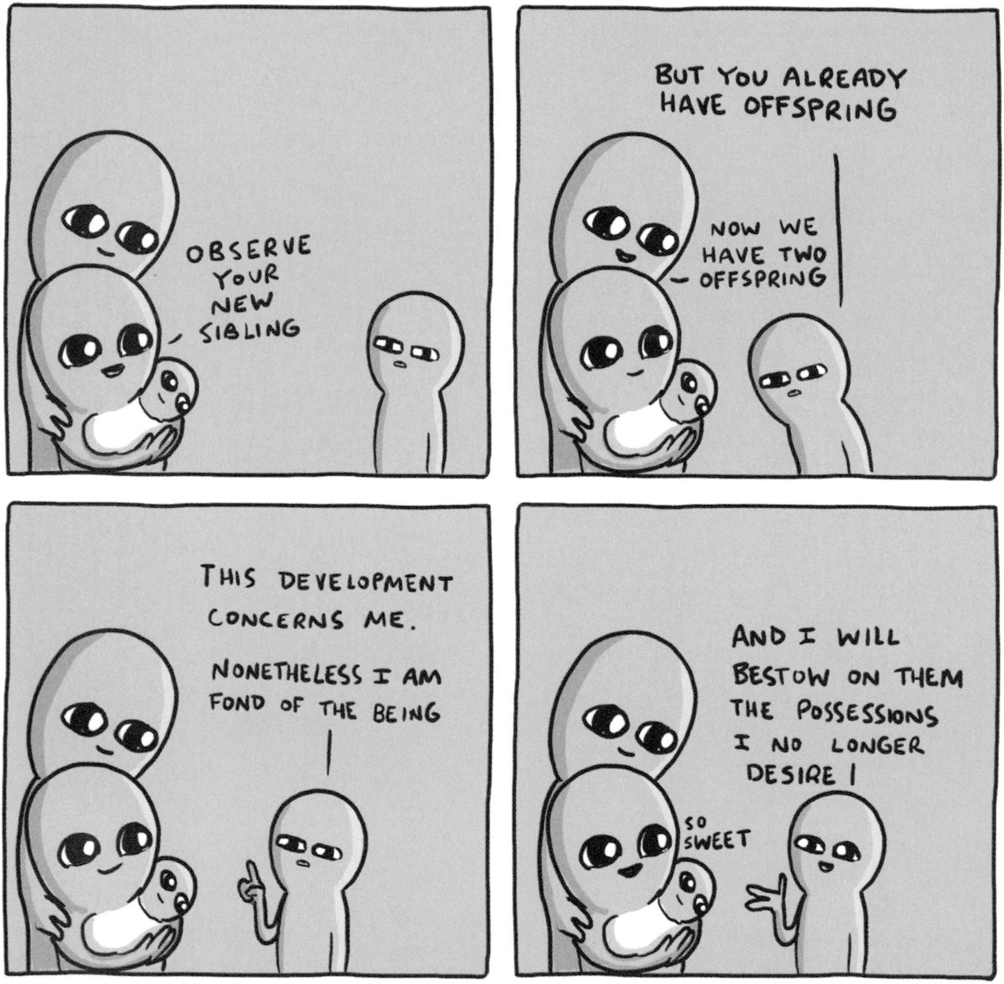
OBSERVE YOUR NEW SIBLING
BUT YOU ALREADY HAVE OFFSPRING
NOW WE HAVE TWO OFFSPRING
THIS DEVELOPMENT CONCERNS ME.
NONETHELESS I AM FOND OF THE BEING
AND I WILL BESTOW ON THEM THE POSSESSIONS I NO LONGER DESIRE!
SO SWEET

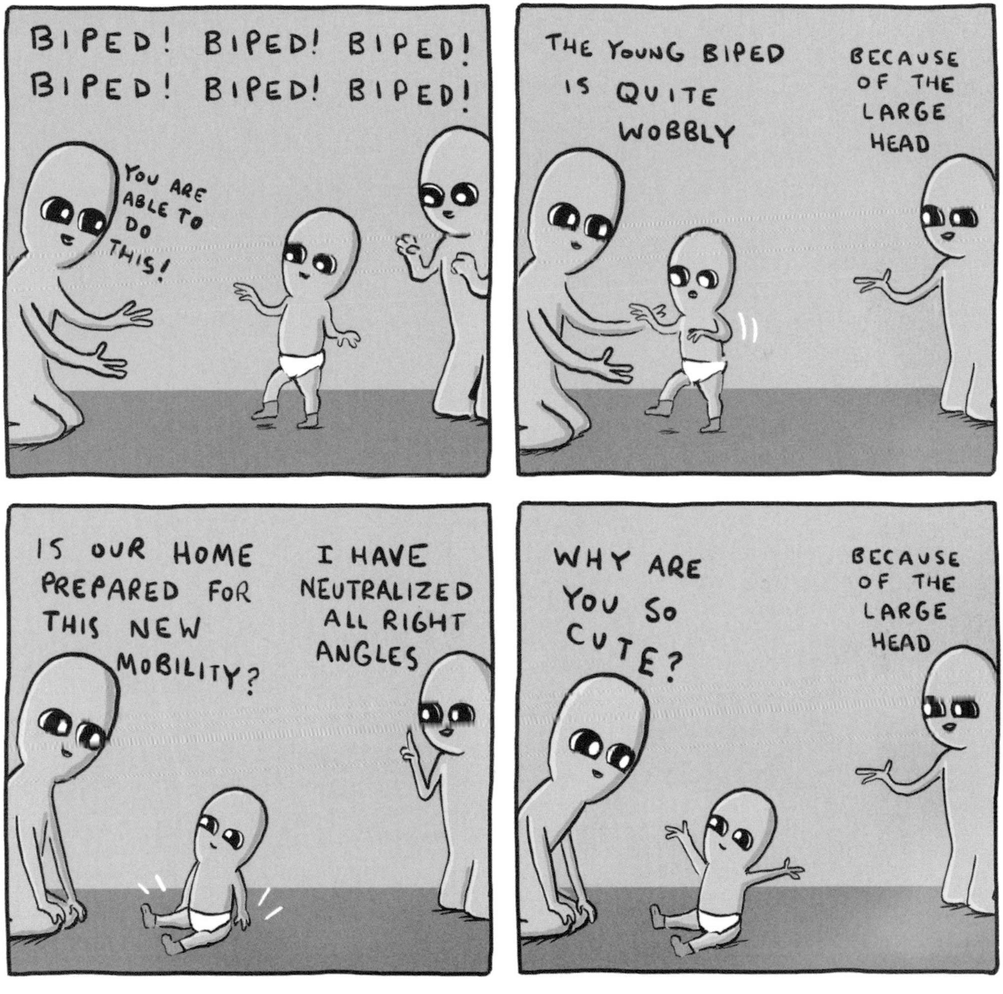
BIPED! BIPED! BIPED! BIPED! BIPED! BIPED!
YOU ARE ABLE TO DO THIS!
THE YOUNG BIPED IS QUITE WOBBLY
BECAUSE OF THE LARGE HEAD
IS OUR HOME PREPARED FOR THIS NEW MOBILITY?
I HAVE NEUTRALIZED ALL RIGHT ANGLES
WHY ARE YOU SO CUTE?
BECAUSE OF THE LARGE HEAD

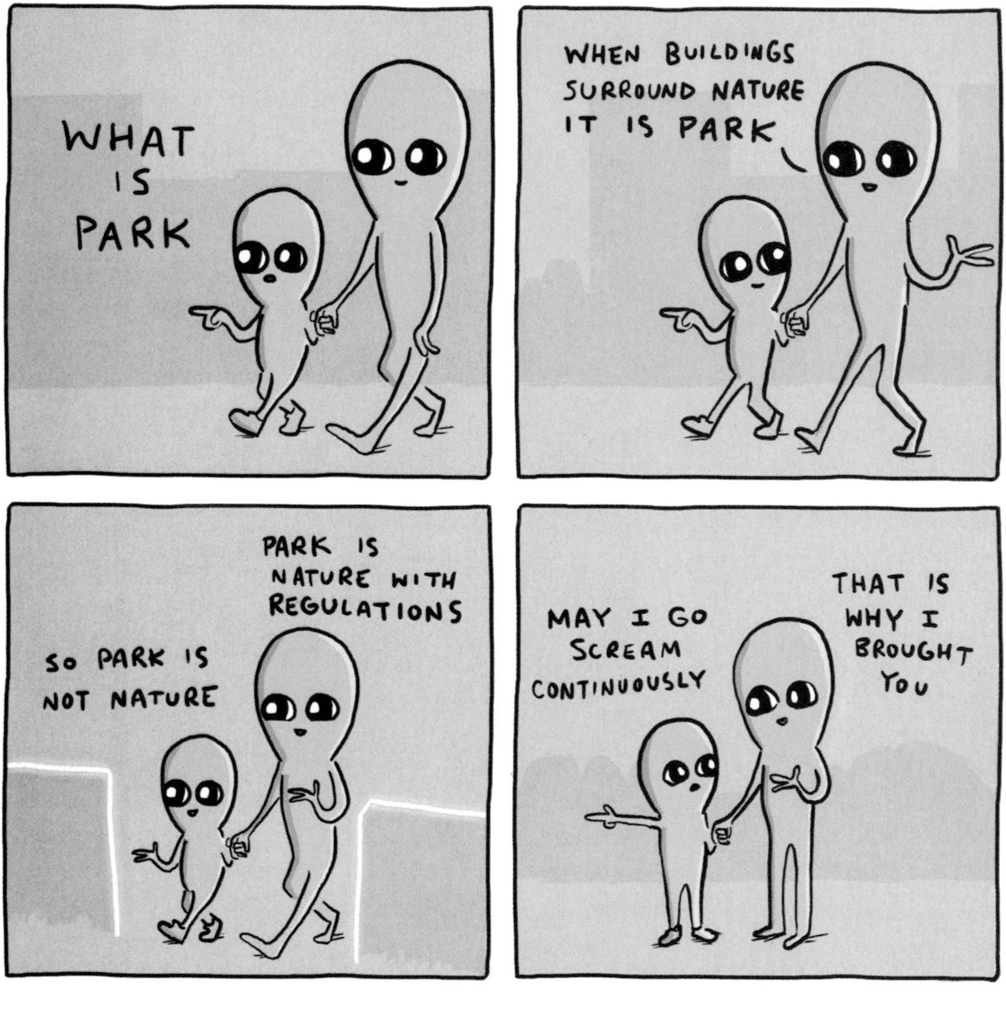
WHAT IS PARK
WHEN BUILDINGS SURROUND NATURE IT IS PARK
PARK IS NATURE WITH REGULATIONS
SO PARK IS NOT NATURE
MAY I GO SCREAM CONTINUOUSLY
THAT IS WHY I BROUGHT YOU

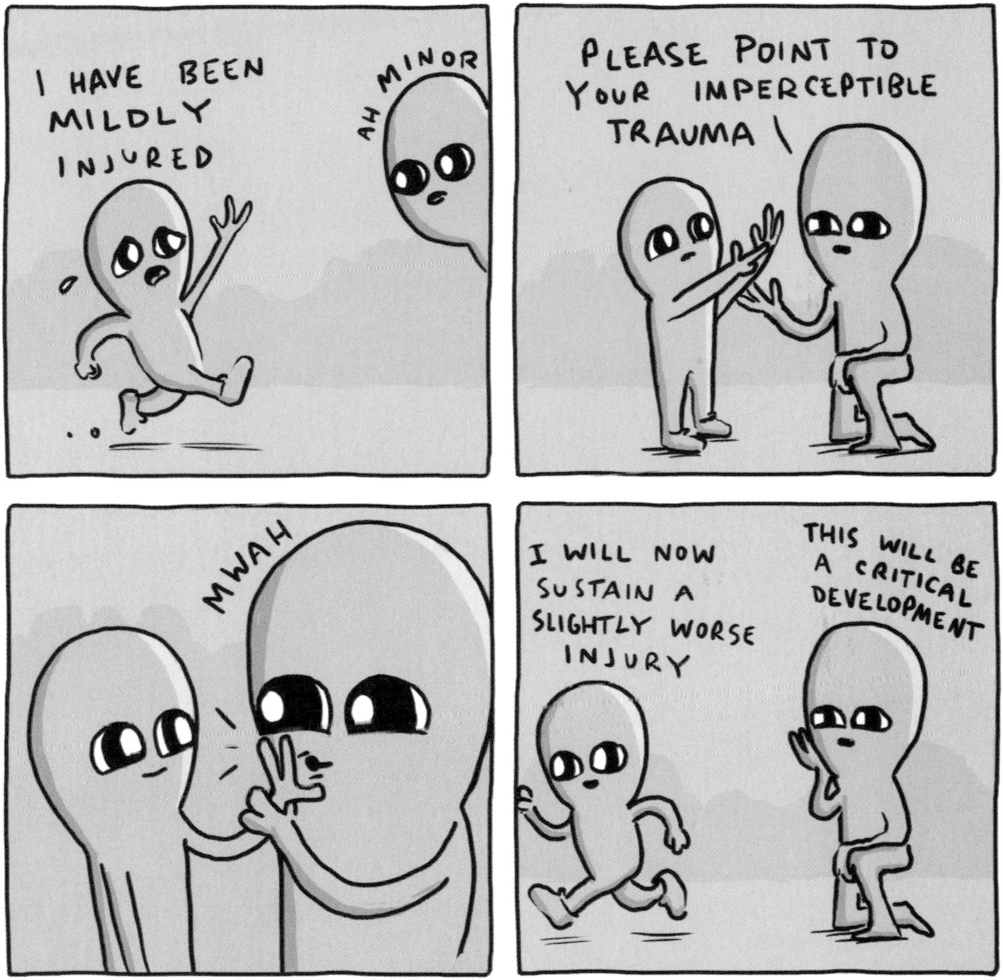
I HAVE BEEN MILDLY INJURED
AH MINOR
PLEASE POINT TO YOUR IMPERCEPTIBLE TRAUMA
MWAH
I WILL NOW SUSTAIN A SLIGHTLY WORSE INJURY
THIS WILL BE A CRITICAL DEVELOPMENT

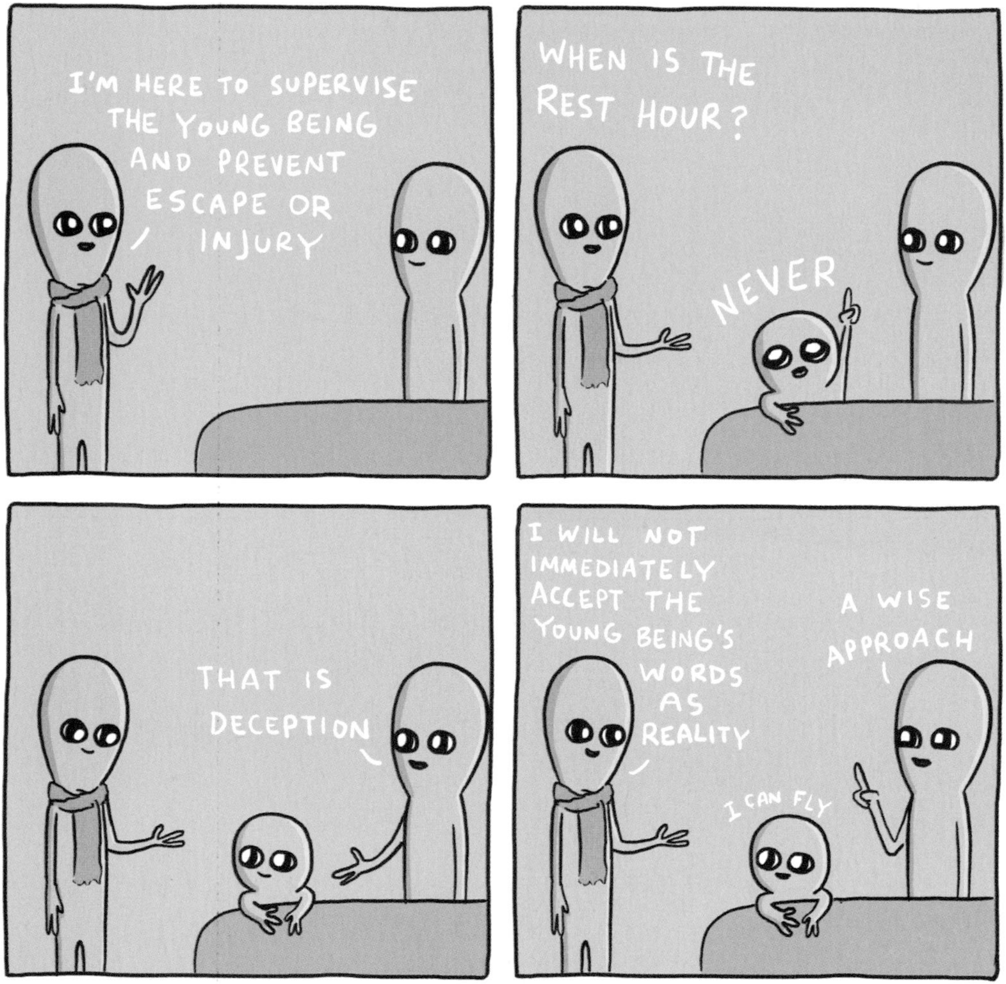
I'M HERE TO SUPERVISE THE YOUNG BEING AND PREVENT ESCAPE OR INJURY
WHEN IS THE REST HOUR?
NEVER
THAT IS DECEPTION
I WILL NOT IMMEDIATELY ACCEPT THE YOUNG BEING'S WORDS AS REALITY
A WISE APPROACH
I CAN FLY

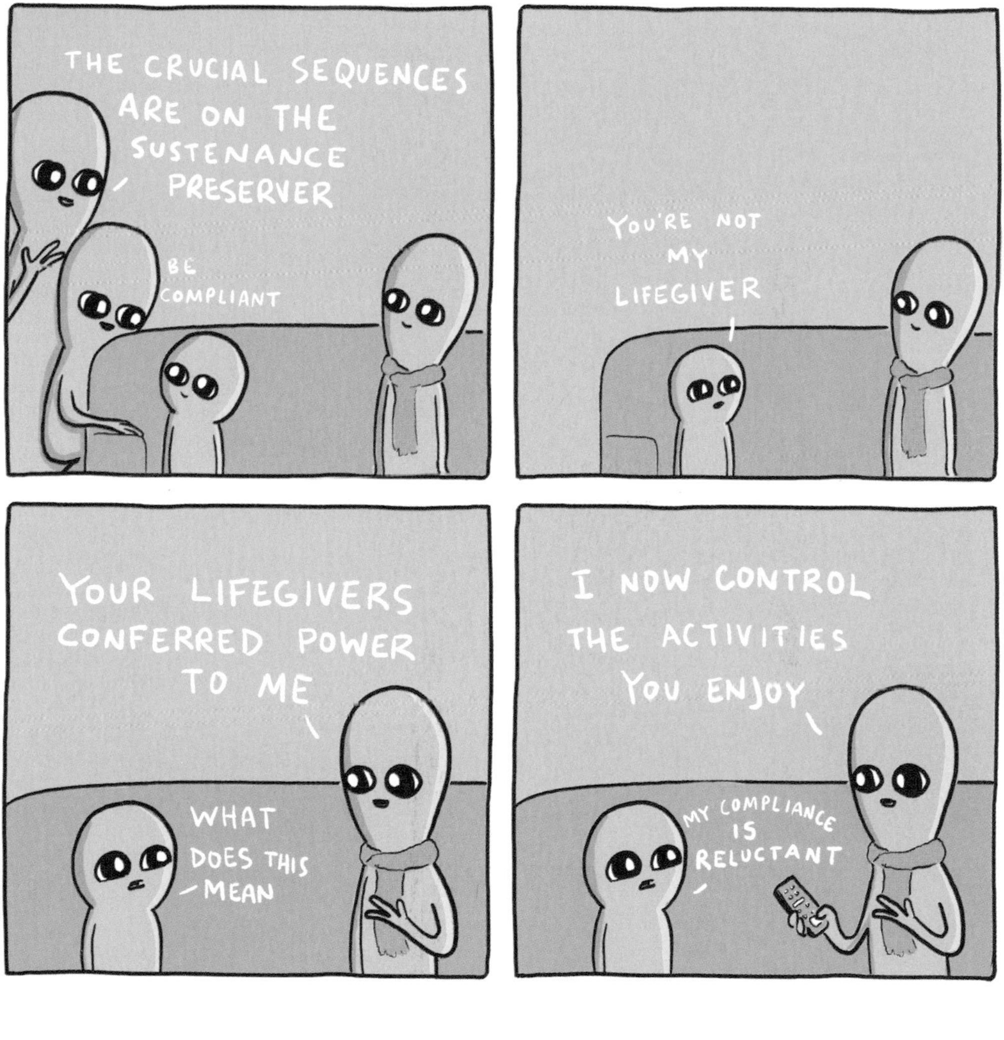
THE CRUCIAL SEQUENCES ARE ON THE SUSTENANCE PRESERVER
BE COMPLIANT
YOU'RE NOT MY LIFEGIVER
YOUR LIFEGIVERS CONFERRED POWER TO ME
WHAT DOES THIS MEAN
I NOW CONTROL THE ACTIVITIES YOU ENJOY
MY COMPLIANCE IS RELUCTANT

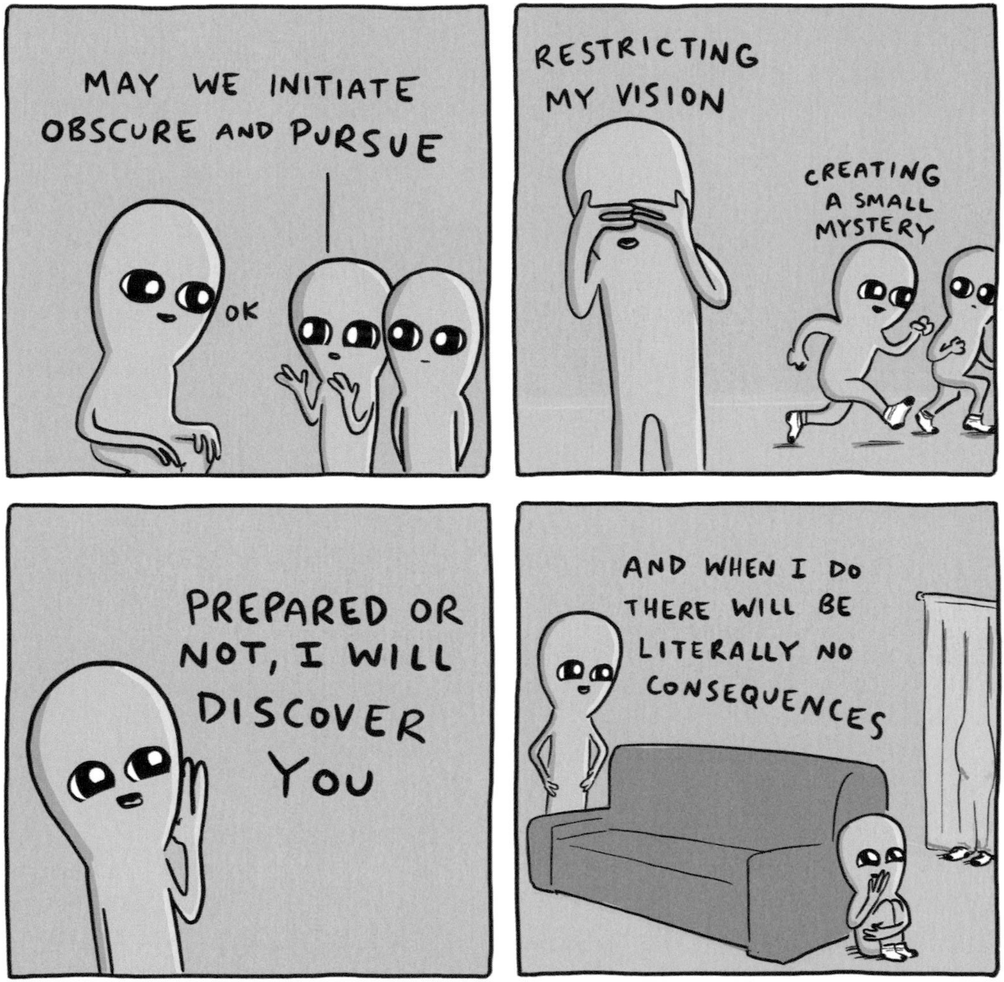

MAY WE INITIATE OBSCURE AND PURSUE
OK
RESTRICTING MY VISION
CREATING A SMALL MYSTERY
PREPARED OR NOT, I WILL DISCOVER YOU
AND WHEN I DO THERE WILL BE LITERALLY NO CONSEQUENCES

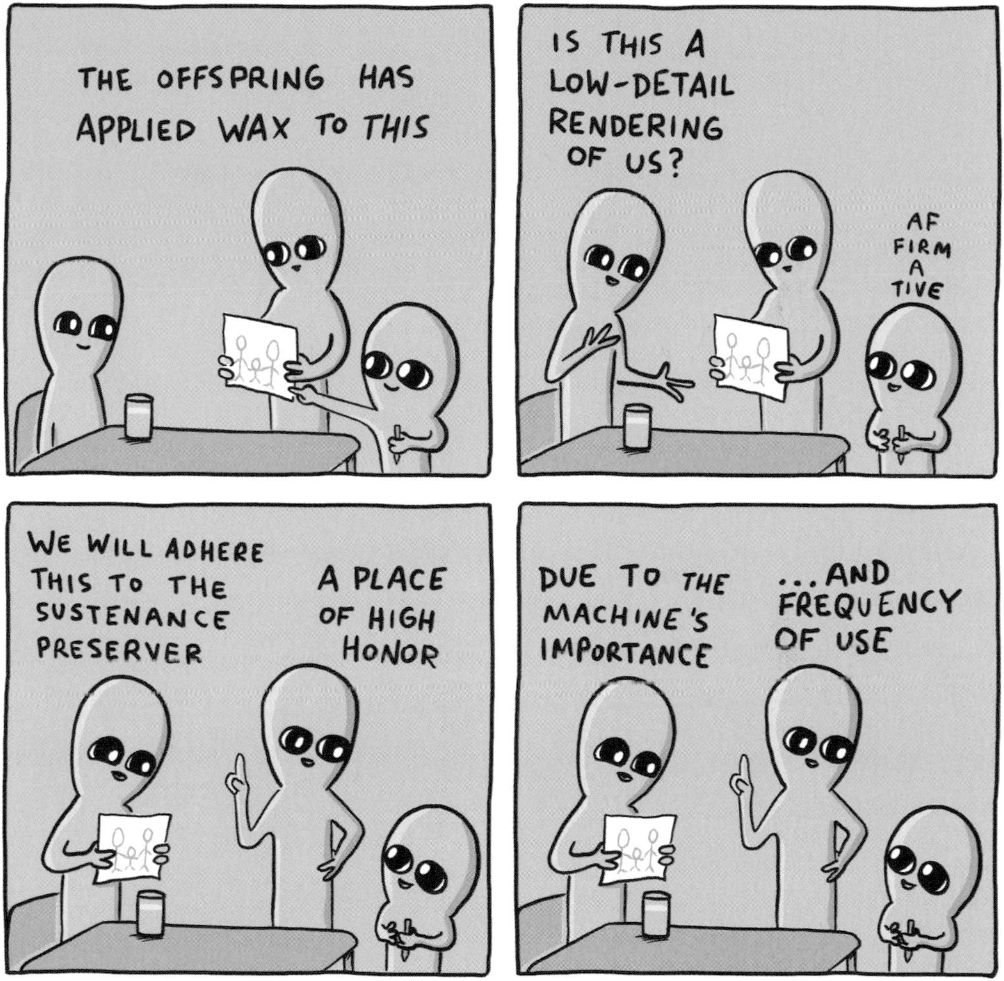
THE OFFSPRING HAS APPLIED WAX TO THIS
IS THIS A LOW-DETAIL RENDERING OF US?
AF FIRM A TIVE
WE WILL ADHERE THIS TO THE SUSTENANCE PRESERVER
A PLACE OF HIGH HONOR
DUE TO THE MACHINE'S IMPORTANCE
...AND FREQUENCY OF USE

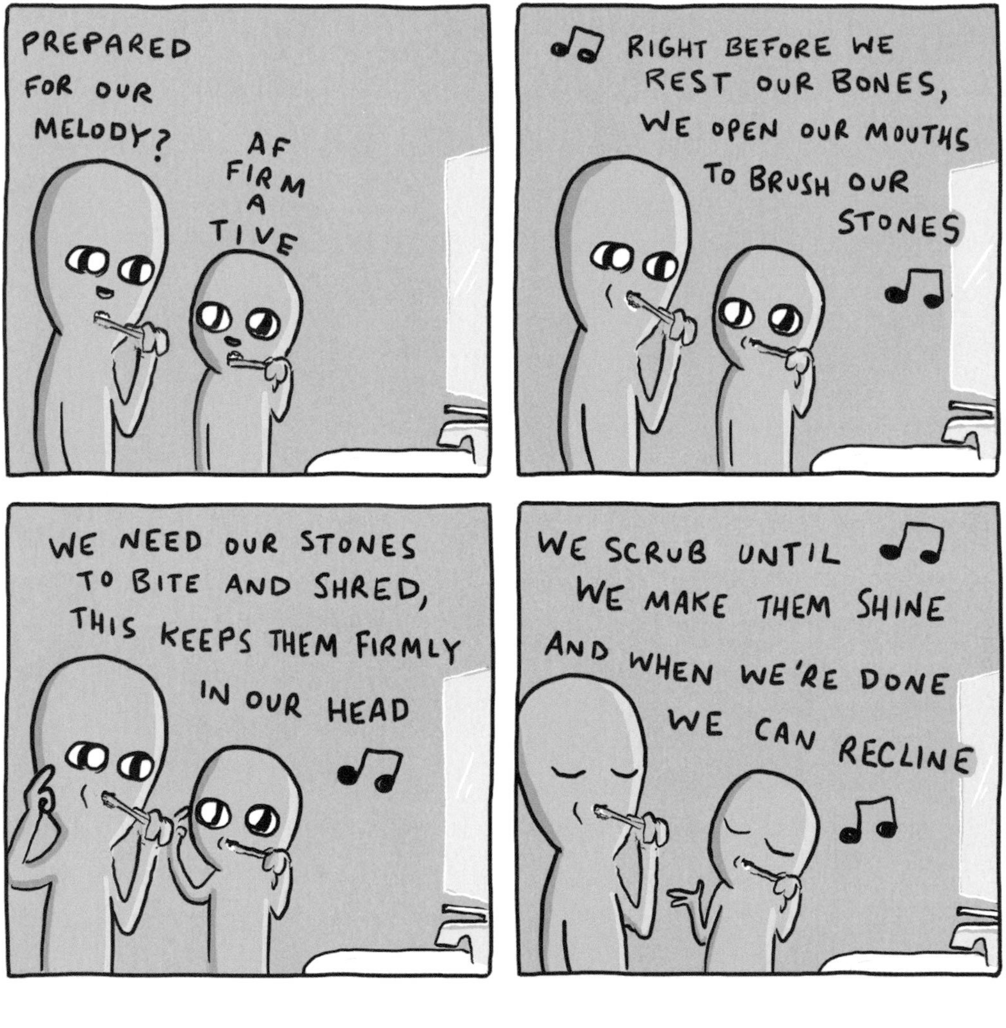
PREPARED FOR OUR MELODY?
AF FIRM A TIVE
RIGHT BEFORE WE REST OUR BONES, WE OPEN OUR MOUTHS TO BRUSH OUR STONES
WE NEED OUR STONES TO BITE AND SHRED, THIS KEEPS THEM FIRMLY IN OUR HEAD
WE SCRUB UNTIL WE MAKE THEM SHINE AND WHEN WE'RE DONE WE CAN RECLINE

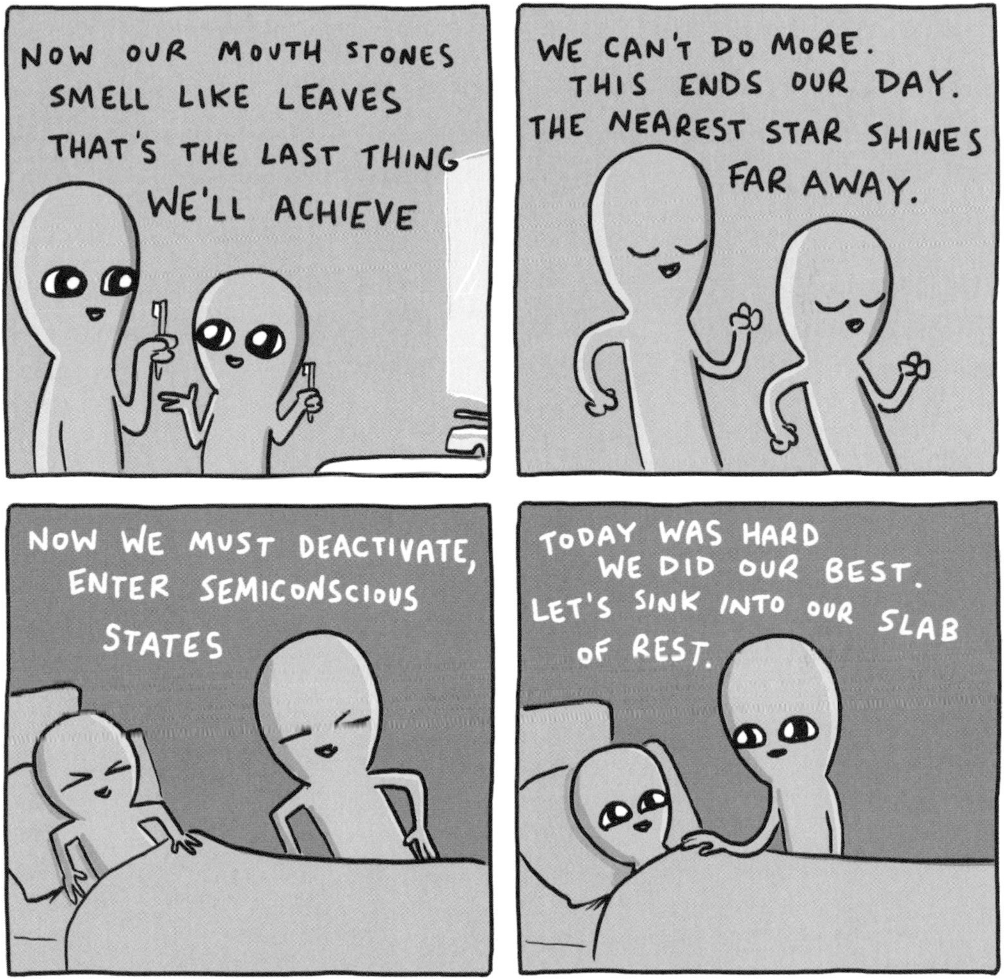
NOW OUR MOUTH STONES SMELL LIKE LEAVES
THAT'S THE LAST THING WE'LL ACHIEVE
WE CAN'T DO MORE. THIS ENDS OUR DAY.
THE NEAREST STAR SHINES FAR AWAY.
NOW WE MUST DEACTIVATE, ENTER SEMICONSCIOUS STATES
TODAY WAS HARD WE DID OUR BEST.
LET'S SINK INTO OUR SLAB OF REST.

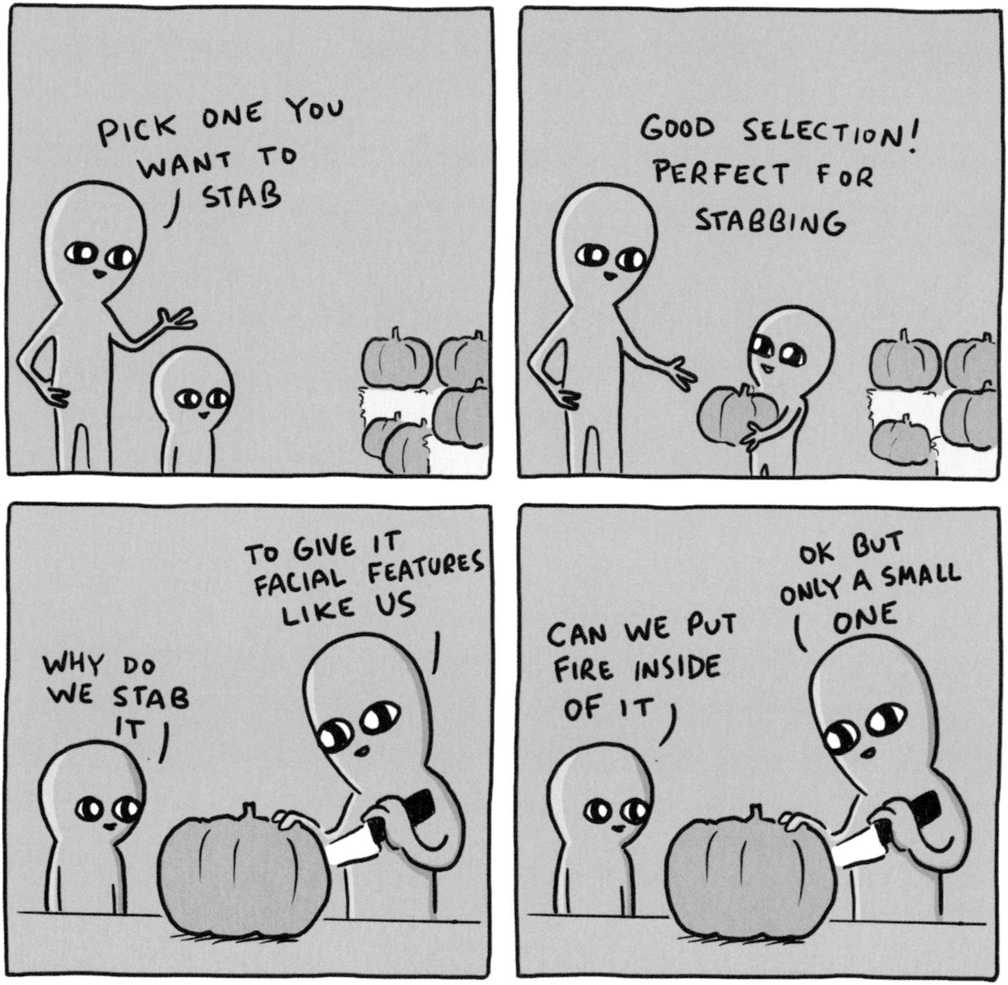
PICK ONE YOU WANT TO STAB
GOOD SELECTION! PERFECT FOR STABBING
WHY DO WE STAB IT
TO GIVE IT FACIAL FEATURES LIKE US
CAN WE PUT FIRE INSIDE OF IT
OK BUT ONLY A SMALL ONE

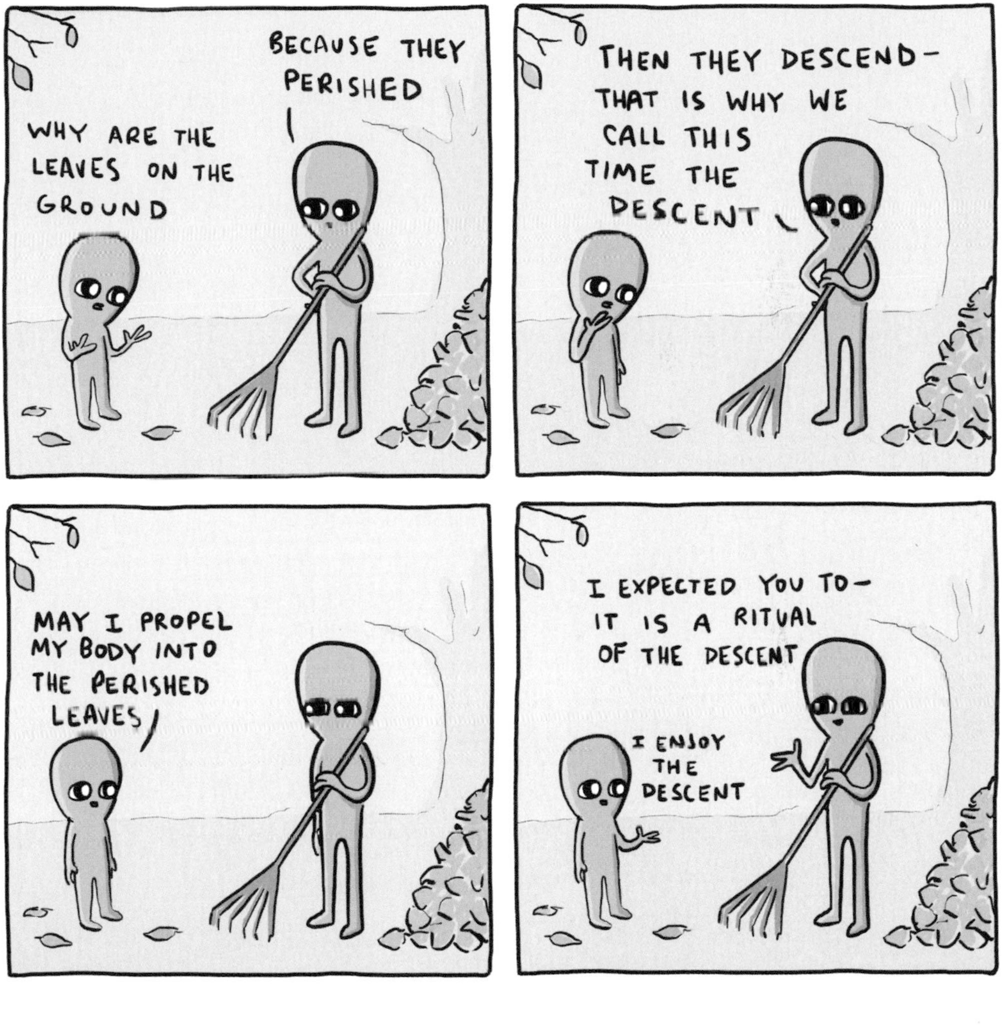

WHY ARE THE LEAVES ON THE GROUND
BECAUSE THEY PERISHED
THEN THEY DESCEND- THAT IS WHY WE CALL THIS TIME THE DESCENT
MAY I PROPEL MY BODY INTO THE PERISHED LEAVES
I EXPECTED YOU TO- IT IS A RITUAL OF THE DESCENT
I ENJOY THE DESCENT

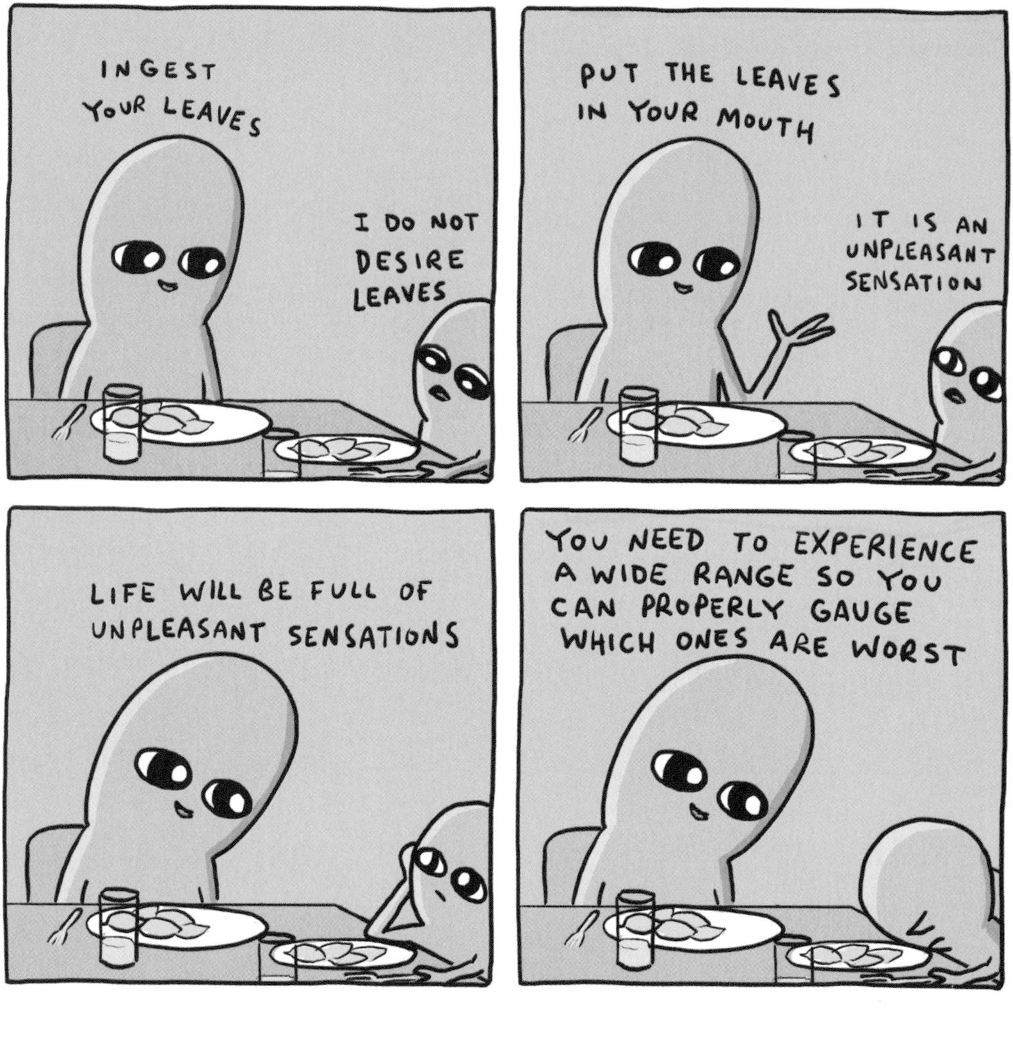
INGEST YOUR LEAVES
I DO NOT DESIRE LEAVES
PUT THE LEAVES IN YOUR MOUTH
IT IS AN UNPLEASANT SENSATION
LIFE WILL BE FULL OF UNPLEASANT SENSATIONS
YOU NEED TO EXPERIENCE A WIDE RANGE SO YOU CAN PROPERLY GAUGE WHICH ONES ARE WORST

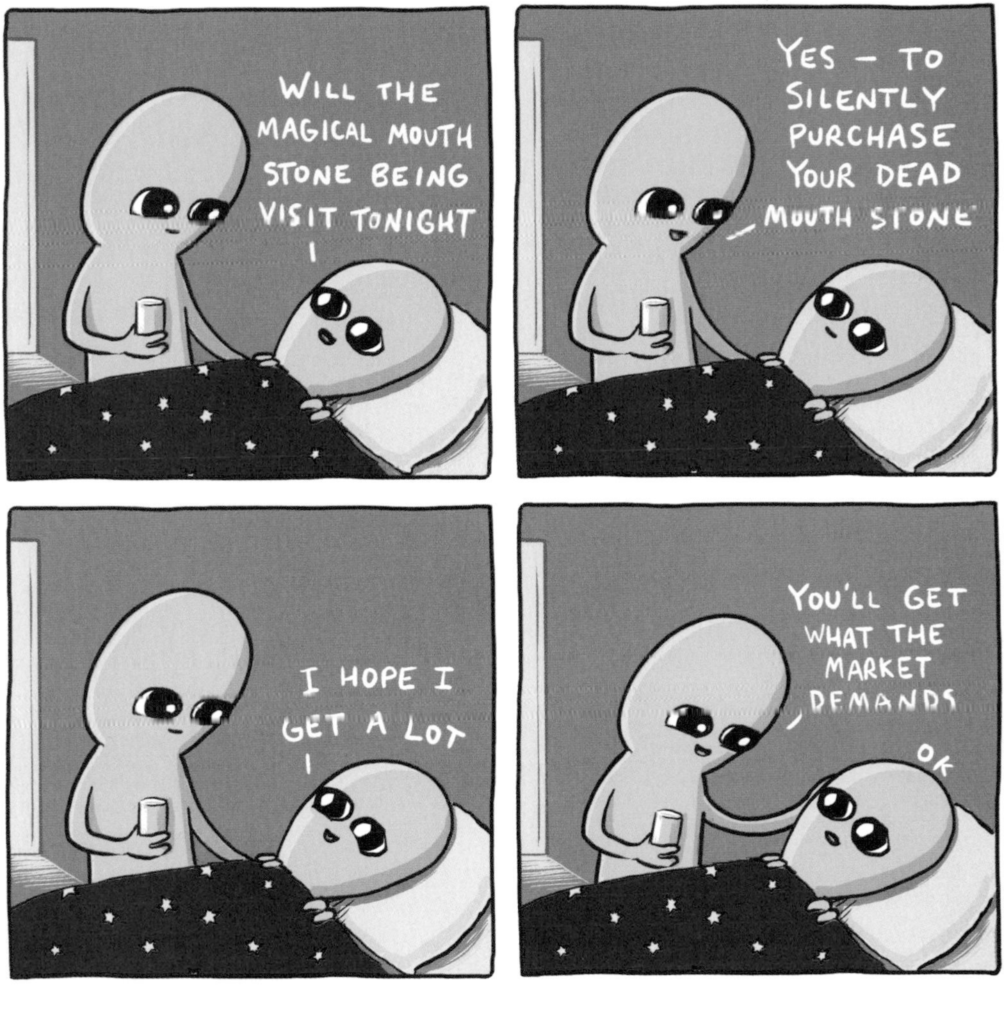
WILL THE MAGICAL MOUTH STONE BEING VISIT TONIGHT
YES — TO SILENTLY PURCHASE YOUR DEAD MOUTH STONE
I HOPE I GET A LOT
YOU'LL GET WHAT THE MARKET DEMANDS
OK

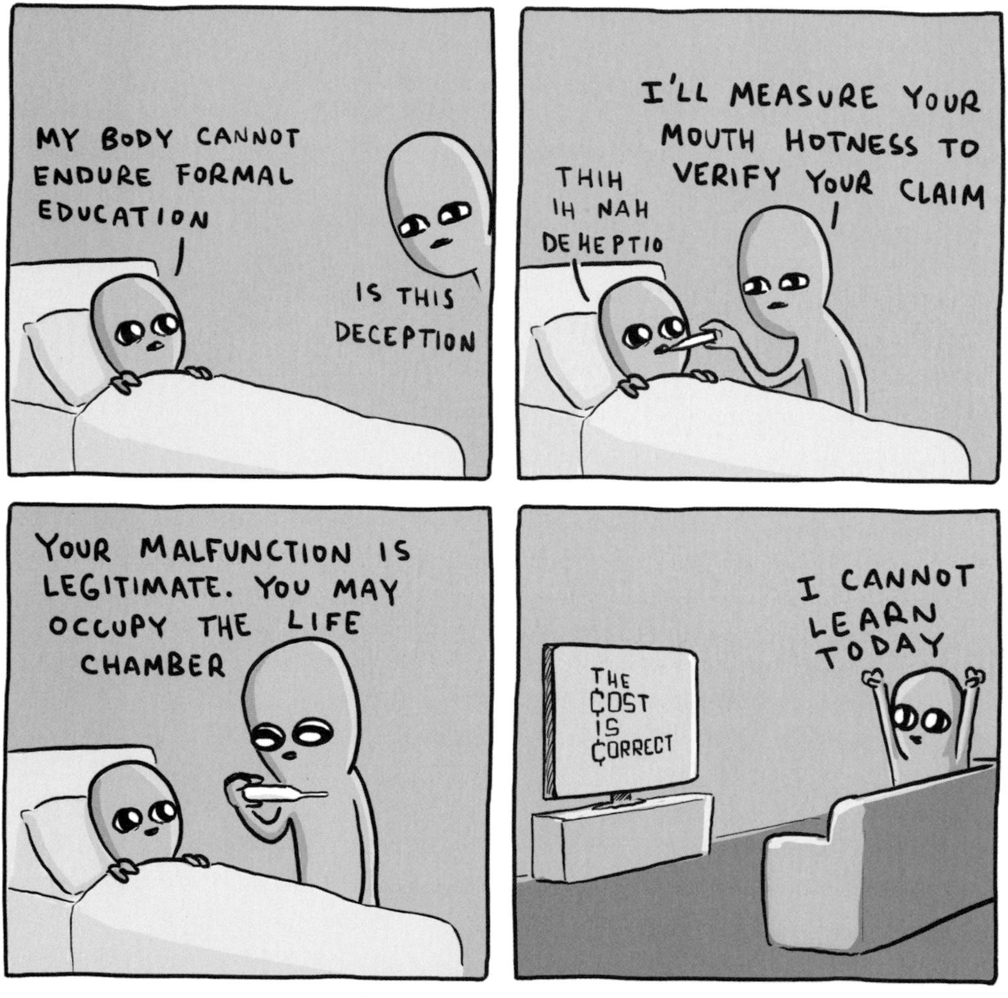
MY BODY CANNOT ENDURE FORMAL EDUCATION
IS THIS DECEPTION
THIH IH NAH DEHEPTIO
I'LL MEASURE YOUR MOUTH HOTNESS TO VERIFY YOUR CLAIM
YOUR MALFUNCTION IS LEGITIMATE. YOU MAY OCCUPY THE LIFE CHAMBER
THE ¢OST IS ¢ORRECT
I CANNOT LEARN TODAY

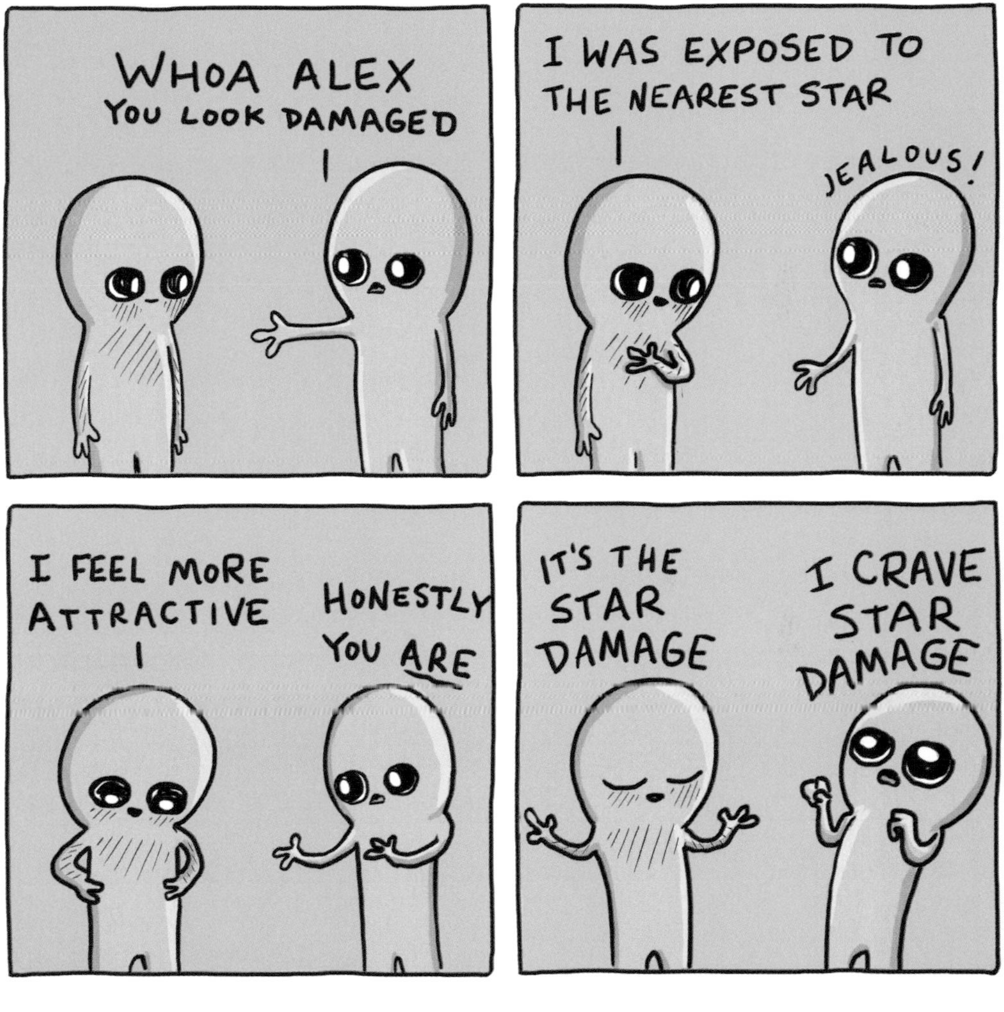
WHOA ALEX
YOU LOOK DAMAGED
I WAS EXPOSED TO THE NEAREST STAR
JEALOUS!
I FEEL MORE ATTRACTIVE
HONESTLY YOU ARE
IT'S THE STAR DAMAGE
I CRAVE STAR DAMAGE

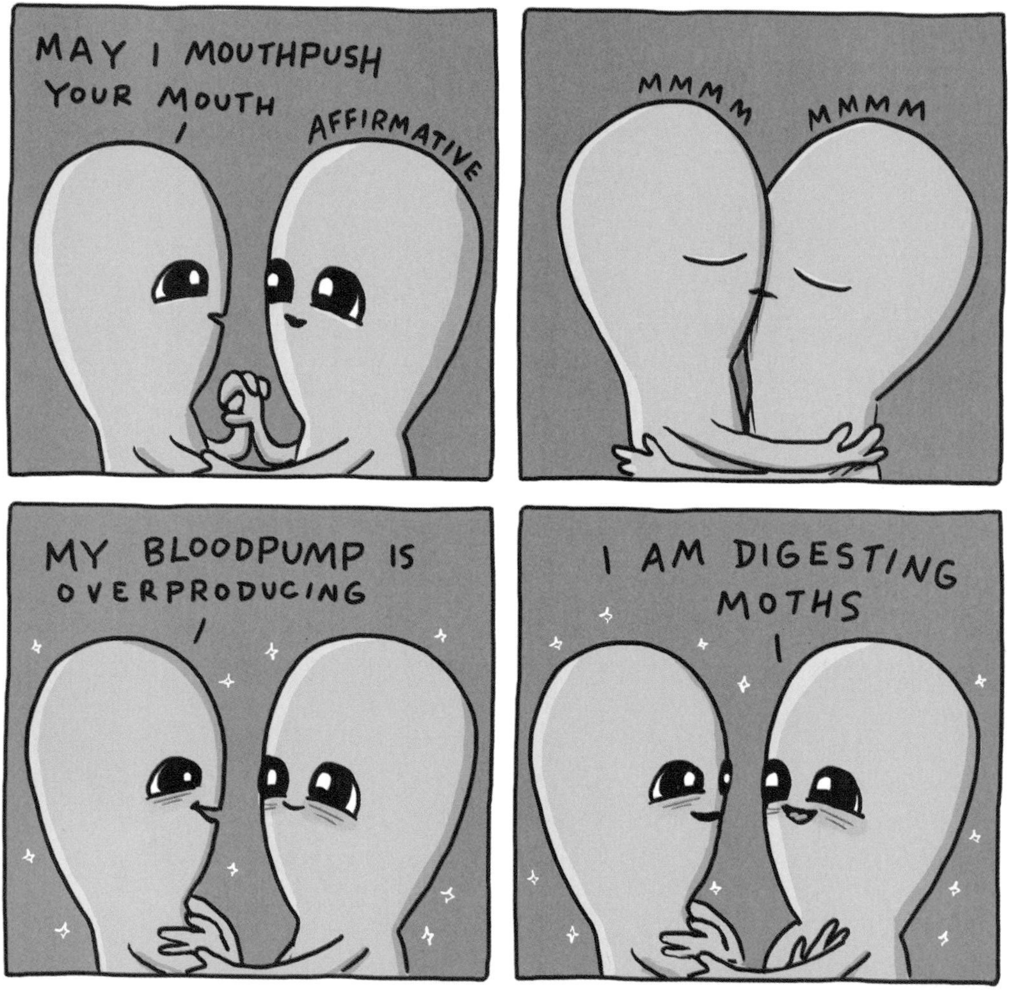
MAY I MOUTHPUSH YOUR MOUTH
AFFIRMATIVE
MMMM
MMMM
MY BLOODPUMP IS OVERPRODUCING
I AM DIGESTING MOTHS

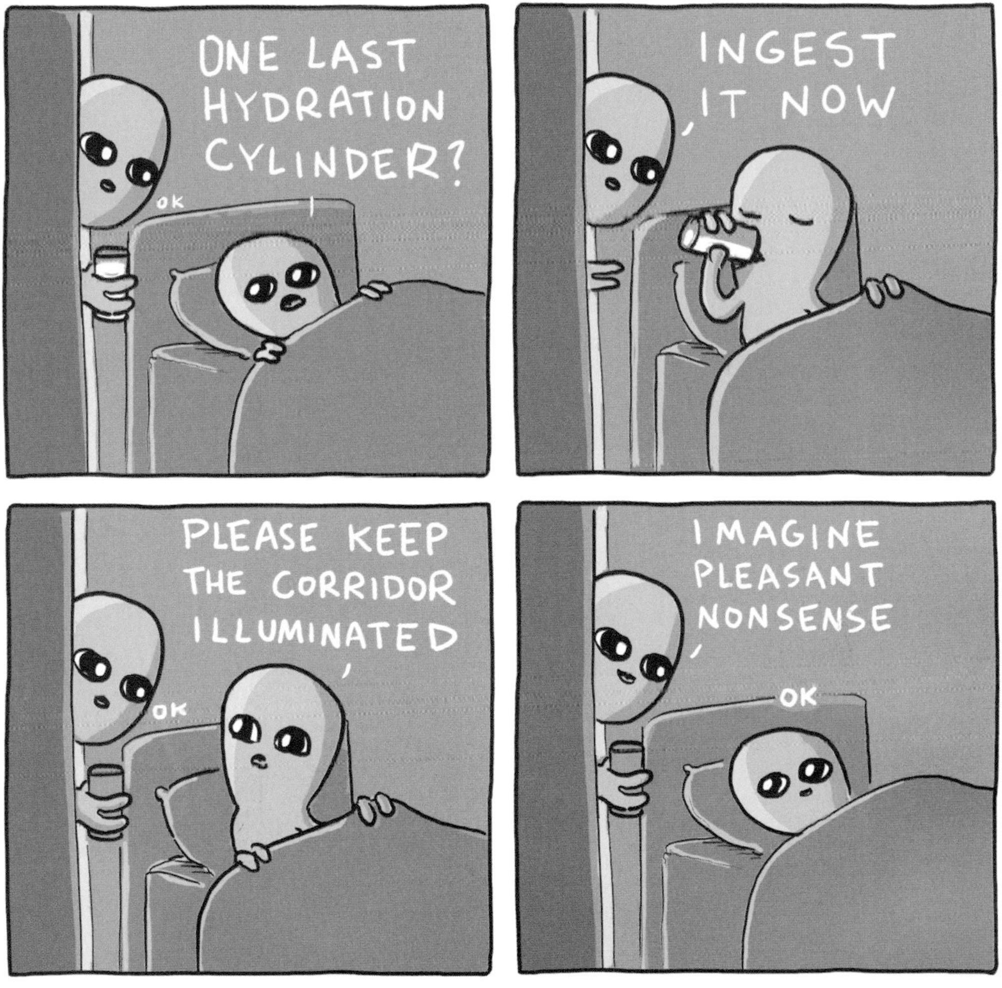
ONE LAST HYDRATION CYLINDER?
OK
INGEST IT NOW
PLEASE KEEP THE CORRIDOR ILLUMINATED
OK
IMAGINE PLEASANT NONSENSE
OK

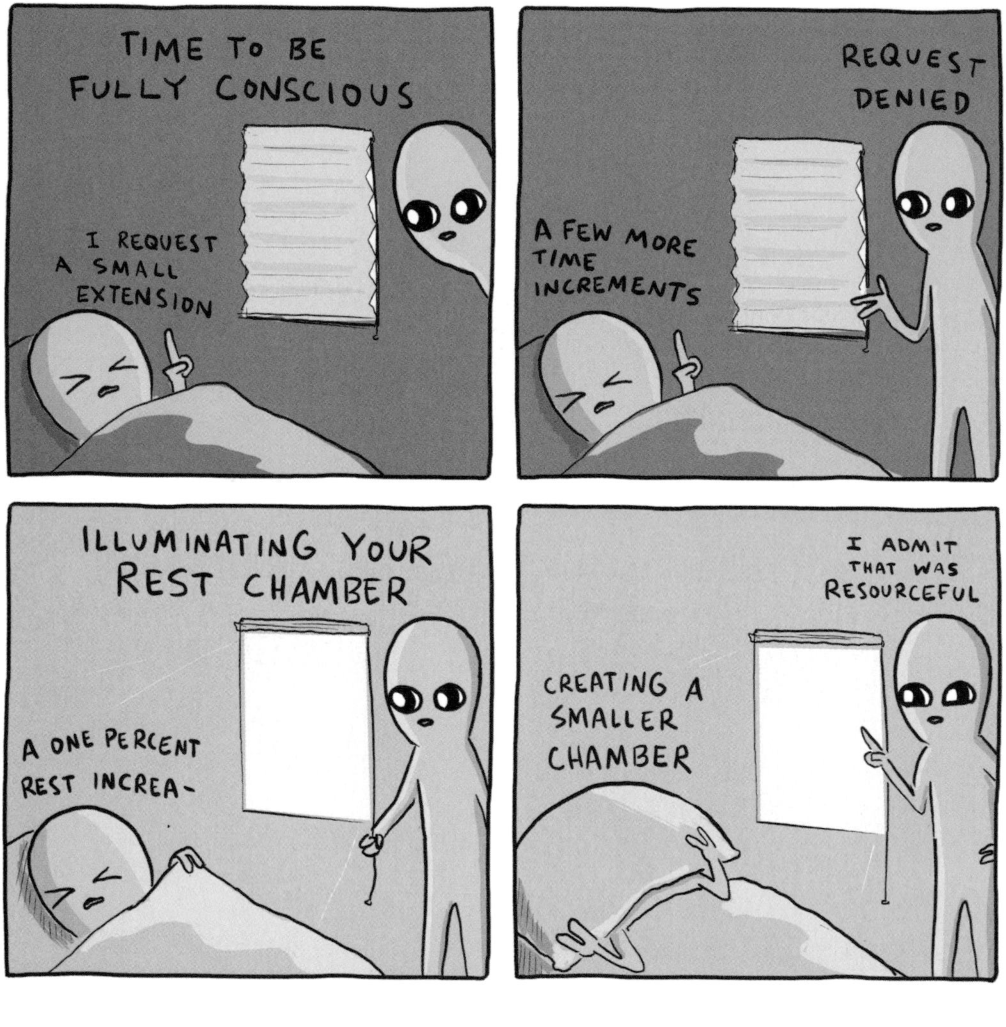
TIME TO BE FULLY CONSCIOUS
I REQUEST A SMALL EXTENSION
REQUEST DENIED
A FEW MORE TIME INCREMENTS
ILLUMINATING YOUR REST CHAMBER
A ONE PERCENT REST INCREA-
I ADMIT THAT WAS RESOURCEFUL
CREATING A SMALLER CHAMBER

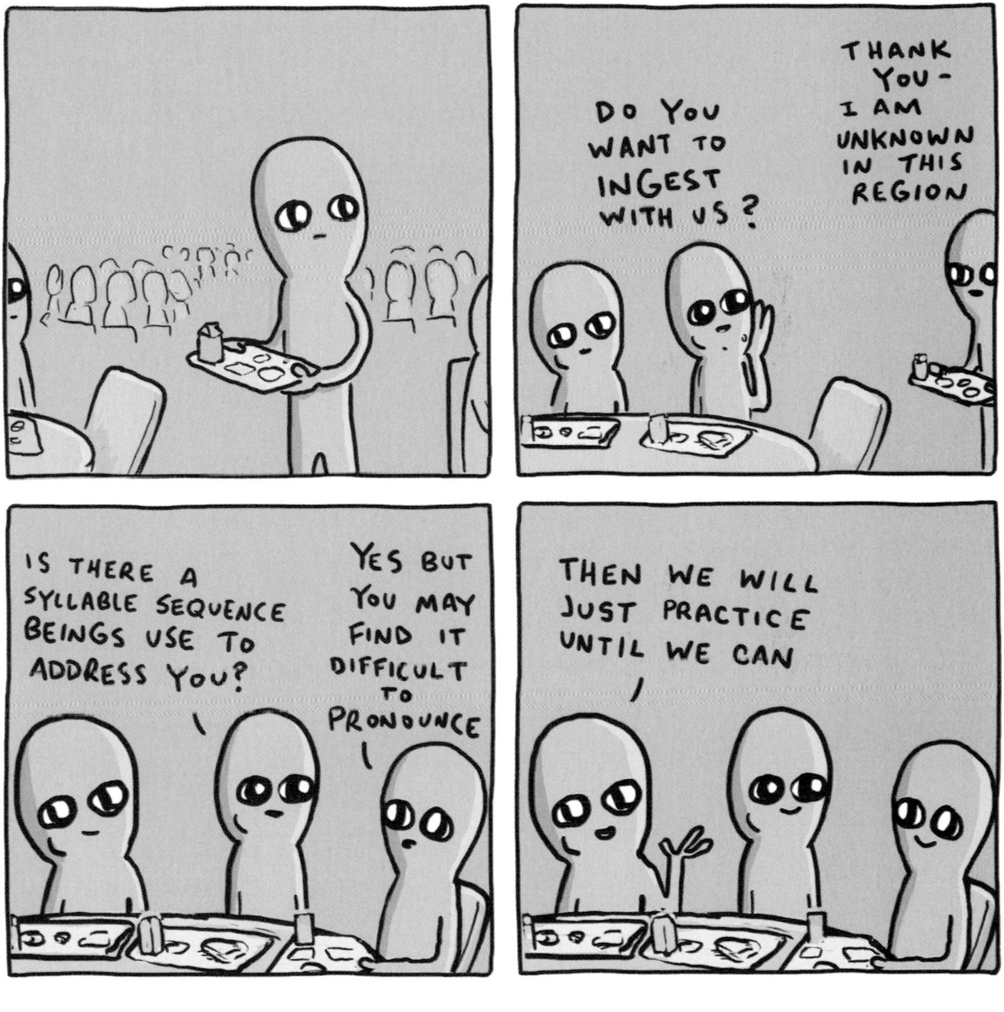
DO YOU WANT TO INGEST WITH US?
THANK YOU - I AM UNKNOWN IN THIS REGION
IS THERE A SYLLABLE SEQUENCE BEINGS USE TO ADDRESS YOU?
YES BUT YOU MAY FIND IT DIFFICULT TO PRONOUNCE
THEN WE WILL JUST PRACTICE UNTIL WE CAN

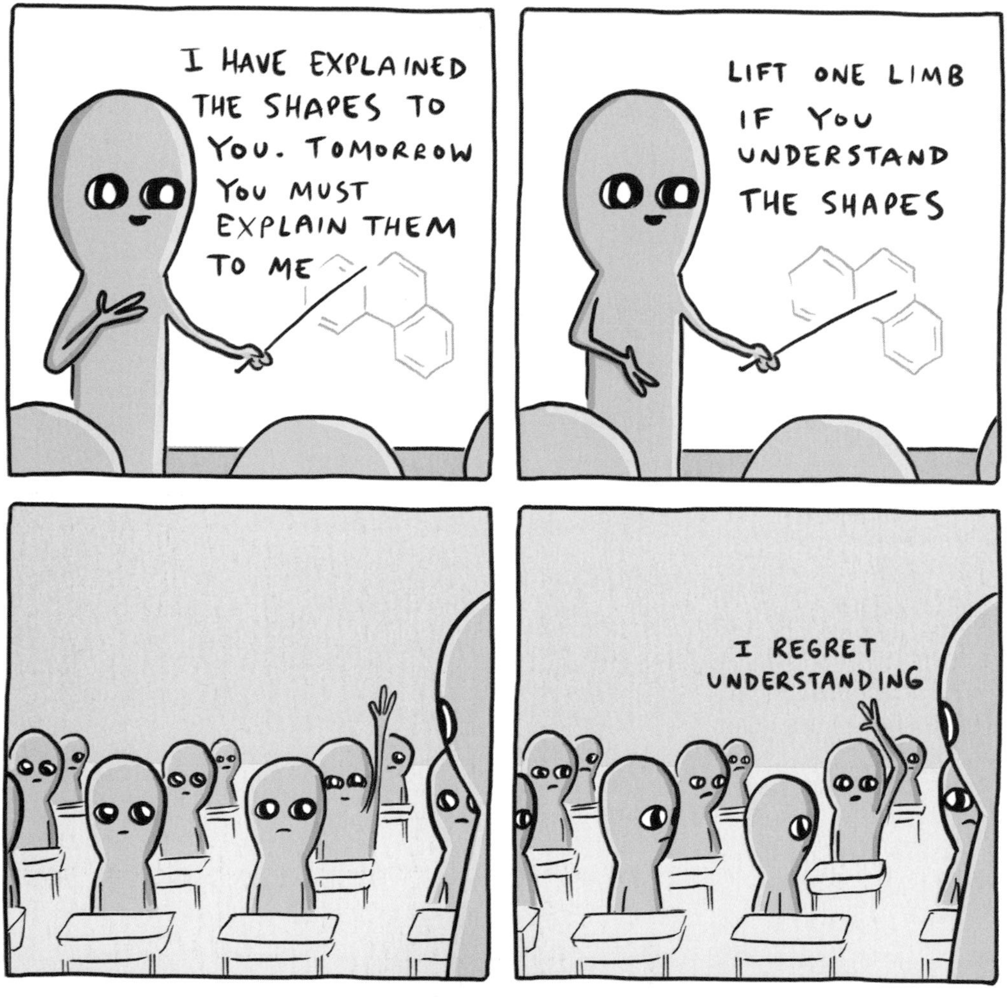
I HAVE EXPLAINED THE SHAPES TO YOU. TOMORROW YOU MUST EXPLAIN THEM TO ME
LIFT ONE LIMB IF YOU UNDERSTAND THE SHAPES
I REGRET UNDERSTANDING

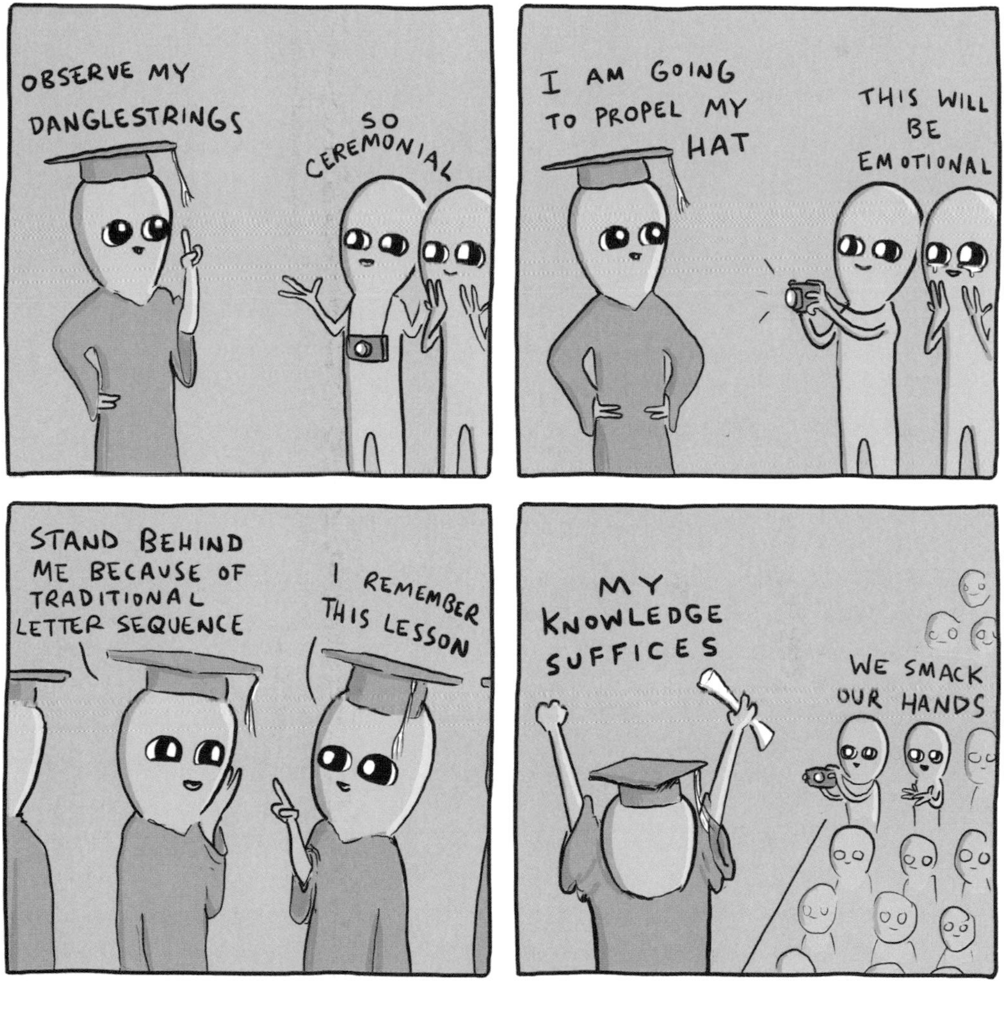
OBSERVE MY DANGLESTRINGS
SO CEREMONIAL
I AM GOING TO PROPEL MY HAT
THIS WILL BE EMOTIONAL
STAND BEHIND ME BECAUSE OF TRADITIONAL LETTER SEQUENCE
I REMEMBER THIS LESSON
MY KNOWLEDGE SUFFICES
WE SMACK OUR HANDS

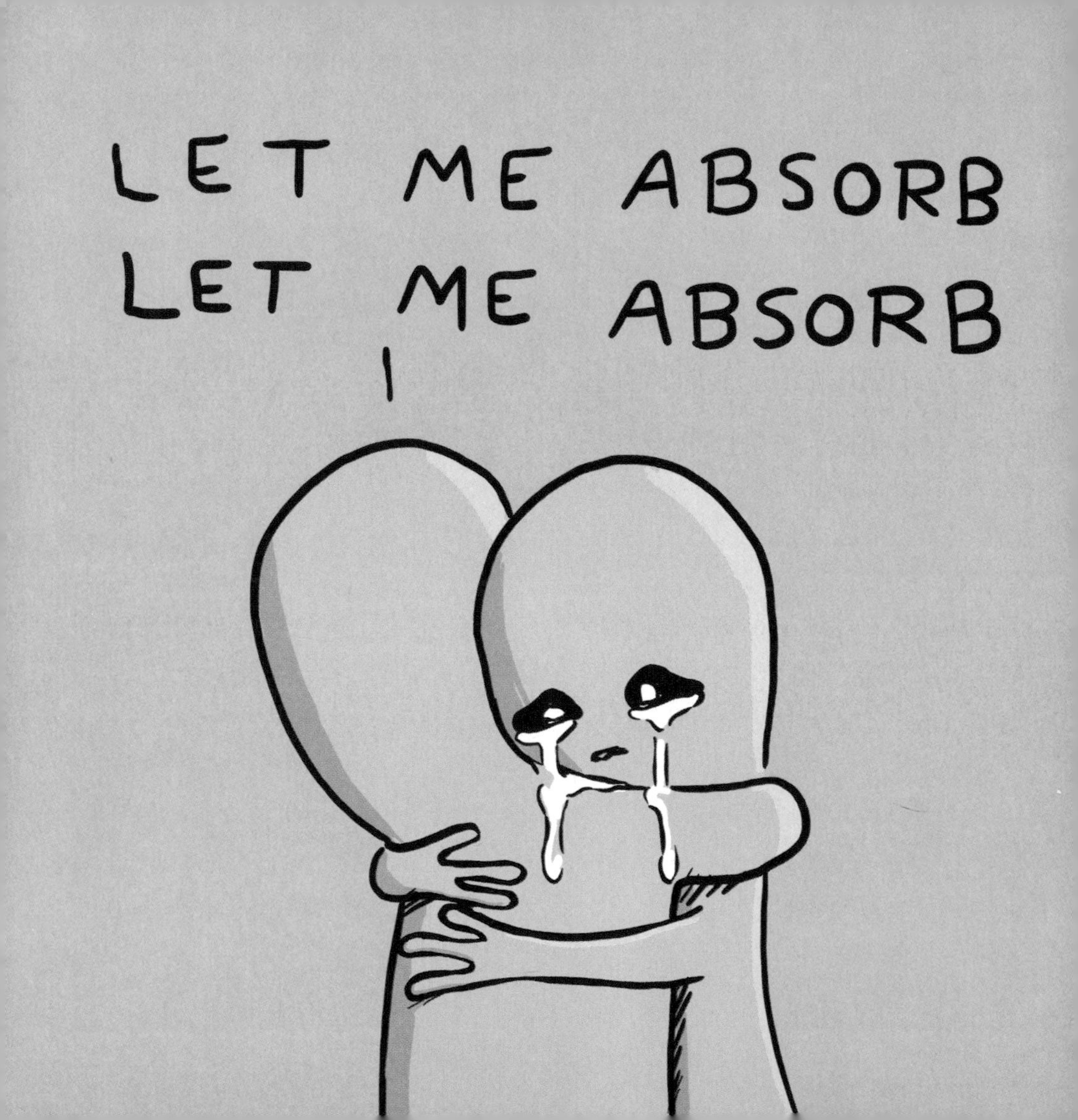
LET ME ABSORB
LET ME ABSORB

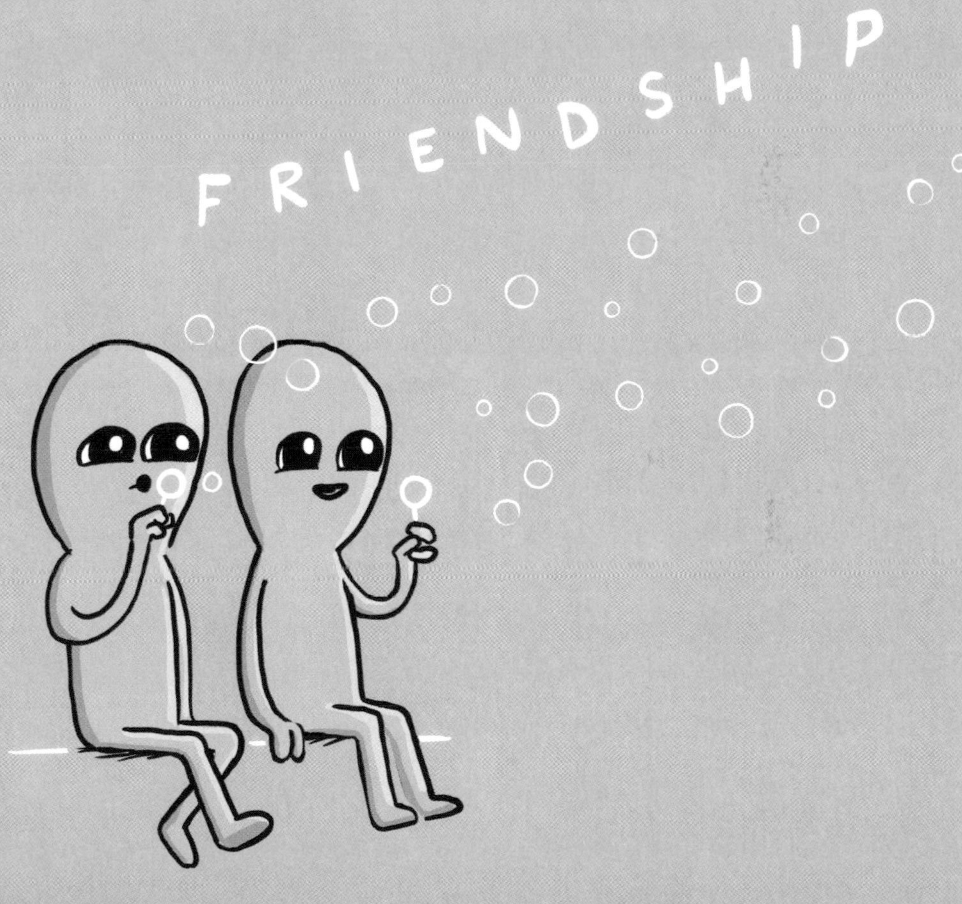
FRIENDSHIP

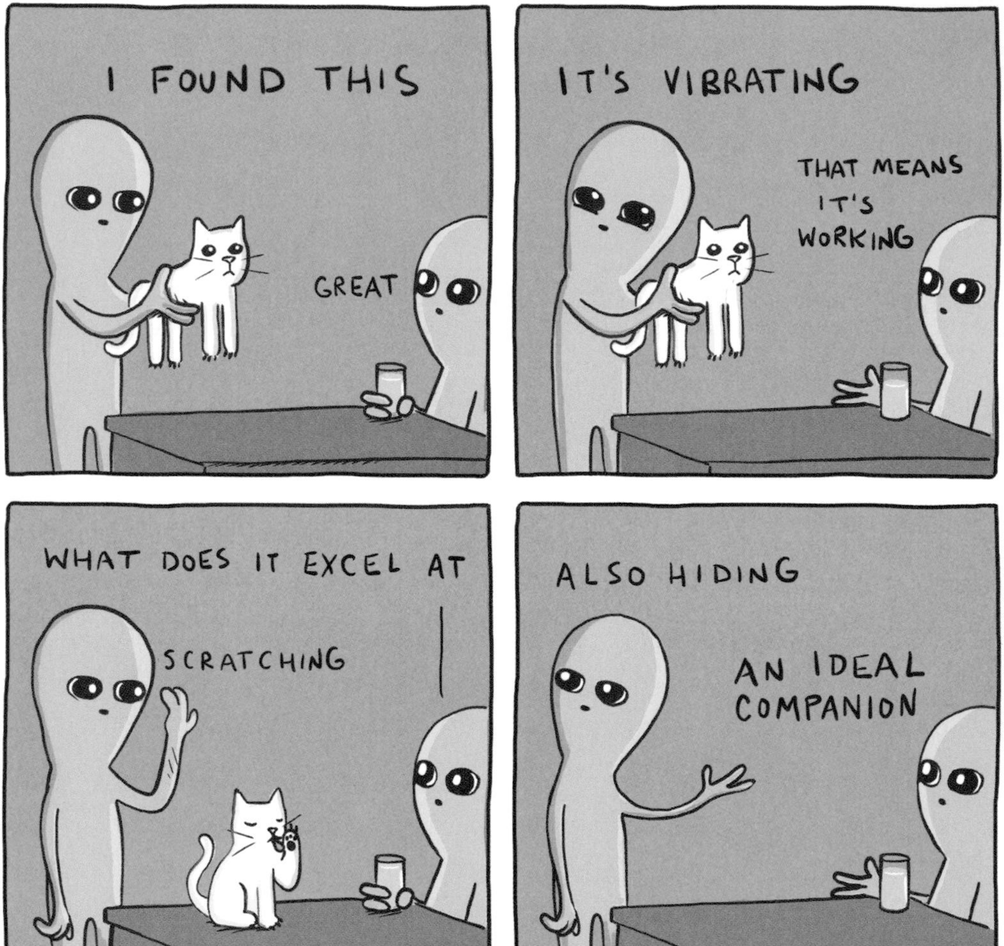
I FOUND THIS
GREAT
IT'S VIBRATING
THAT MEANS IT'S WORKING
WHAT DOES IT EXCEL AT
SCRATCHING
ALSO HIDING
AN IDEAL COMPANION

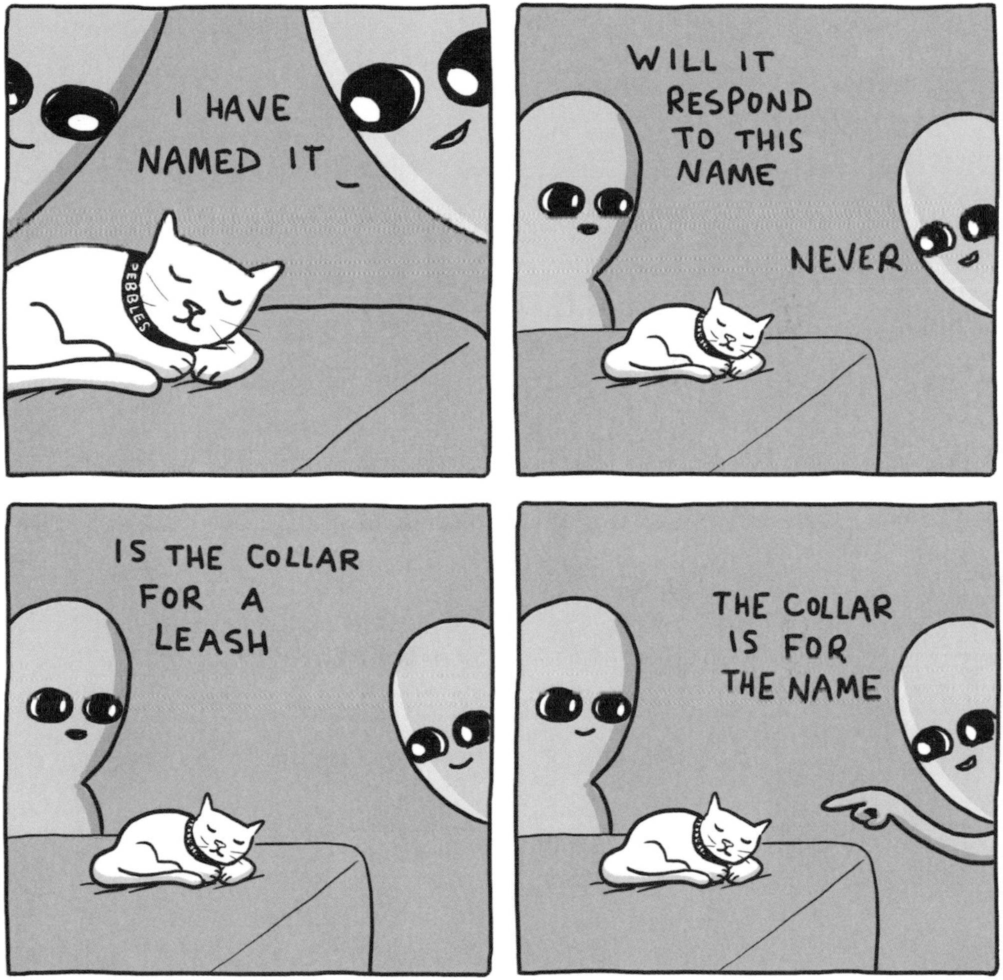
I HAVE NAMED IT
WILL IT RESPOND TO THIS NAME
NEVER
IS THE COLLAR FOR A LEASH
THE COLLAR IS FOR THE NAME

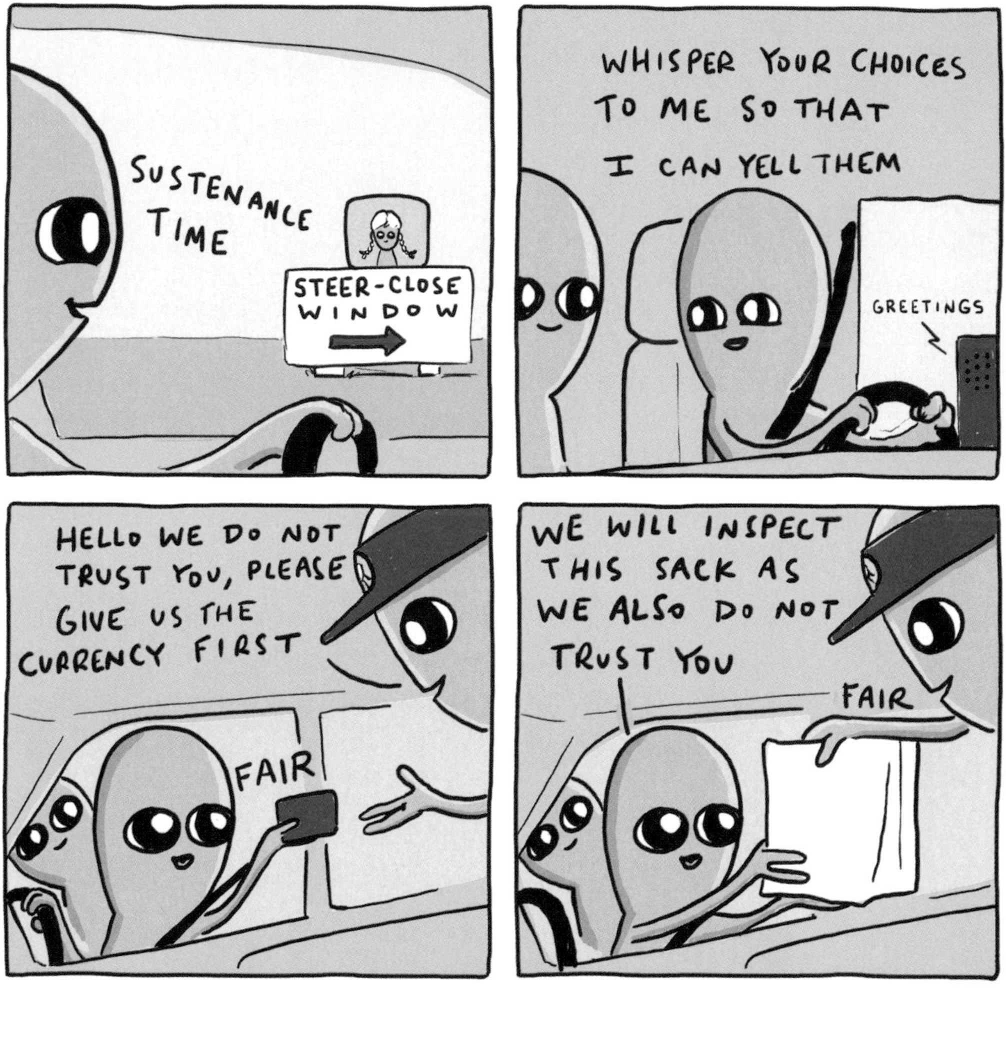
SUSTENANCE TIME
STEER-CLOSE WINDOW
WHISPER YOUR CHOICES TO ME SO THAT I CAN YELL THEM
GREETINGS
HELLO WE DO NOT TRUST YOU, PLEASE GIVE US THE CURRENCY FIRST
FAIR
WE WILL INSPECT THIS SACK AS WE ALSO DO NOT TRUST YOU
FAIR

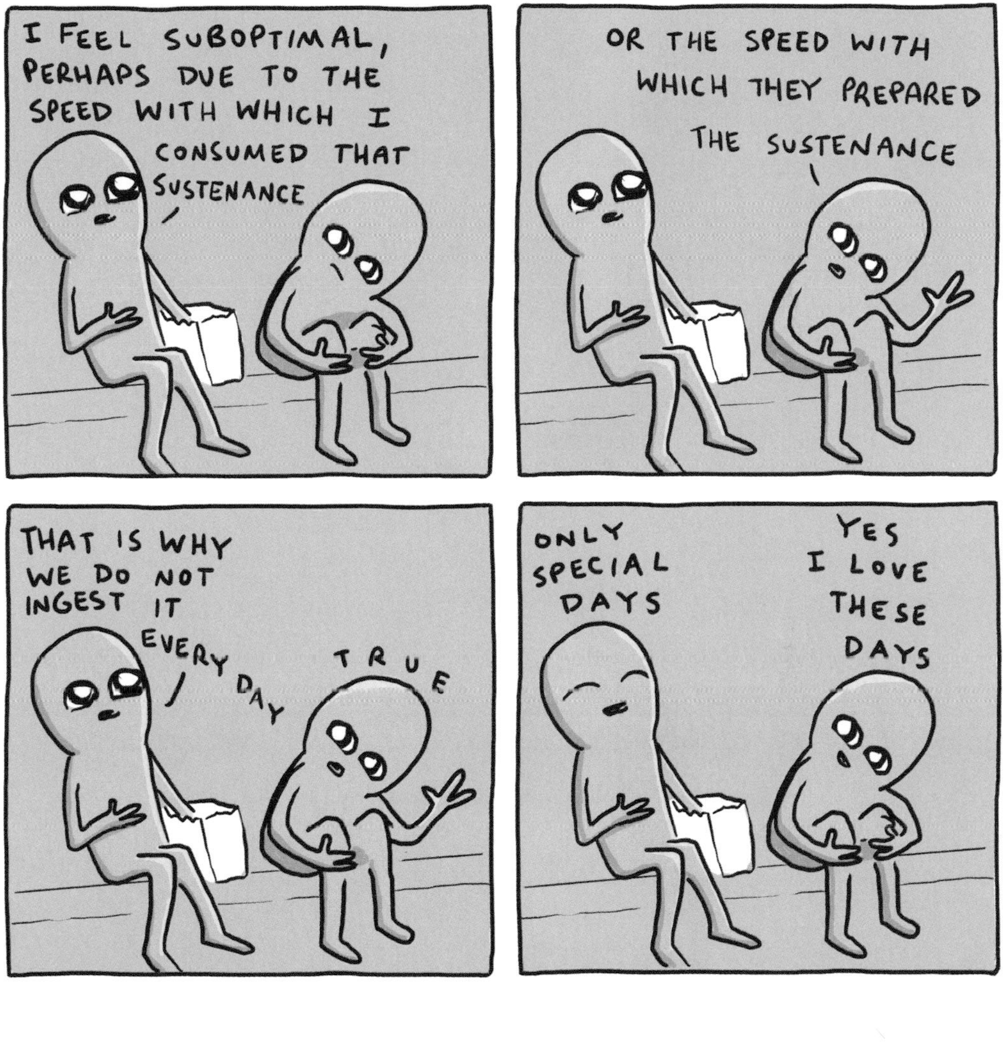
I FEEL SUBOPTIMAL, PERHAPS DUE TO THE SPEED WITH WHICH I CONSUMED THAT SUSTENANCE
OR THE SPEED WITH WHICH THEY PREPARED THE SUSTENANCE
THAT IS WHY WE DO NOT INGEST IT EVERY DAY
TRUE
ONLY SPECIAL DAYS
YES I LOVE THESE DAYS

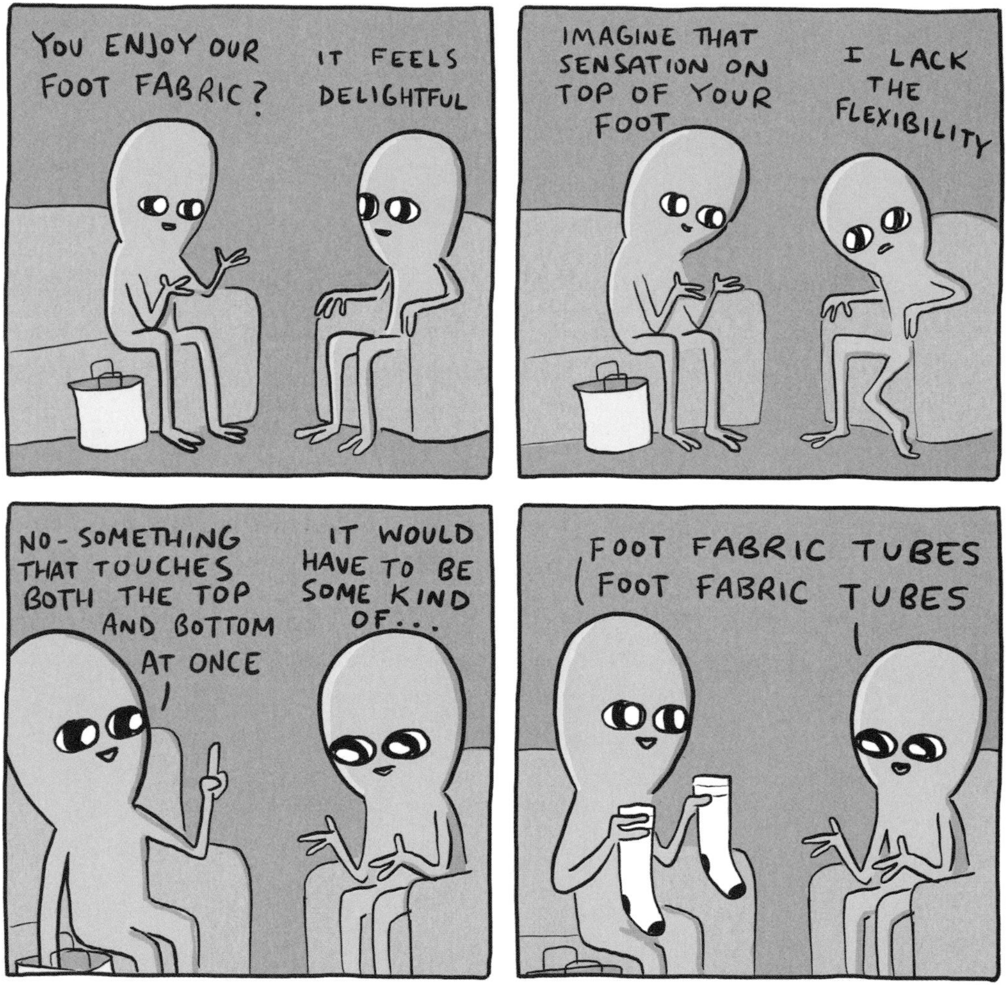
YOU ENJOY OUR FOOT FABRIC?
IT FEELS DELIGHTFUL
IMAGINE THAT SENSATION ON TOP OF YOUR FOOT
I LACK THE FLEXIBILITY
NO-SOMETHING THAT TOUCHES BOTH THE TOP AND BOTTOM AT ONCE
IT WOULD HAVE TO BE SOME KIND OF...
FOOT FABRIC TUBES
FOOT FABRIC TUBES

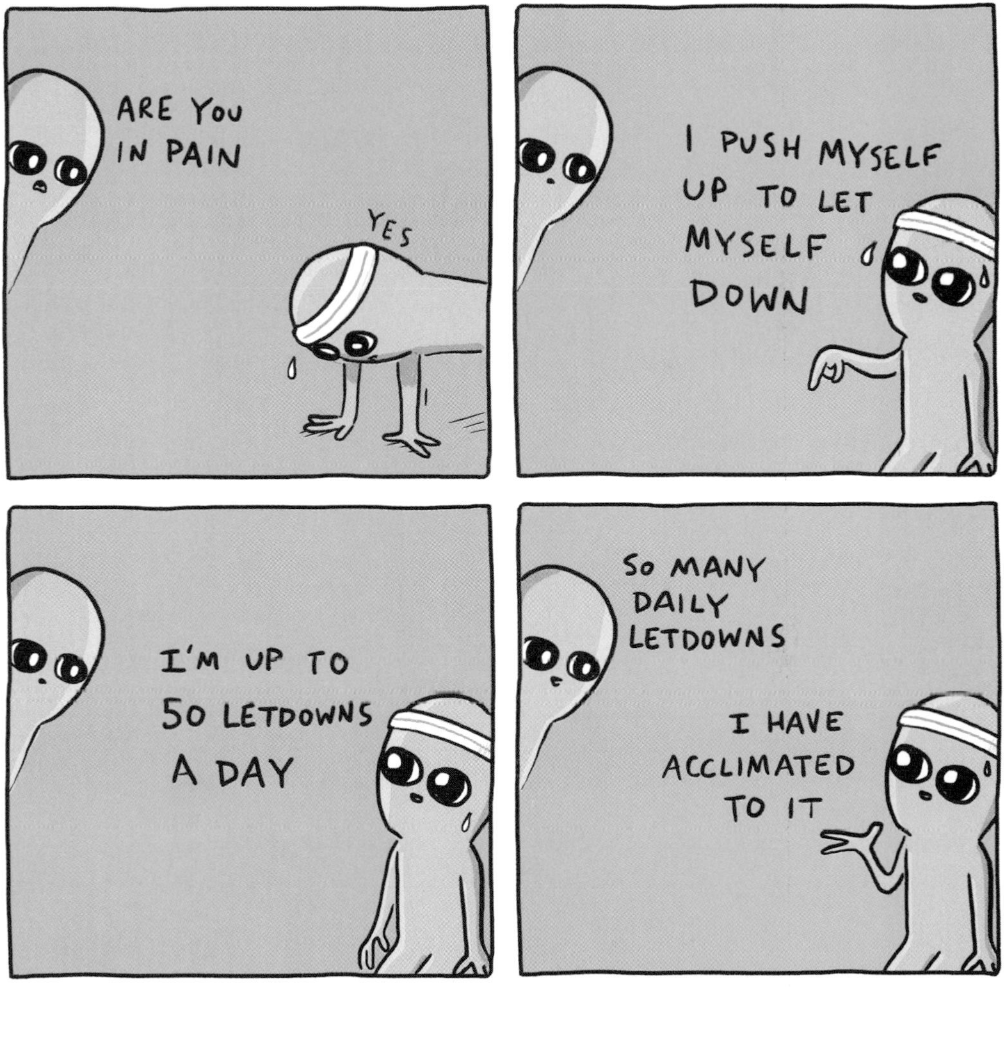
ARE YOU IN PAIN
YES
I PUSH MYSELF UP TO LET MYSELF DOWN
I'M UP TO 50 LETDOWNS A DAY
SO MANY DAILY LETDOWNS
I HAVE ACCLIMATED TO IT

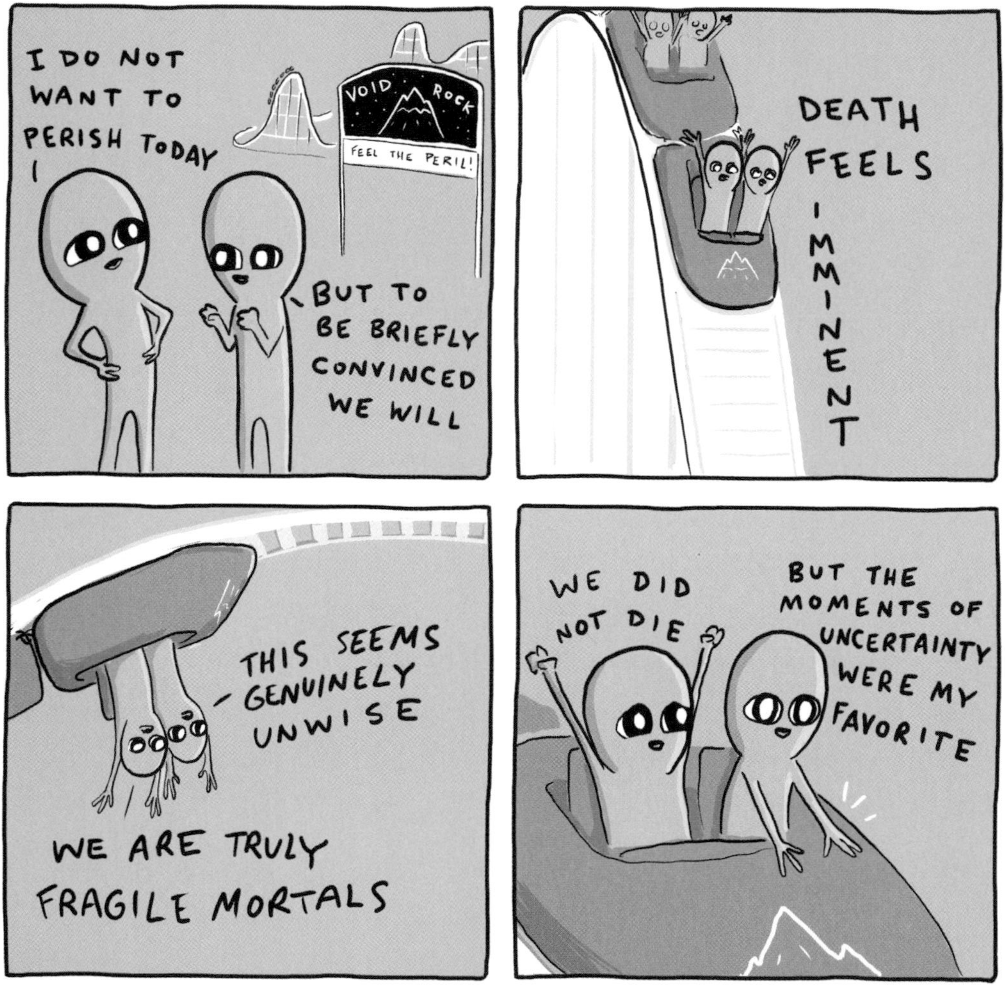
I DO NOT WANT TO PERISH TODAY
VOID ROCK
FEEL THE PERIL!
BUT TO BE BRIEFLY CONVINCED WE WILL
DEATH FEELS IMMINENT
THIS SEEMS GENUINELY UNWISE
WE ARE TRULY FRAGILE MORTALS
WE DID NOT DIE
BUT THE MOMENTS OF UNCERTAINTY WERE MY FAVORITE

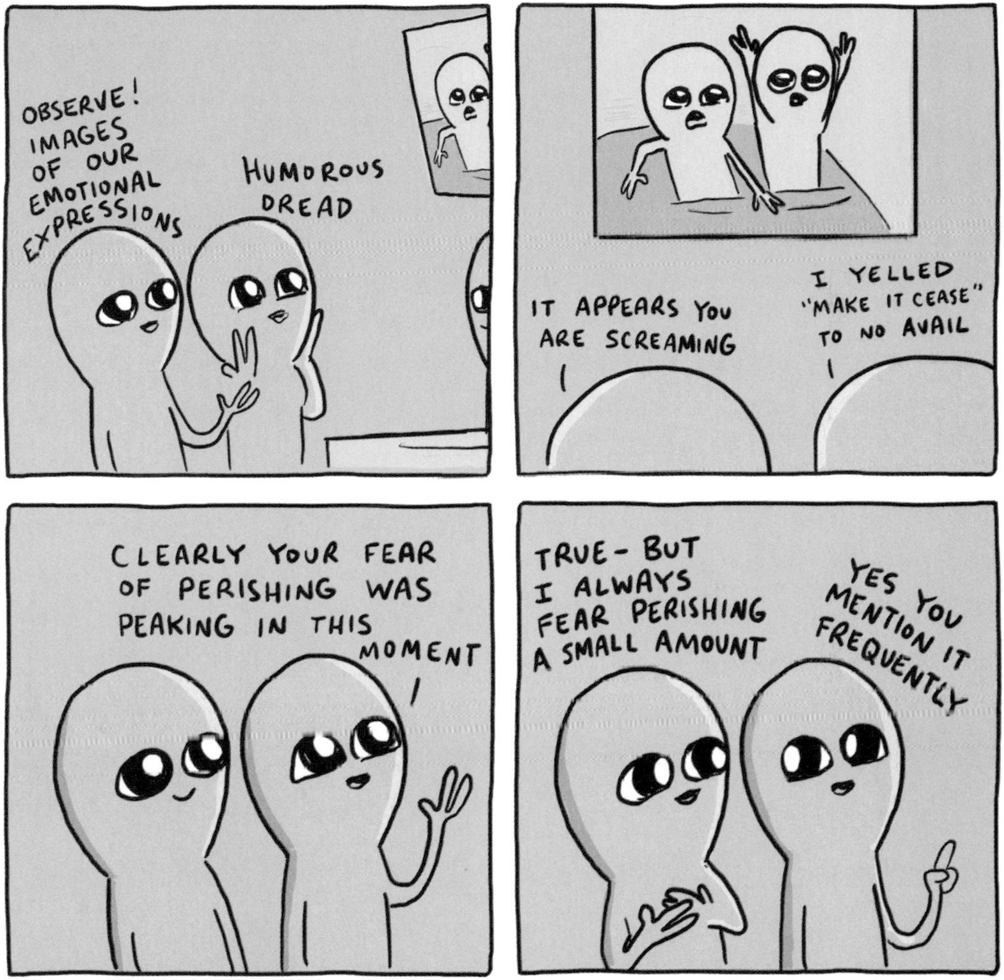
OBSERVE! IMAGES OF OUR EMOTIONAL EXPRESSIONS
HUMOROUS DREAD
IT APPEARS YOU ARE SCREAMING
I YELLED "MAKE IT CEASE" TO NO AVAIL
CLEARLY YOUR FEAR OF PERISHING WAS PEAKING IN THIS MOMENT
TRUE- BUT I ALWAYS FEAR PERISHING A SMALL AMOUNT
YES YOU MENTION IT FREQUENTLY

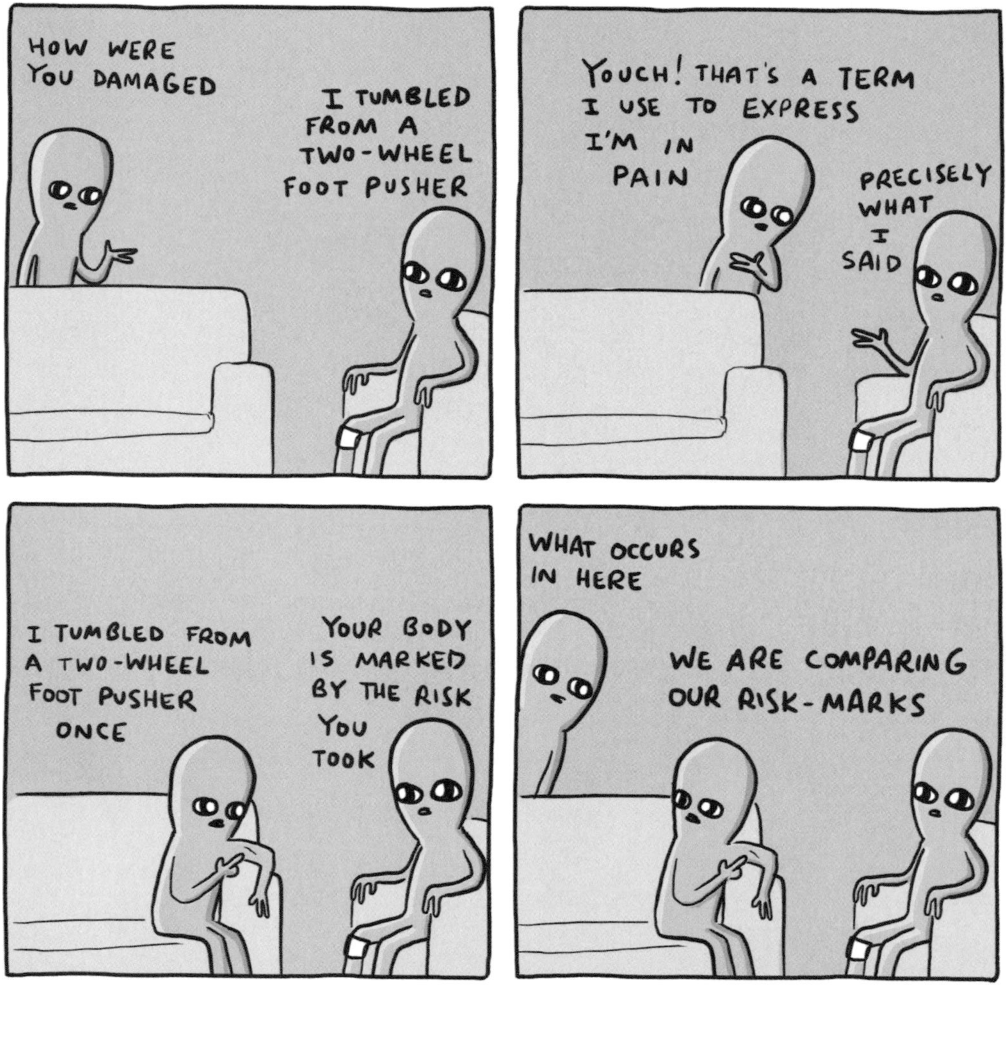
HOW WERE YOU DAMAGED
I TUMBLED FROM A TWO-WHEEL FOOT PUSHER
YOUCH! THAT'S A TERM I USE TO EXPRESS I'M IN PAIN
PRECISELY WHAT I SAID
I TUMBLED FROM A TWO-WHEEL FOOT PUSHER ONCE
YOUR BODY IS MARKED BY THE RISK YOU TOOK
WHAT OCCURS IN HERE
WE ARE COMPARING OUR RISK-MARKS

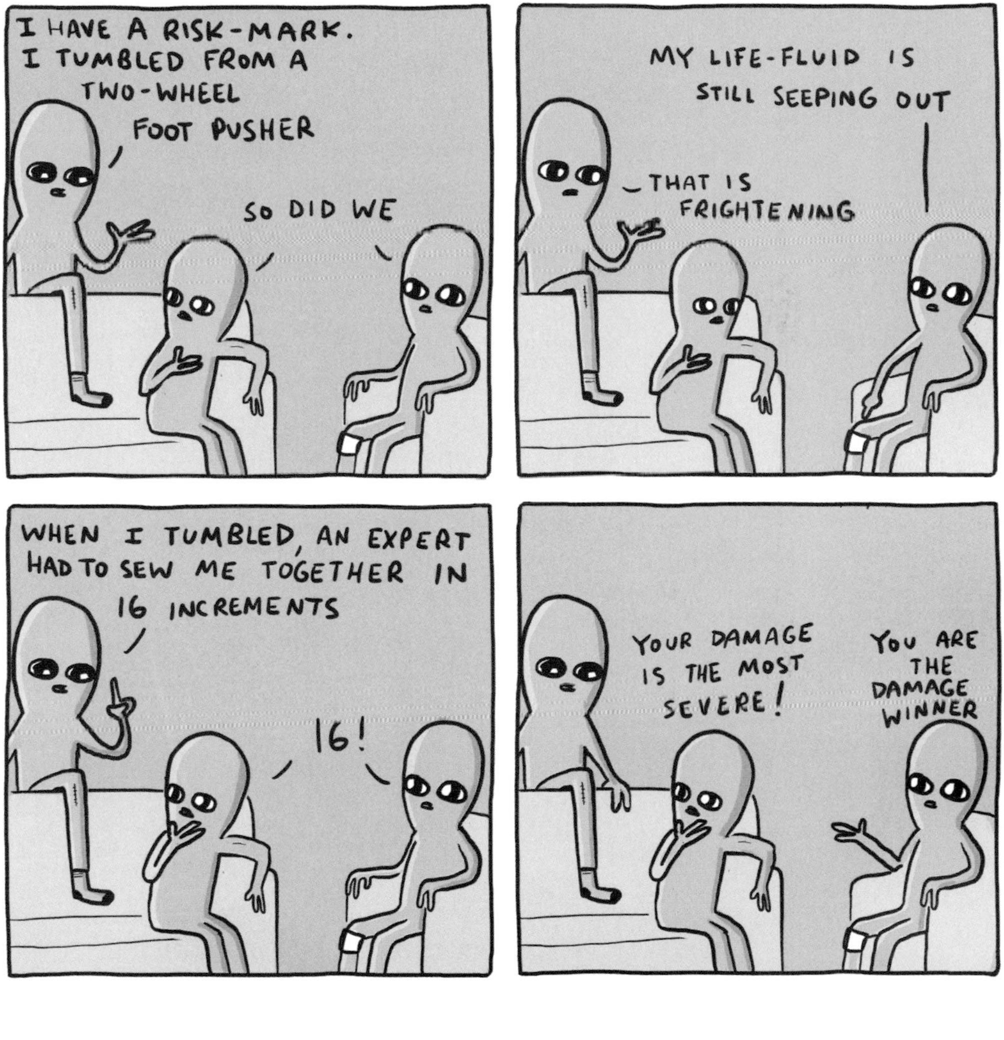
I HAVE A RISK-MARK. I TUMBLED FROM A TWO-WHEEL FOOT PUSHER
SO DID WE
MY LIFE-FLUID IS STILL SEEPING OUT
THAT IS FRIGHTENING
WHEN I TUMBLED, AN EXPERT HAD TO SEW ME TOGETHER IN 16 INCREMENTS
16!
YOUR DAMAGE IS THE MOST SEVERE!
YOU ARE THE DAMAGE WINNER

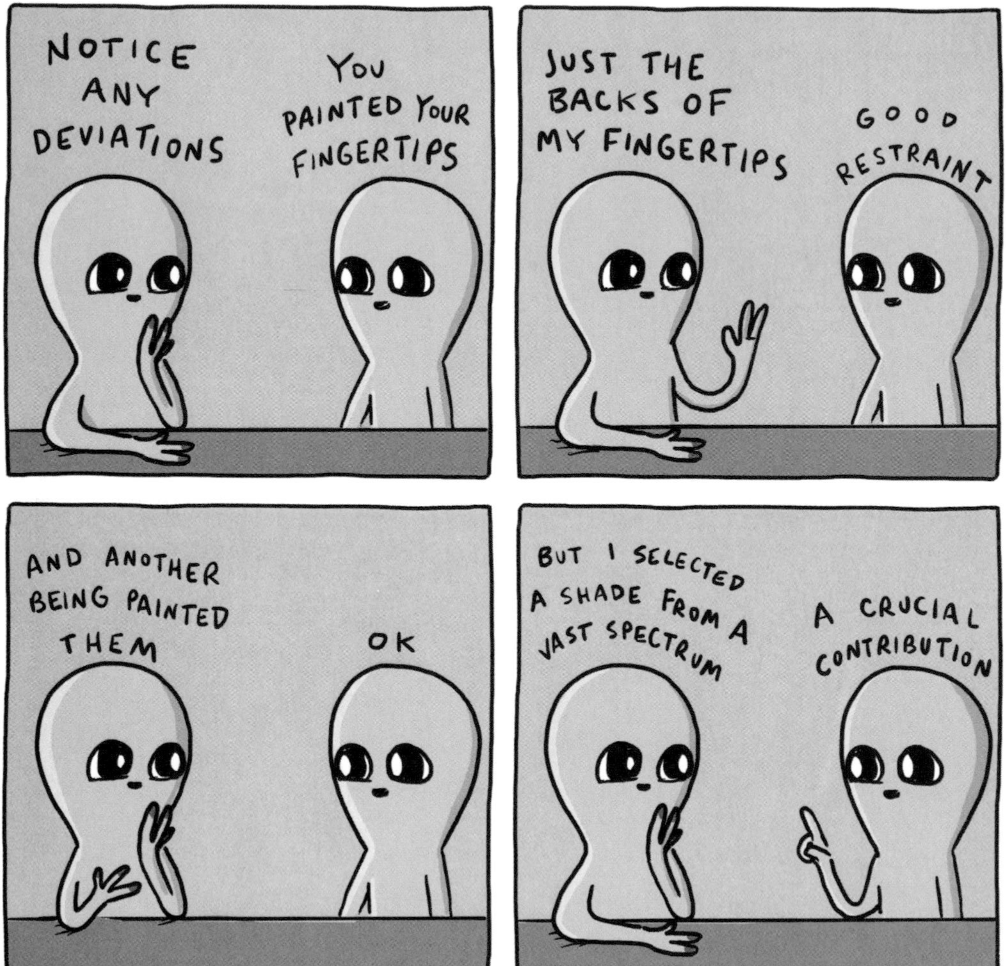
NOTICE ANY DEVIATIONS
YOU PAINTED YOUR FINGERTIPS
JUST THE BACKS OF MY FINGERTIPS
GOOD RESTRAINT
AND ANOTHER BEING PAINTED THEM
OK
BUT I SELECTED A SHADE FROM A VAST SPECTRUM
A CRUCIAL CONTRIBUTION

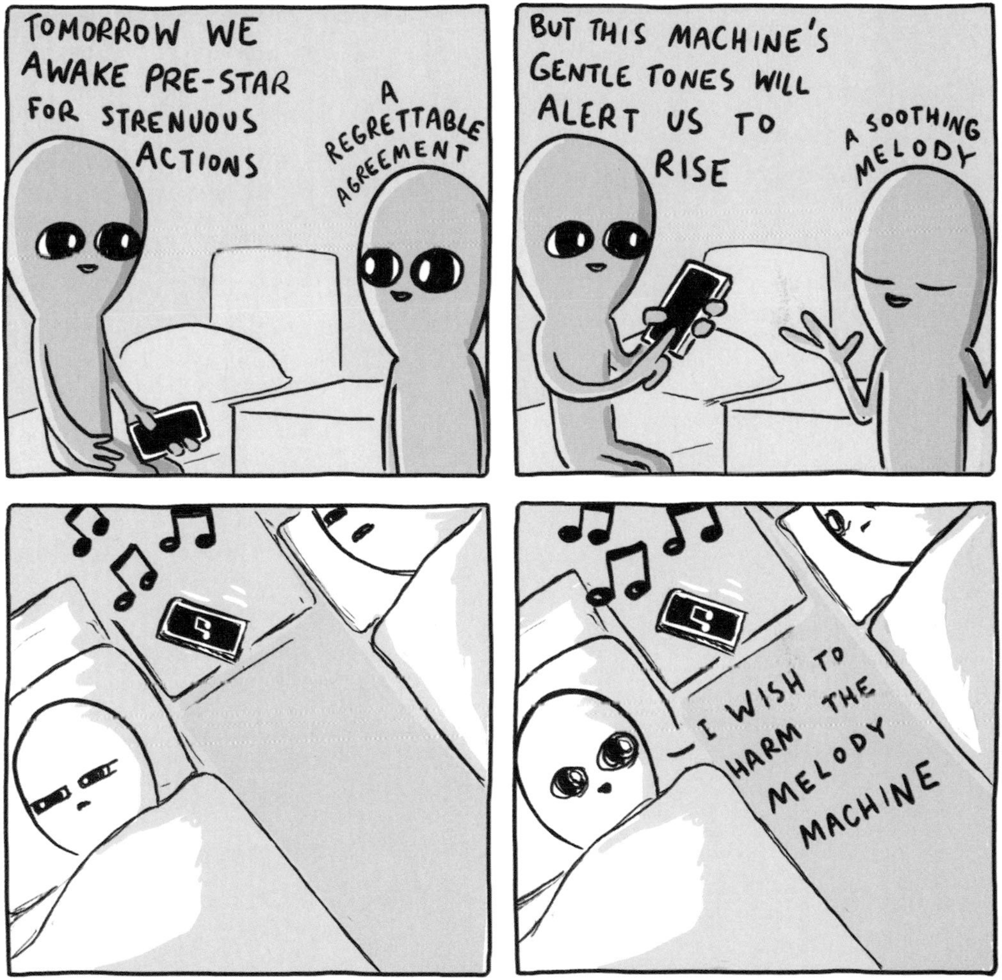
TOMORROW WE AWAKE PRE-STAR FOR STRENUOUS ACTIONS
A REGRETTABLE AGREEMENT
BUT THIS MACHINE'S GENTLE TONES WILL ALERT US TO RISE
A SOOTHING MELODY
I WISH TO HARM THE MELODY MACHINE

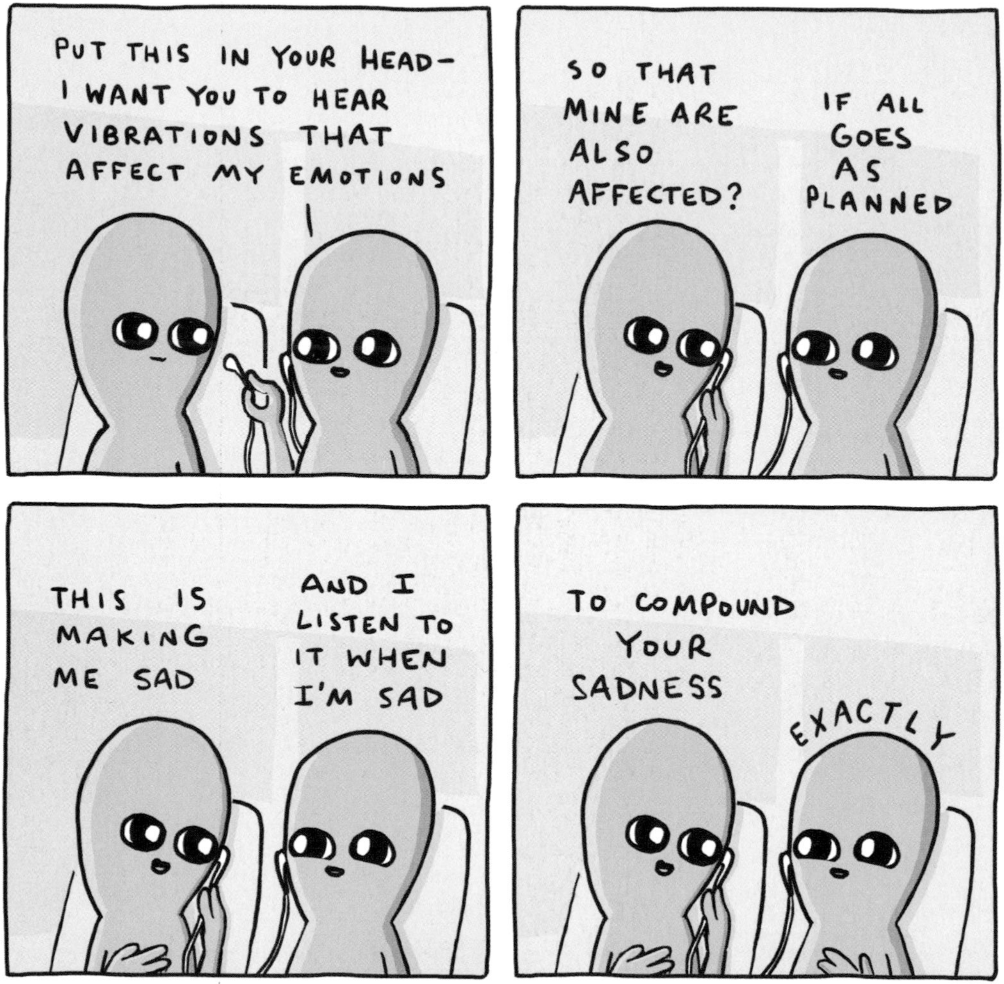
PUT THIS IN YOUR HEAD-
I WANT YOU TO HEAR VIBRATIONS THAT AFFECT MY EMOTIONS
SO THAT MINE ARE ALSO AFFECTED?
IF ALL GOES AS PLANNED
THIS IS MAKING ME SAD
AND I LISTEN TO IT WHEN I'M SAD
TO COMPOUND YOUR SADNESS
EXACTLY

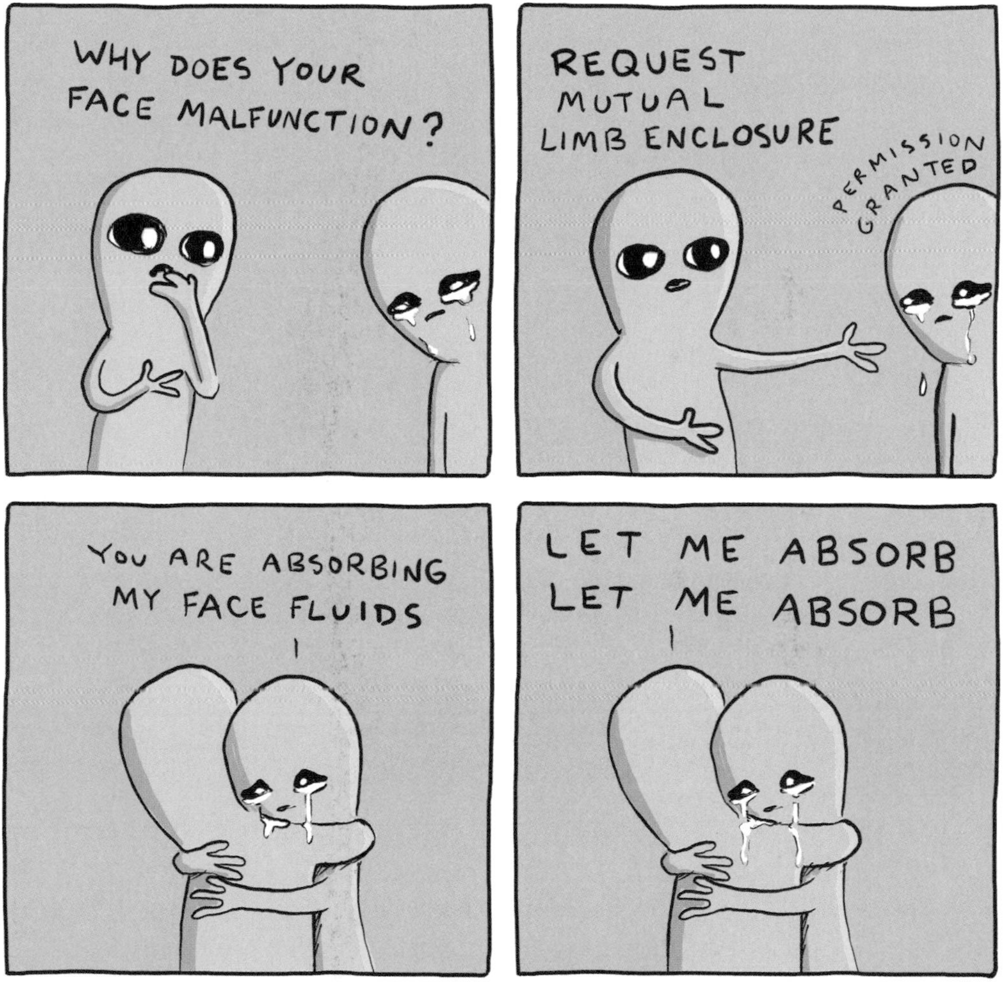
WHY DOES YOUR FACE MALFUNCTION?
REQUEST MUTUAL LIMB ENCLOSURE
PERMISSION GRANTED
YOU ARE ABSORBING MY FACE FLUIDS
LET ME ABSORB LET ME ABSORB

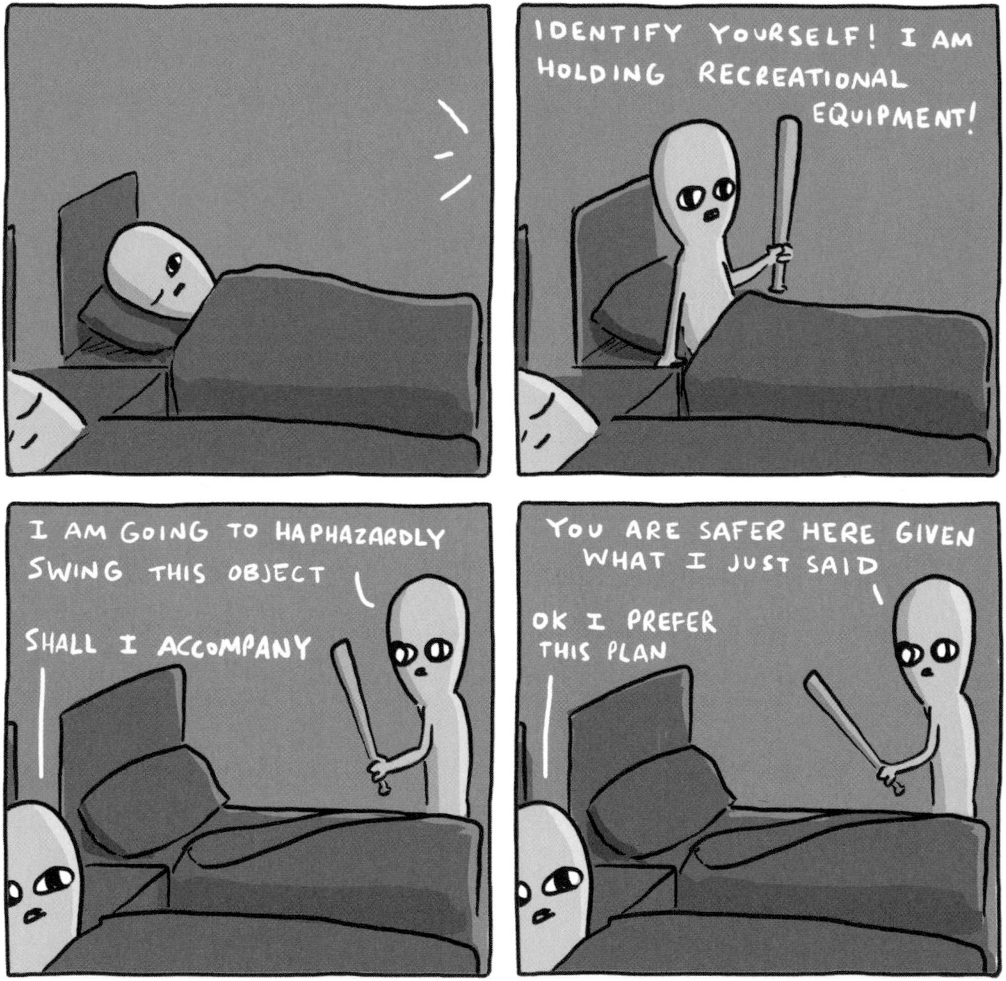
IDENTIFY YOURSELF! I AM HOLDING RECREATIONAL EQUIPMENT!
I AM GOING TO HAPHAZARDLY SWING THIS OBJECT
SHALL I ACCOMPANY
YOU ARE SAFER HERE GIVEN WHAT I JUST SAID
OK I PREFER THIS PLAN

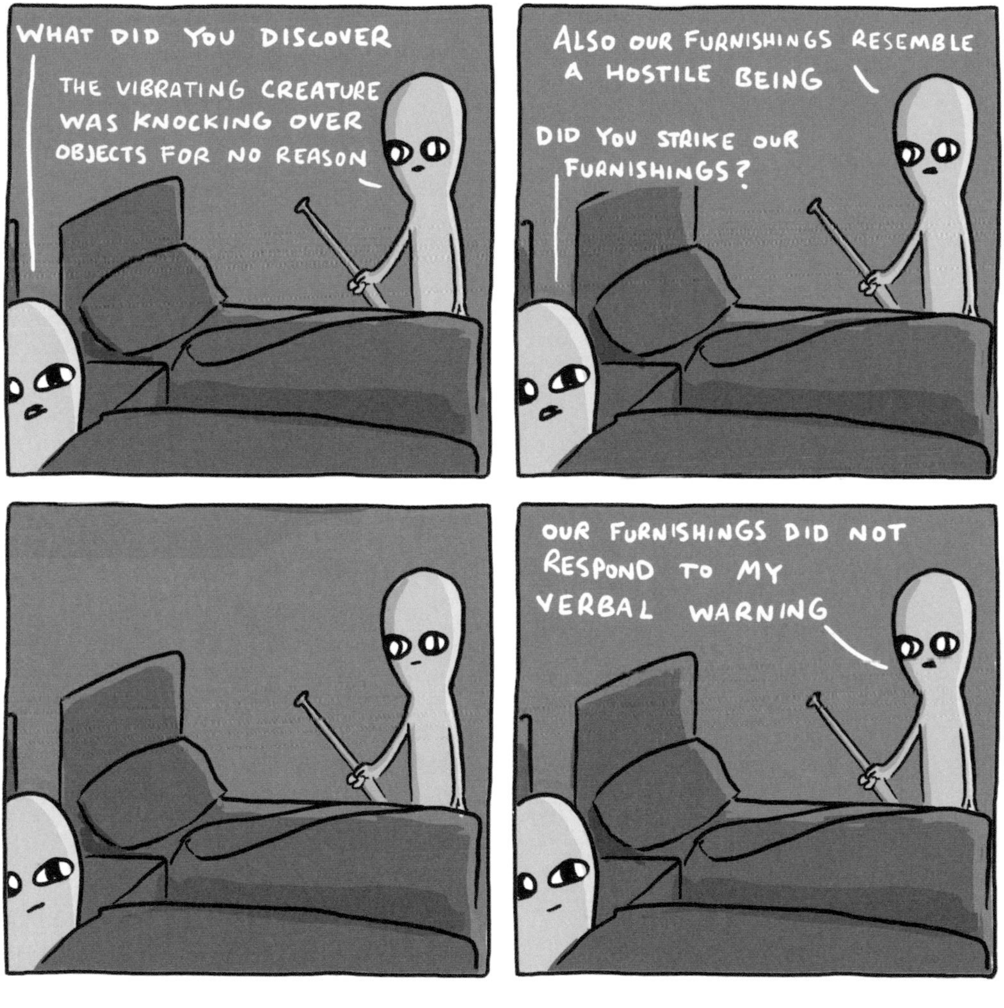
WHAT DID YOU DISCOVER
THE VIBRATING CREATURE WAS KNOCKING OVER OBJECTS FOR NO REASON
ALSO OUR FURNISHINGS RESEMBLE A HOSTILE BEING
DID YOU STRIKE OUR FURNISHINGS?
OUR FURNISHINGS DID NOT RESPOND TO MY VERBAL WARNING

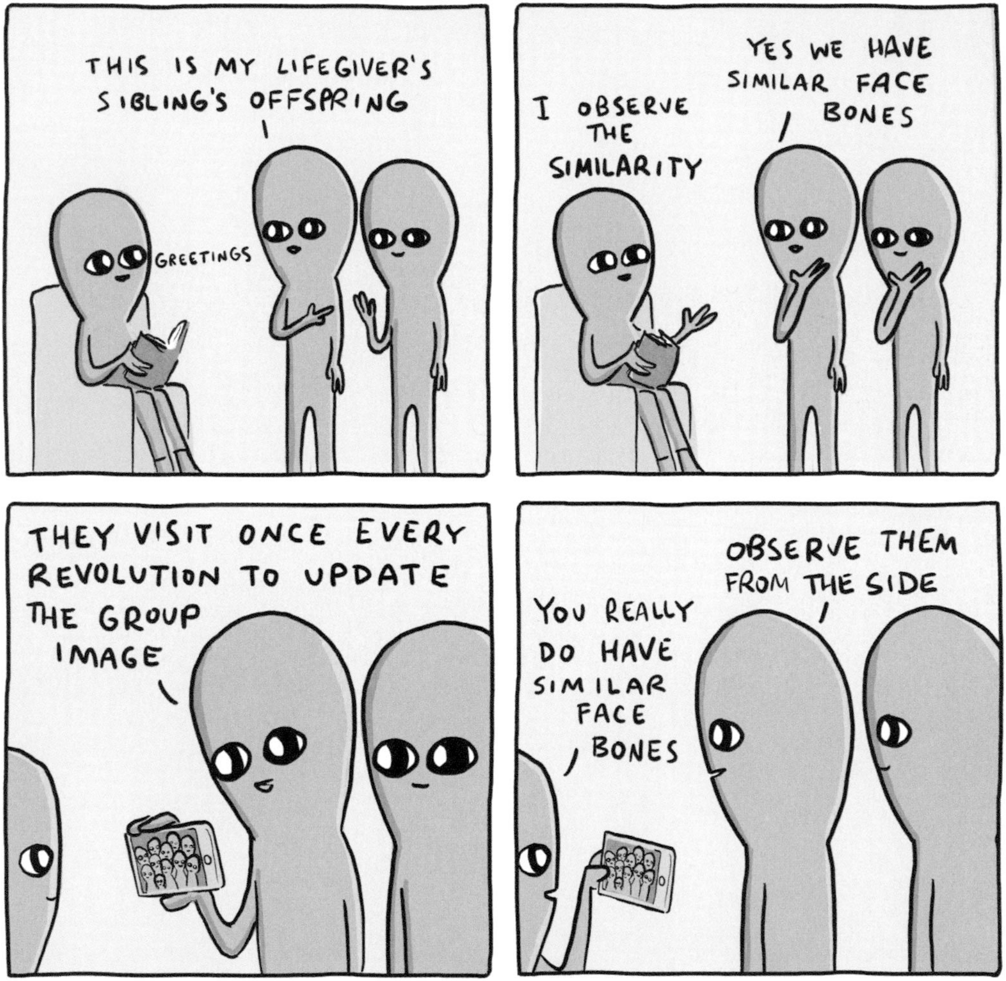
THIS IS MY LIFEGIVER'S SIBLING'S OFFSPRING
GREETINGS
I OBSERVE THE SIMILARITY
YES WE HAVE SIMILAR FACE BONES
THEY VISIT ONCE EVERY REVOLUTION TO UPDATE THE GROUP IMAGE
YOU REALLY DO HAVE SIMILAR FACE BONES
OBSERVE THEM FROM THE SIDE

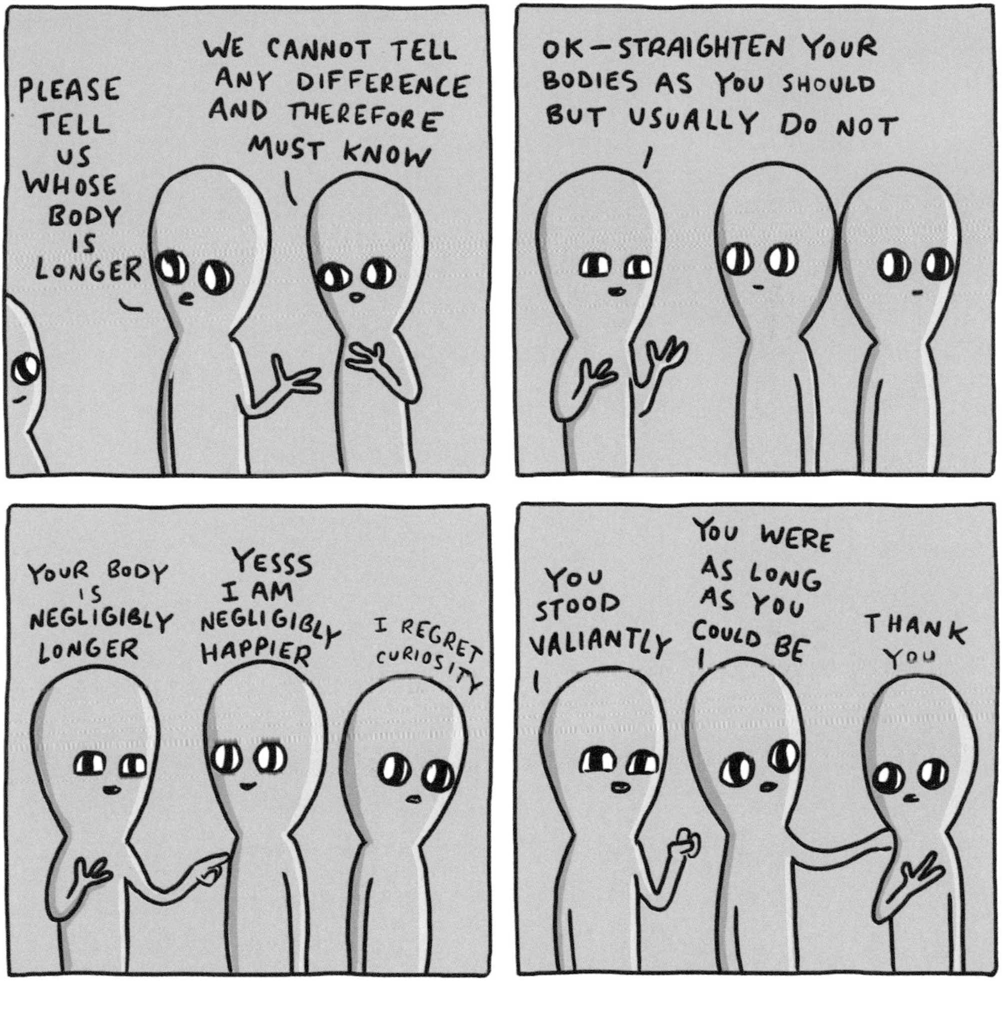
PLEASE TELL US WHOSE BODY IS LONGER
WE CANNOT TELL ANY DIFFERENCE AND THEREFORE MUST KNOW
OK—STRAIGHTEN YOUR BODIES AS YOU SHOULD BUT USUALLY DO NOT
YOUR BODY IS NEGLIGIBLY LONGER
YESSS I AM NEGLIGIBLY HAPPIER
I REGRET CURIOSITY
YOU STOOD VALIANTLY
YOU WERE AS LONG AS YOU COULD BE
THANK YOU

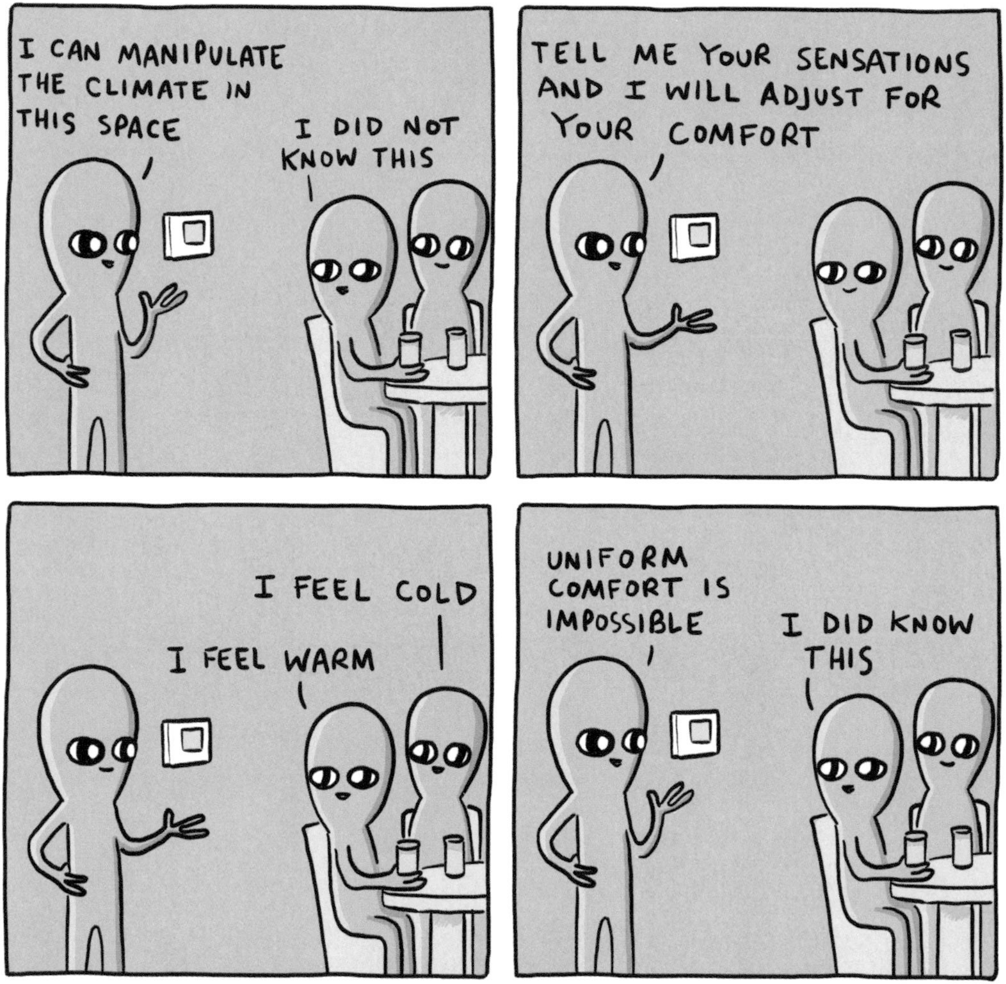
I CAN MANIPULATE THE CLIMATE IN THIS SPACE
I DID NOT KNOW THIS
TELL ME YOUR SENSATIONS AND I WILL ADJUST FOR YOUR COMFORT
I FEEL COLD
I FEEL WARM
UNIFORM COMFORT IS IMPOSSIBLE
I DID KNOW THIS

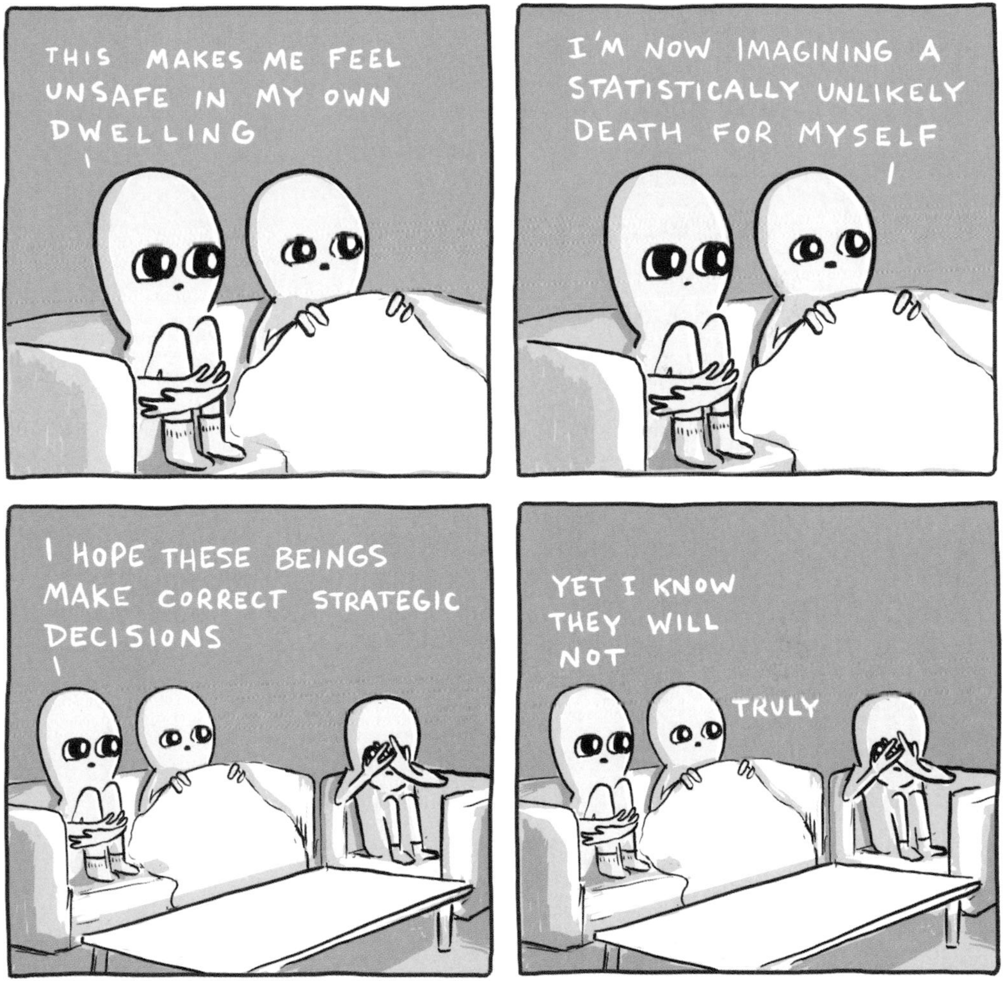
THIS MAKES ME FEEL UNSAFE IN MY OWN DWELLING
I'M NOW IMAGINING A STATISTICALLY UNLIKELY DEATH FOR MYSELF
I HOPE THESE BEINGS MAKE CORRECT STRATEGIC DECISIONS
YET I KNOW THEY WILL NOT
TRULY

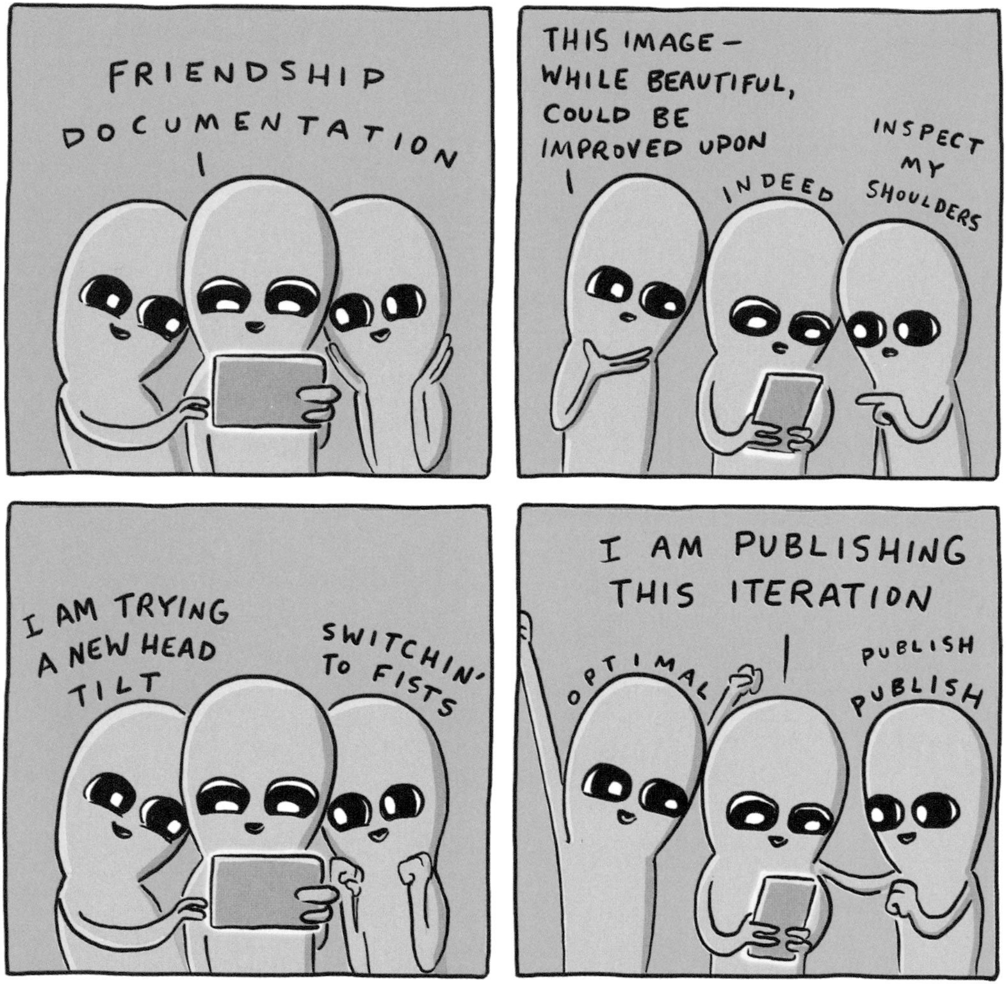
FRIENDSHIP DOCUMENTATION
THIS IMAGE— WHILE BEAUTIFUL, COULD BE IMPROVED UPON
INDEED
INSPECT MY SHOULDERS
I AM TRYING A NEW HEAD TILT
SWITCHIN' TO FISTS
I AM PUBLISHING THIS ITERATION
OPTIMAL
PUBLISH PUBLISH

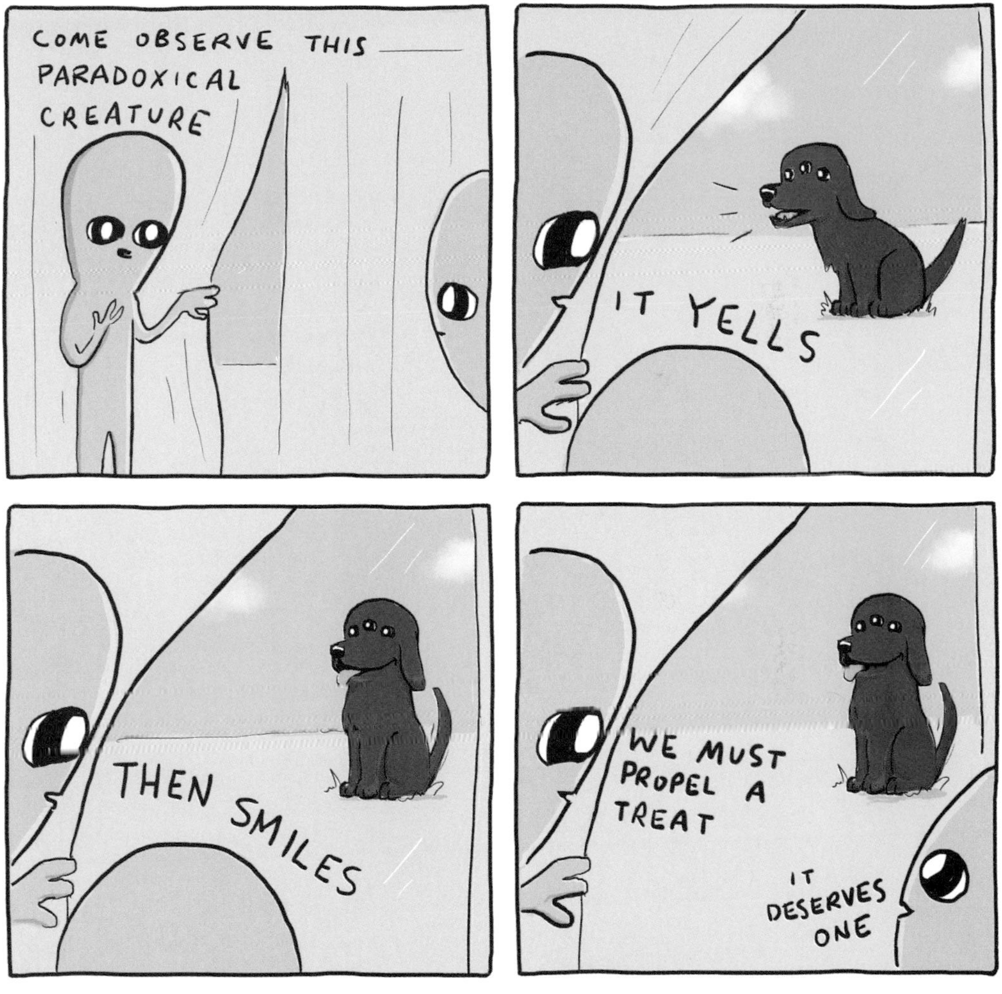
COME OBSERVE THIS PARADOXICAL CREATURE
IT YELLS
THEN SMILES
WE MUST PROPEL A TREAT
IT DESERVES ONE

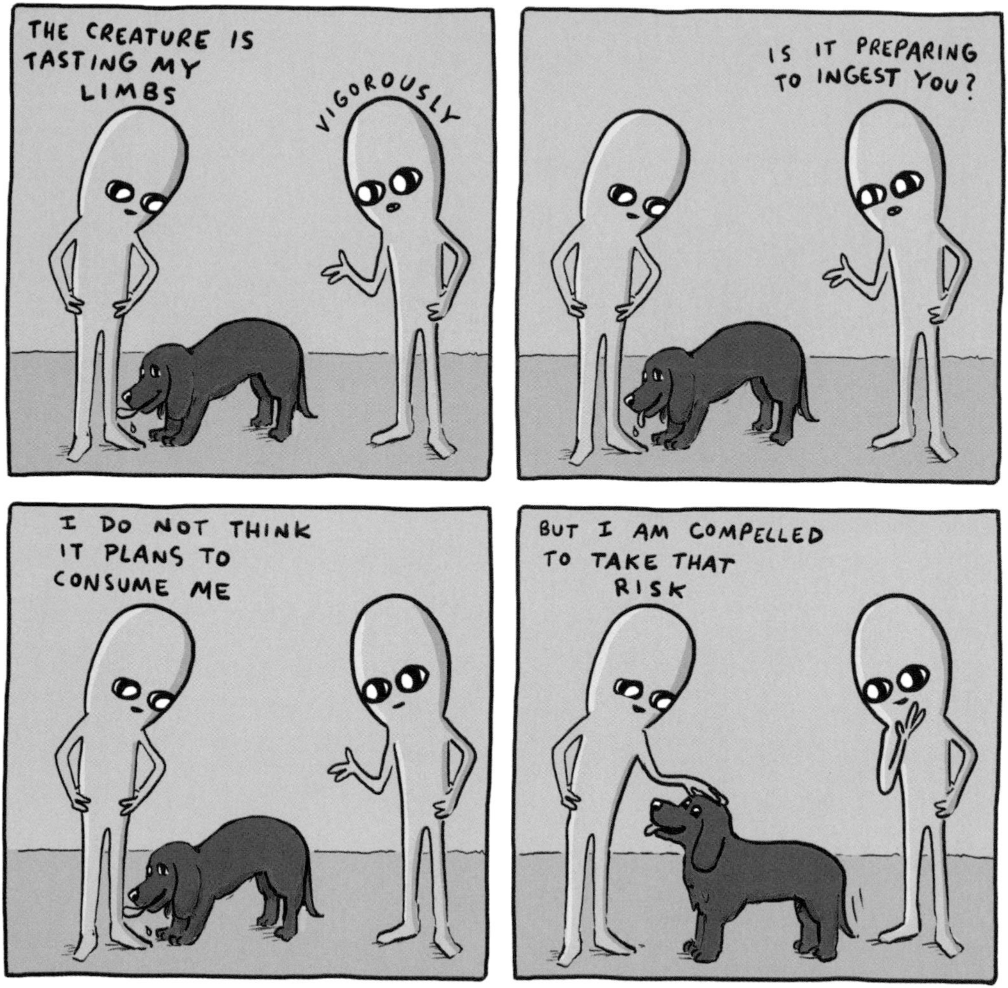
THE CREATURE IS TASTING MY LIMBS
VIGOROUSLY
IS IT PREPARING TO INGEST YOU?
I DO NOT THINK IT PLANS TO CONSUME ME
BUT I AM COMPELLED TO TAKE THAT RISK

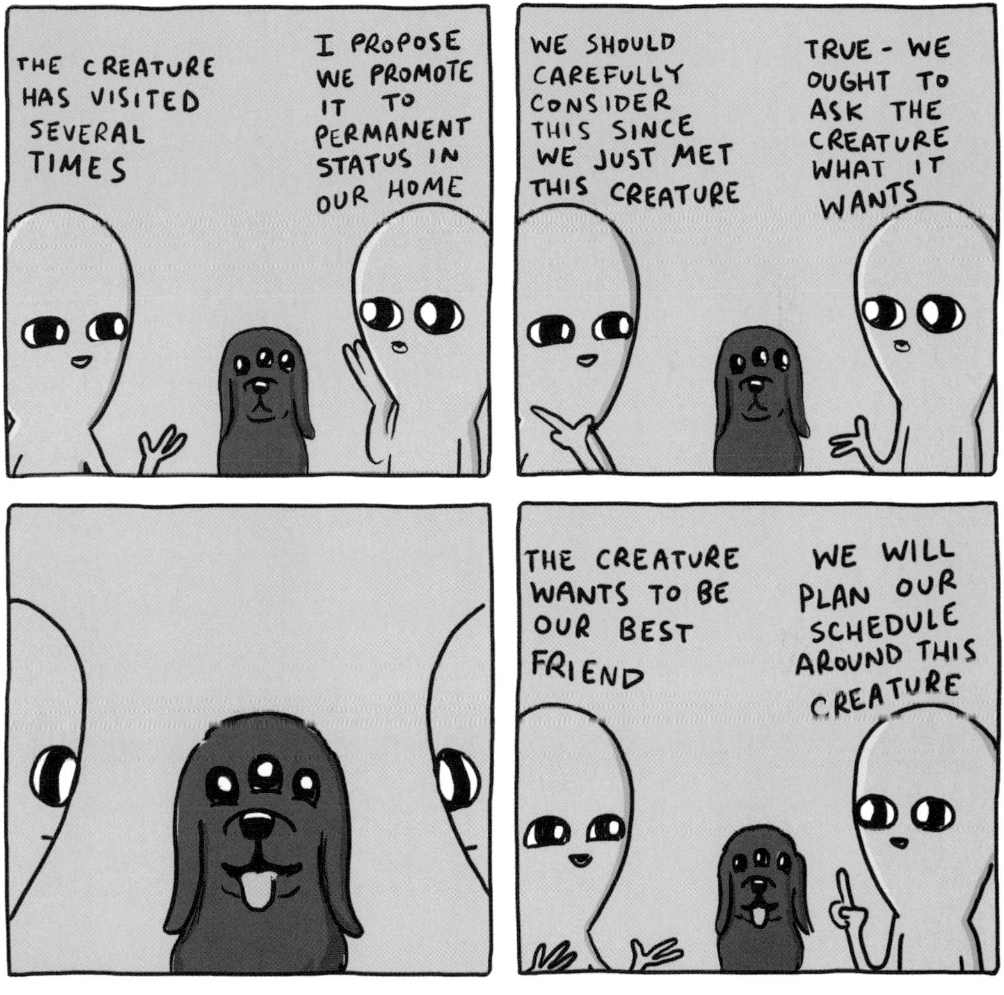
THE CREATURE HAS VISITED SEVERAL TIMES
I PROPOSE WE PROMOTE IT TO PERMANENT STATUS IN OUR HOME
WE SHOULD CAREFULLY CONSIDER THIS SINCE WE JUST MET THIS CREATURE
TRUE - WE OUGHT TO ASK THE CREATURE WHAT IT WANTS
THE CREATURE WANTS TO BE OUR BEST FRIEND
WE WILL PLAN OUR SCHEDULE AROUND THIS CREATURE

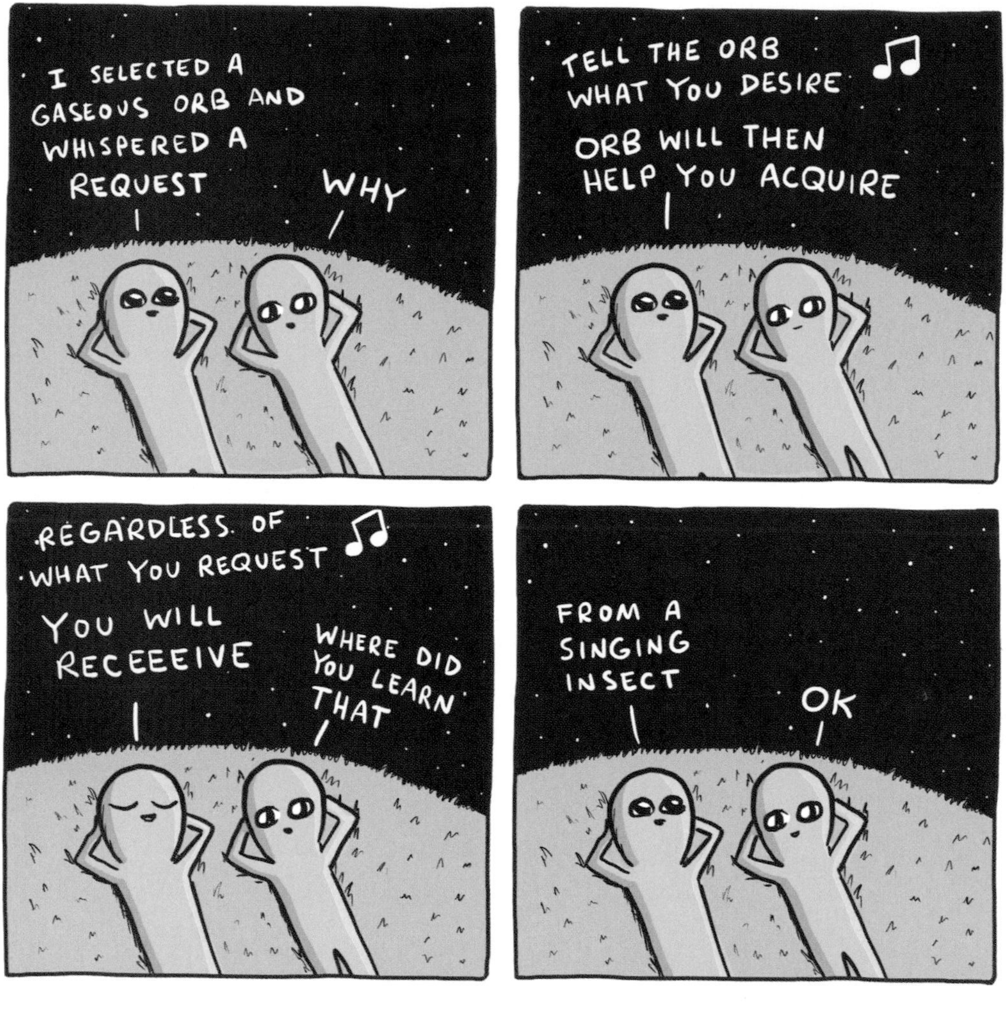
I SELECTED A GASEOUS ORB AND WHISPERED A REQUEST
WHY
TELL THE ORB WHAT YOU DESIRE
ORB WILL THEN HELP YOU ACQUIRE
REGARDLESS OF WHAT YOU REQUEST
YOU WILL RECEEEIVE
WHERE DID YOU LEARN THAT
FROM A SINGING INSECT
OK

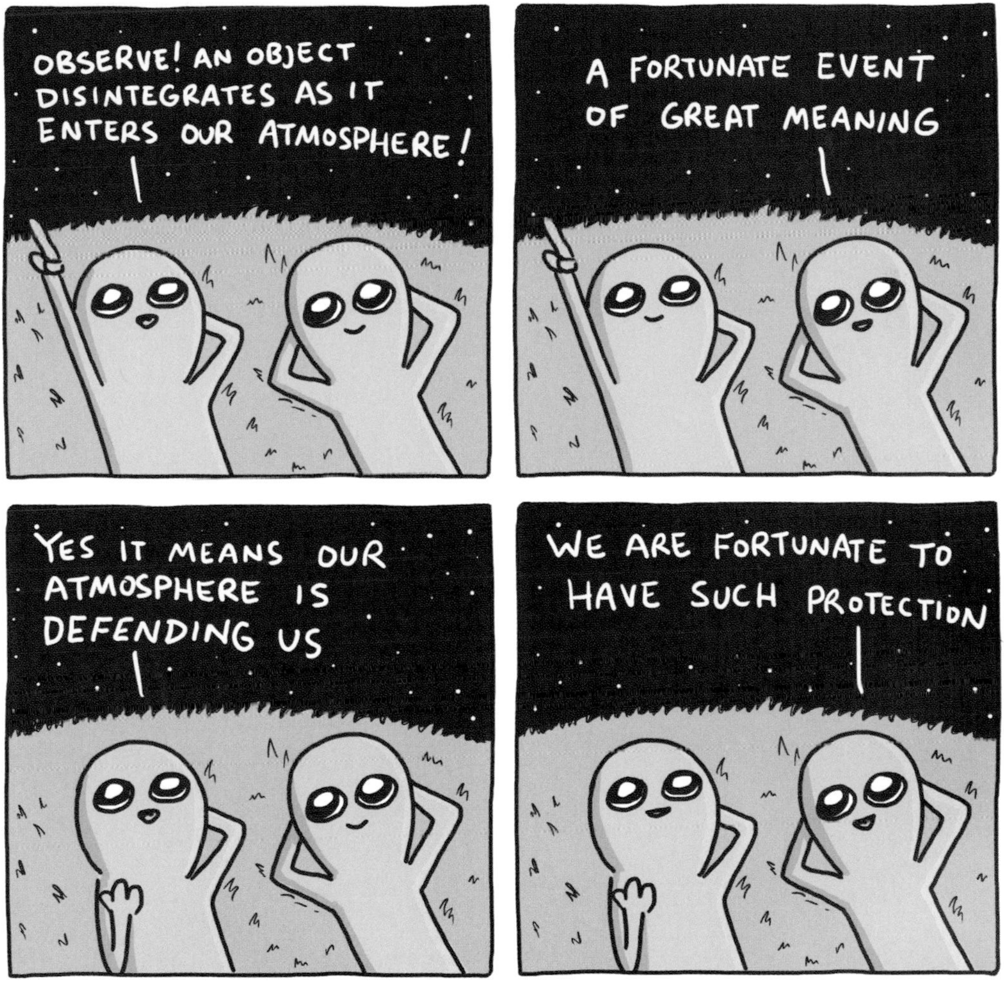
OBSERVE! AN OBJECT DISINTEGRATES AS IT ENTERS OUR ATMOSPHERE!
A FORTUNATE EVENT OF GREAT MEANING
YES IT MEANS OUR ATMOSPHERE IS DEFENDING US
WE ARE FORTUNATE TO HAVE SUCH PROTECTION

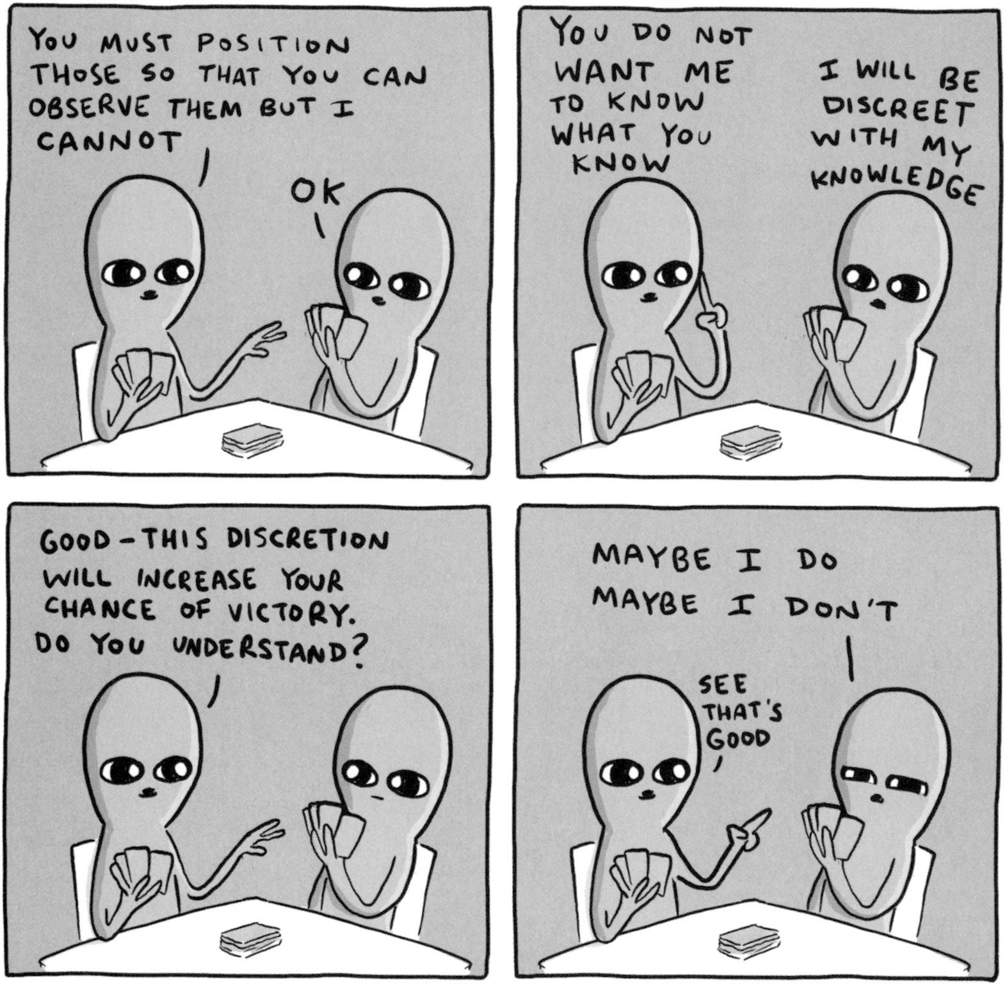
YOU MUST POSITION THOSE SO THAT YOU CAN OBSERVE THEM BUT I CANNOT
OK
YOU DO NOT WANT ME TO KNOW WHAT YOU KNOW
I WILL BE DISCREET WITH MY KNOWLEDGE
GOOD - THIS DISCRETION WILL INCREASE YOUR CHANCE OF VICTORY. DO YOU UNDERSTAND?
MAYBE I DO MAYBE I DON'T
SEE THAT'S GOOD

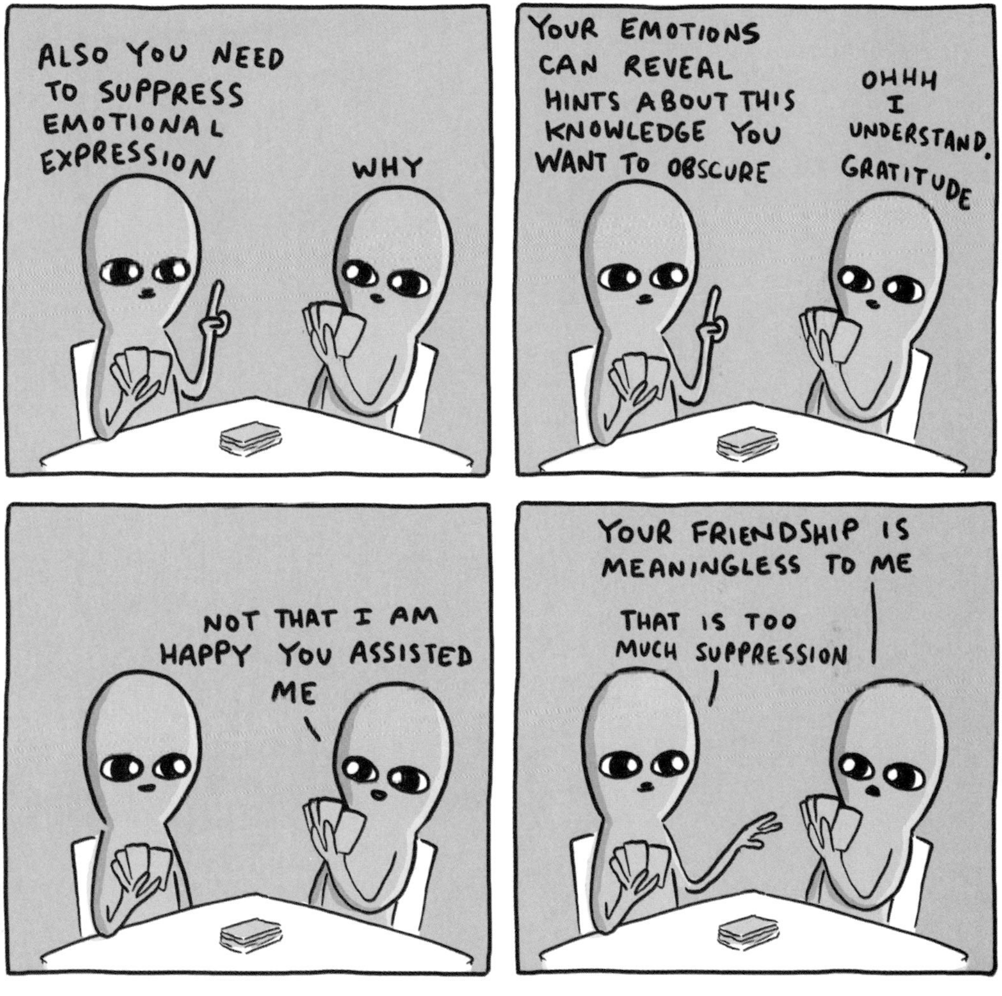
ALSO YOU NEED TO SUPPRESS EMOTIONAL EXPRESSION
WHY
YOUR EMOTIONS CAN REVEAL HINTS ABOUT THIS KNOWLEDGE YOU WANT TO OBSCURE
OHHH I UNDERSTAND.
GRATITUDE
NOT THAT I AM HAPPY YOU ASSISTED ME
YOUR FRIENDSHIP IS MEANINGLESS TO ME
THAT IS TOO MUCH SUPPRESSION

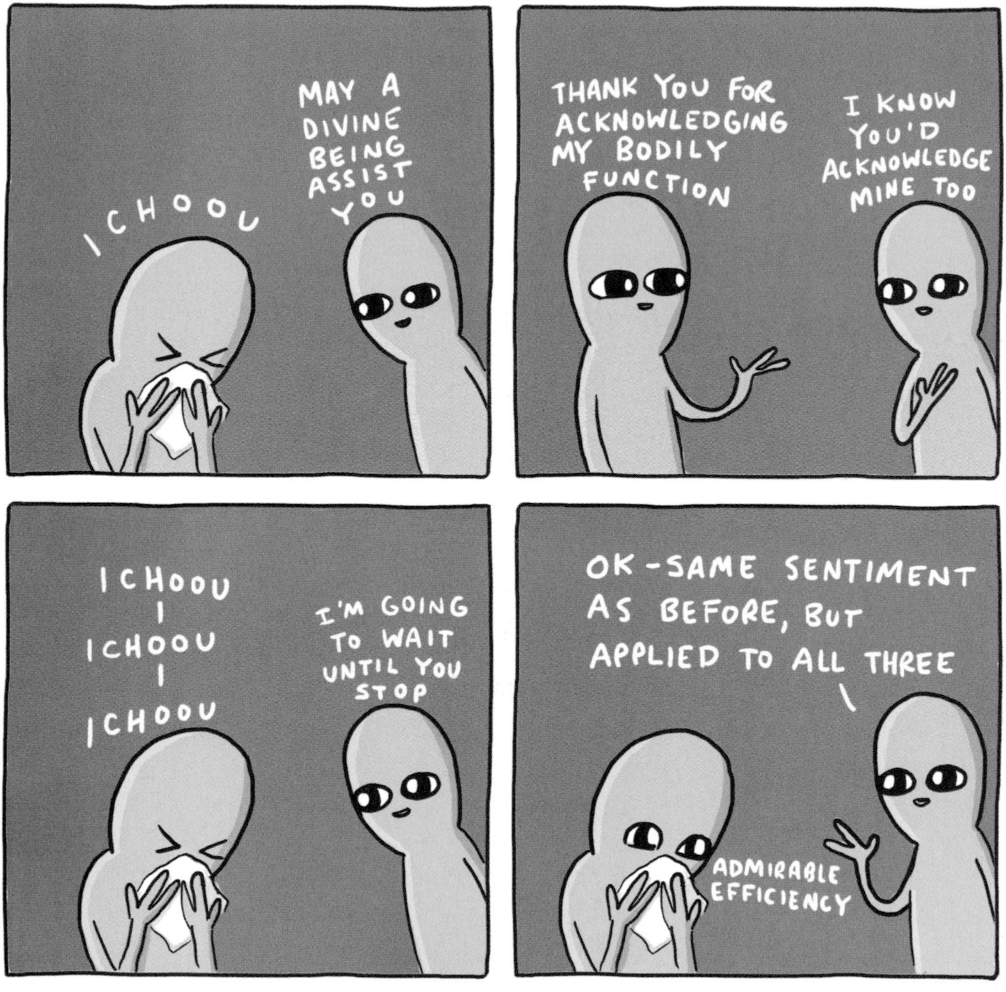
ICHOOU
MAY A DIVINE BEING ASSIST YOU
THANK YOU FOR ACKNOWLEDGING MY BODILY FUNCTION
I KNOW YOU'D ACKNOWLEDGE MINE TOO
ICHOOU
ICHOOU
ICHOOU
I'M GOING TO WAIT UNTIL YOU STOP
OK-SAME SENTIMENT AS BEFORE, BUT APPLIED TO ALL THREE
ADMIRABLE EFFICIENCY

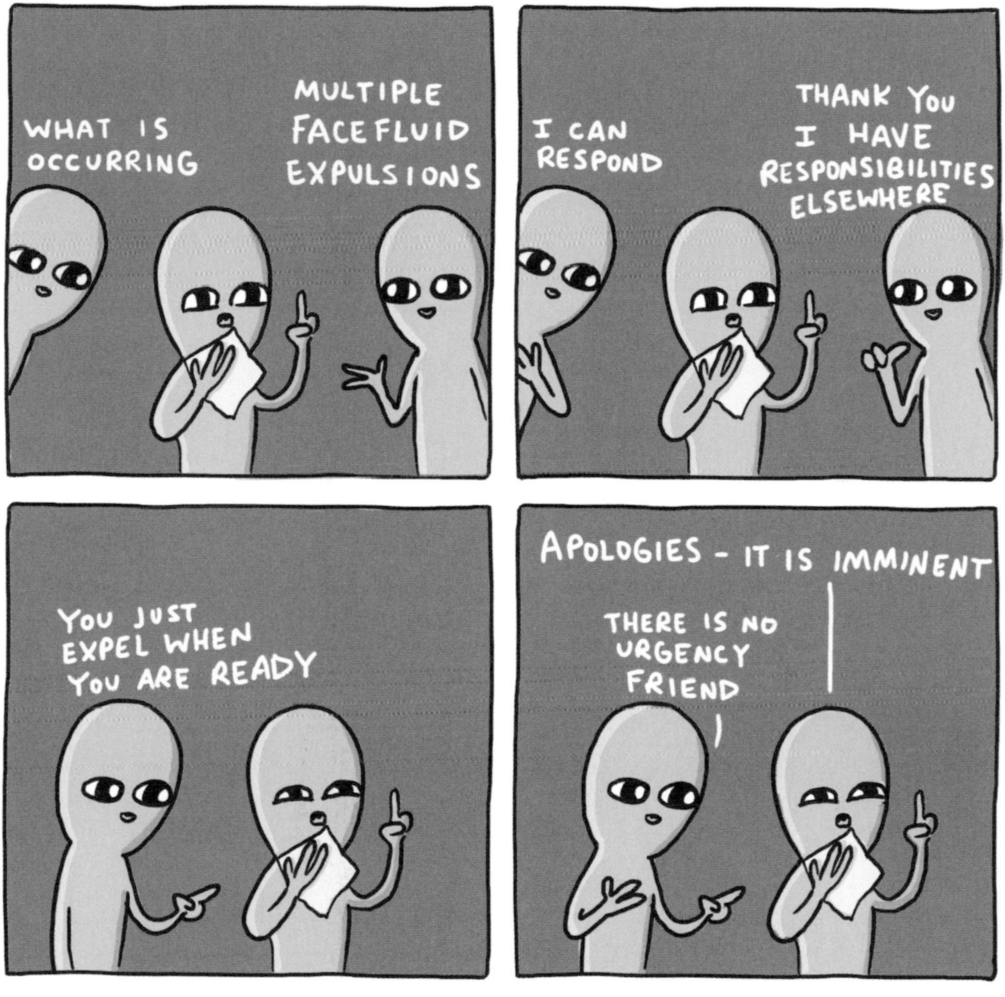
WHAT IS OCCURRING
MULTIPLE FACEFLUID EXPULSIONS
I CAN RESPOND
THANK YOU I HAVE RESPONSIBILITIES ELSEWHERE
YOU JUST EXPEL WHEN YOU ARE READY
APOLOGIES - IT IS IMMINENT
THERE IS NO URGENCY FRIEND

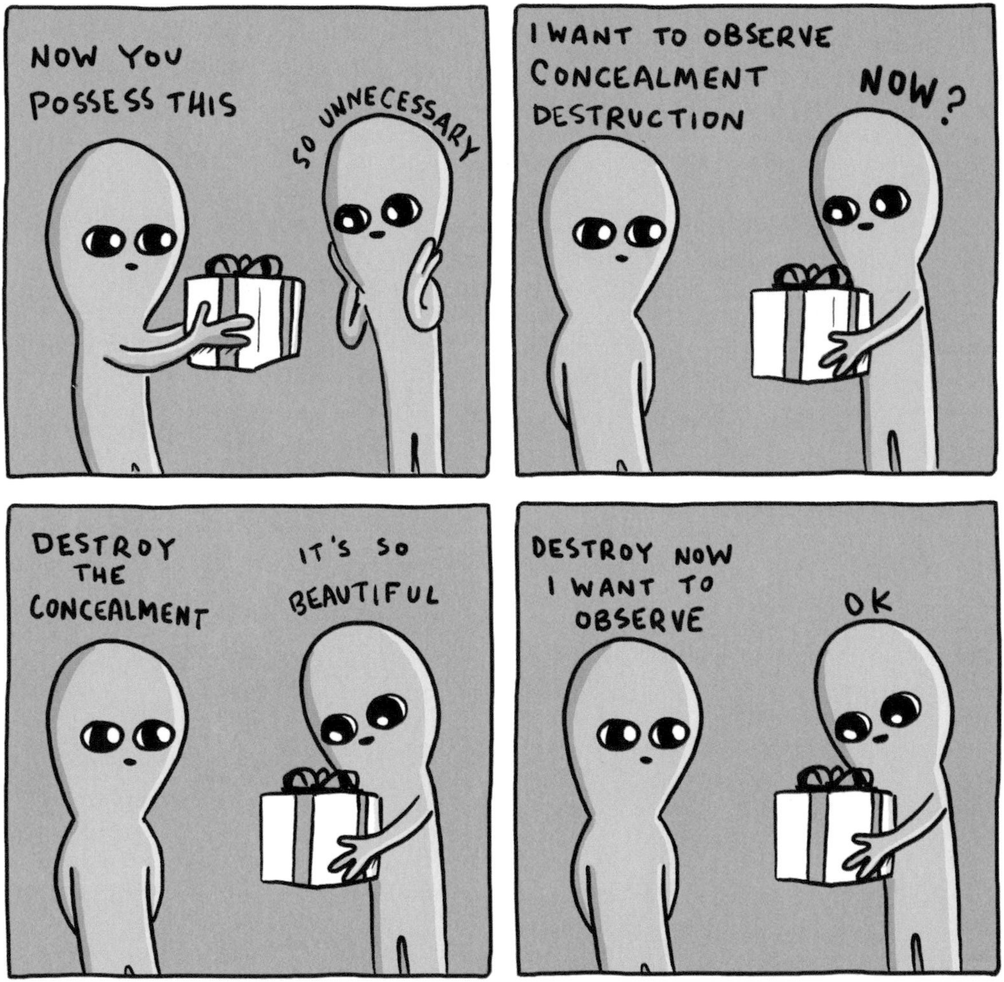
NOW YOU POSSESS THIS
SO UNNECESSARY
I WANT TO OBSERVE CONCEALMENT DESTRUCTION
NOW?
DESTROY THE CONCEALMENT
IT'S SO BEAUTIFUL
DESTROY NOW I WANT TO OBSERVE
OK

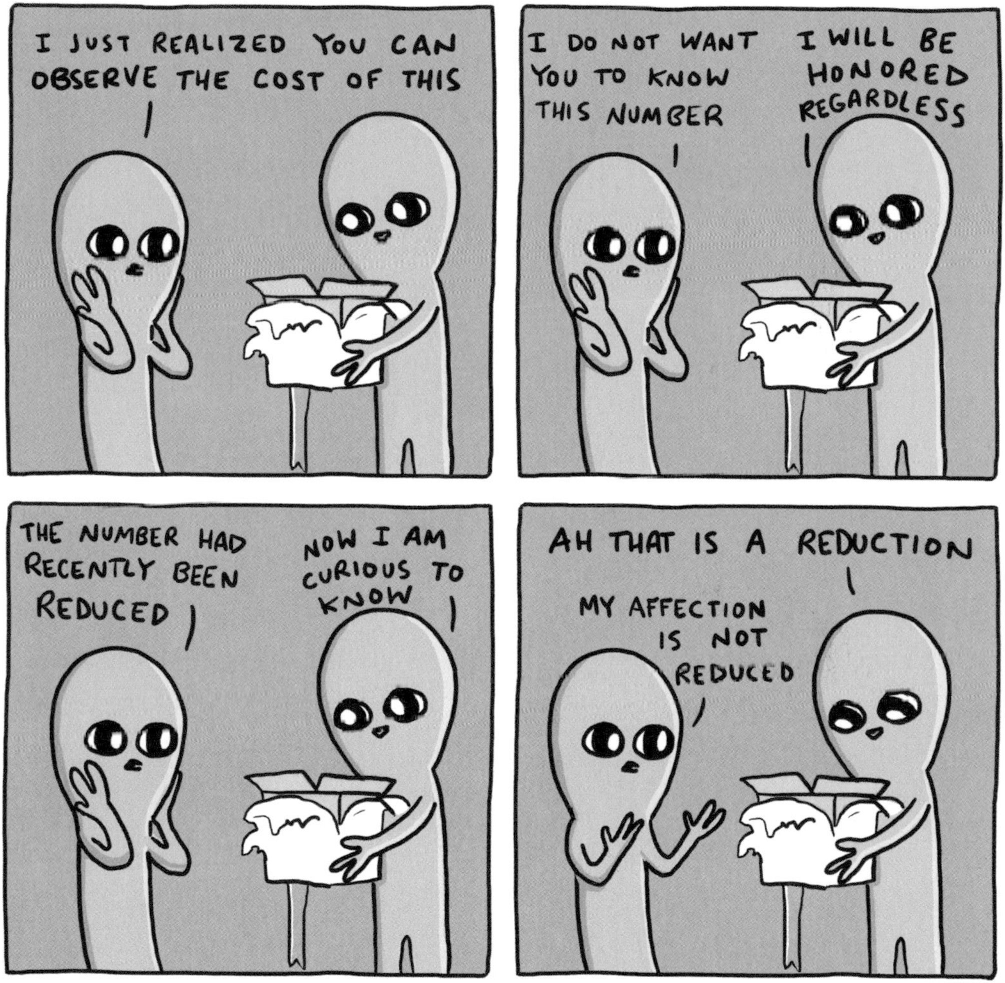
I JUST REALIZED YOU CAN OBSERVE THE COST OF THIS
I DO NOT WANT YOU TO KNOW THIS NUMBER
I WILL BE HONORED REGARDLESS
THE NUMBER HAD RECENTLY BEEN REDUCED
NOW I AM CURIOUS TO KNOW
AH THAT IS A REDUCTION
MY AFFECTION IS NOT REDUCED

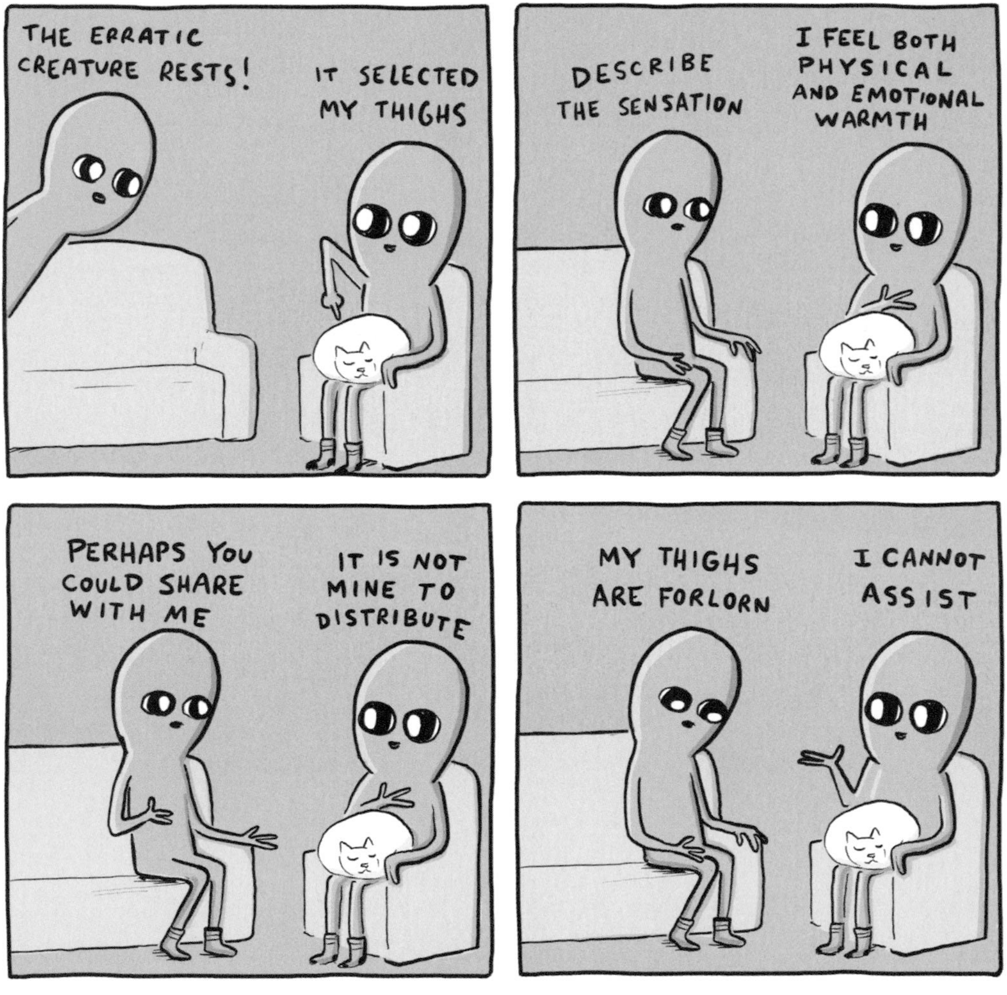
THE ERRATIC CREATURE RESTS!
IT SELECTED MY THIGHS
DESCRIBE THE SENSATION
I FEEL BOTH PHYSICAL AND EMOTIONAL WARMTH
PERHAPS YOU COULD SHARE WITH ME
IT IS NOT MINE TO DISTRIBUTE
MY THIGHS ARE FORLORN
I CANNOT ASSIST

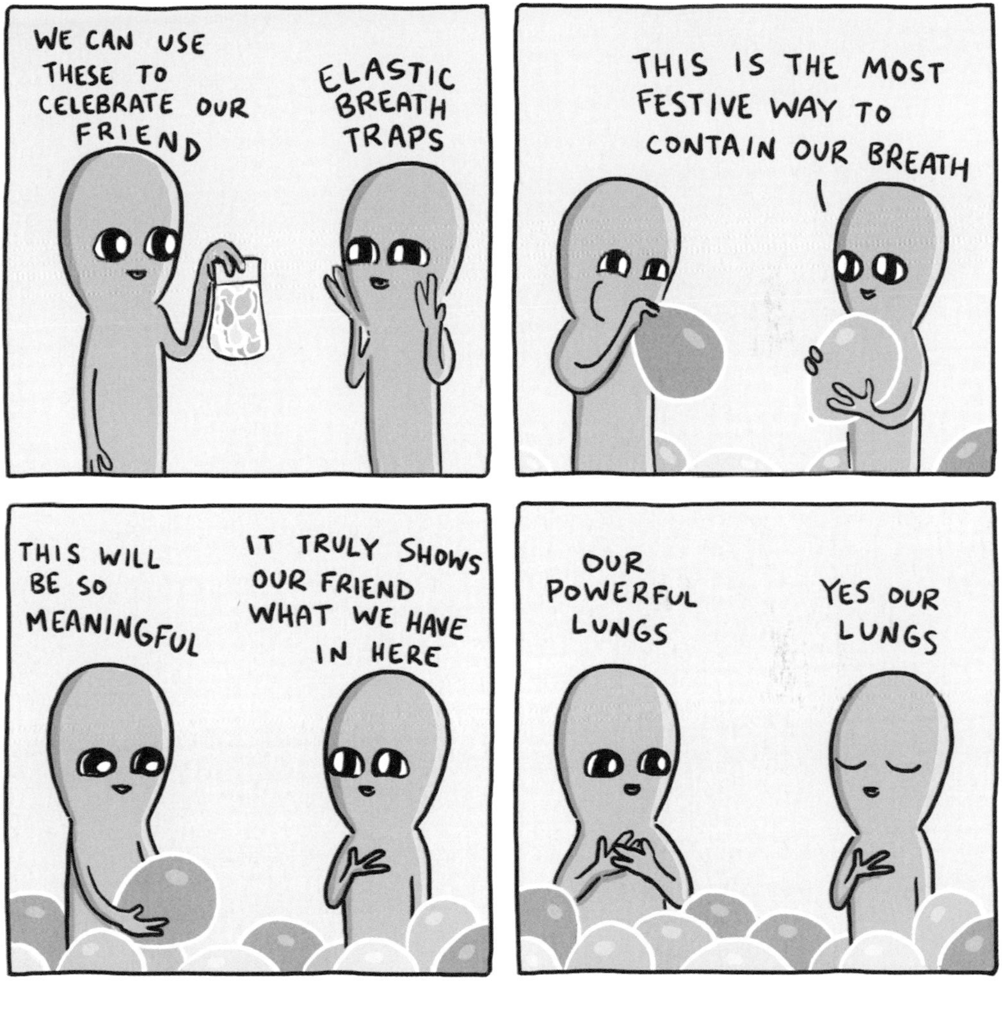
WE CAN USE THESE TO CELEBRATE OUR FRIEND
ELASTIC BREATH TRAPS
THIS IS THE MOST FESTIVE WAY TO CONTAIN OUR BREATH
THIS WILL BE SO MEANINGFUL
IT TRULY SHOWS OUR FRIEND WHAT WE HAVE IN HERE
OUR POWERFUL LUNGS
YES OUR LUNGS

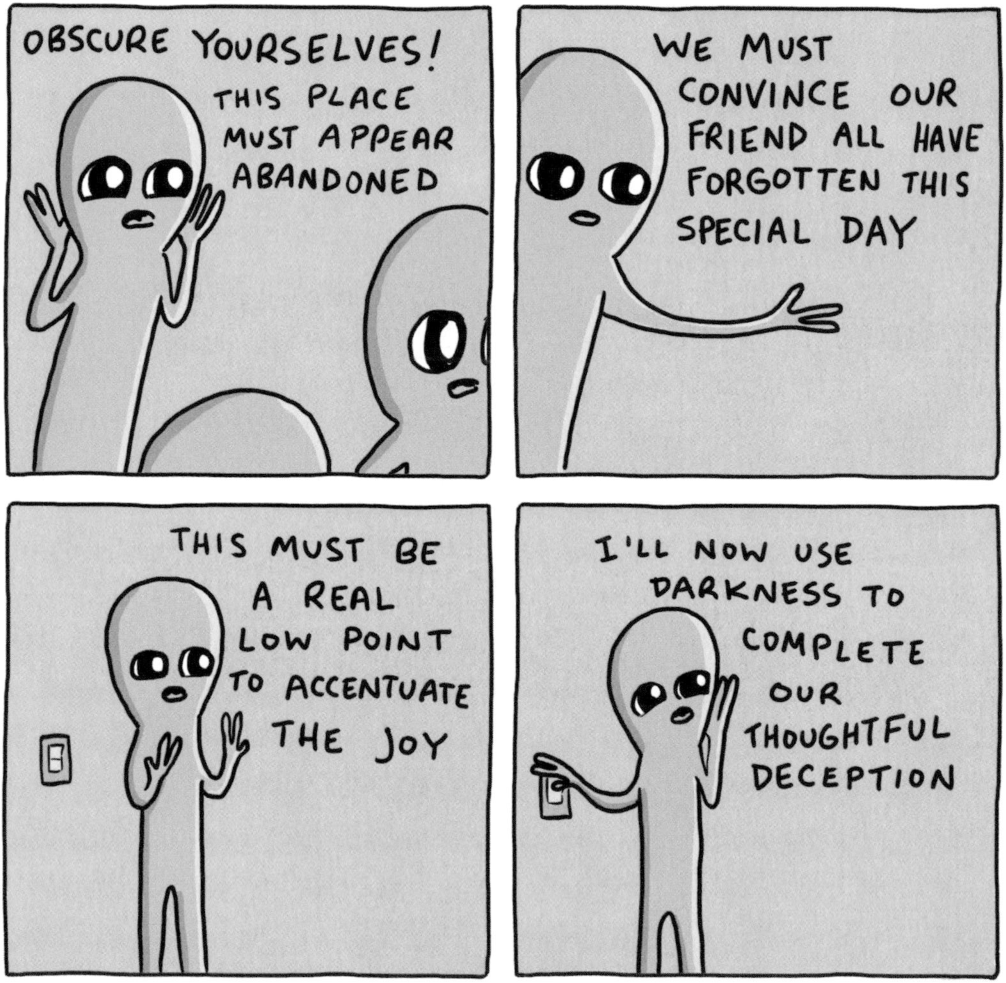
OBSCURE YOURSELVES! THIS PLACE MUST APPEAR ABANDONED
WE MUST CONVINCE OUR FRIEND ALL HAVE FORGOTTEN THIS SPECIAL DAY
THIS MUST BE A REAL LOW POINT TO ACCENTUATE THE JOY
I'LL NOW USE DARKNESS TO COMPLETE OUR THOUGHTFUL DECEPTION

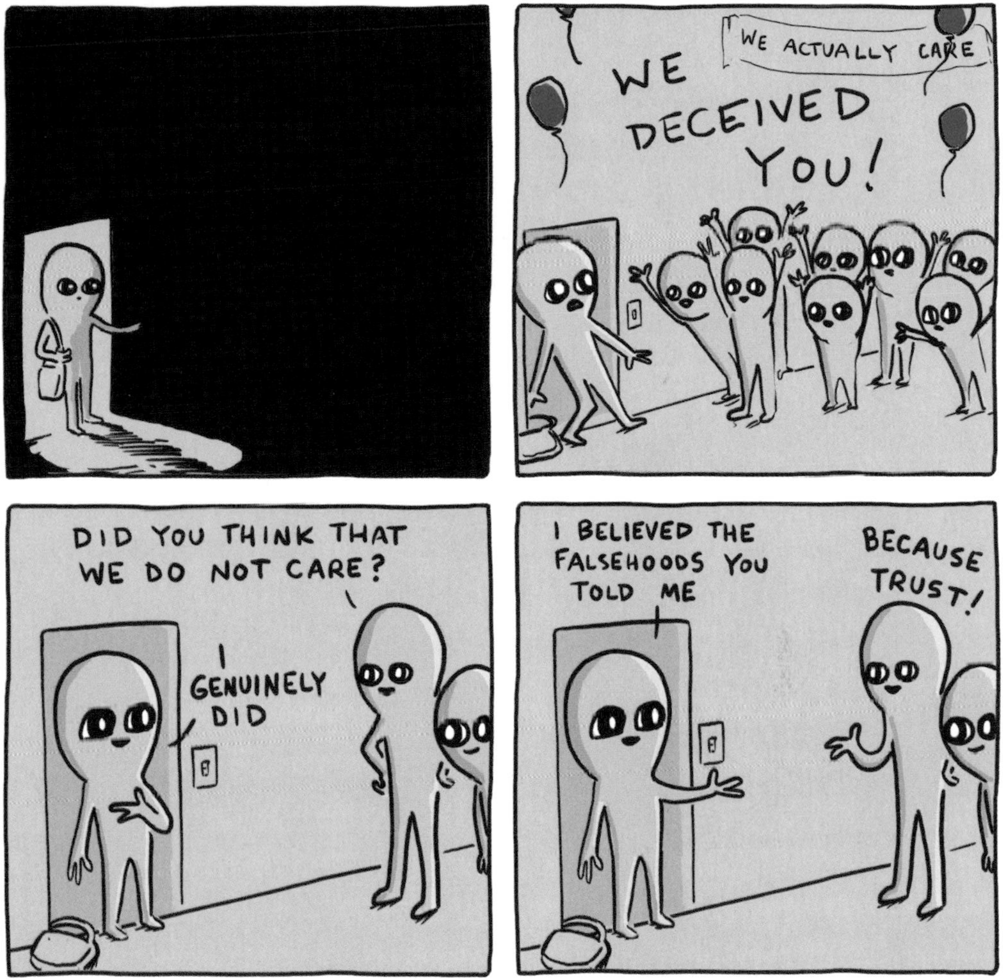
WE ACTUALLY CARE
WE DECEIVED YOU!
DID YOU THINK THAT WE DO NOT CARE?
I GENUINELY DID
I BELIEVED THE FALSEHOODS YOU TOLD ME
BECAUSE TRUST!

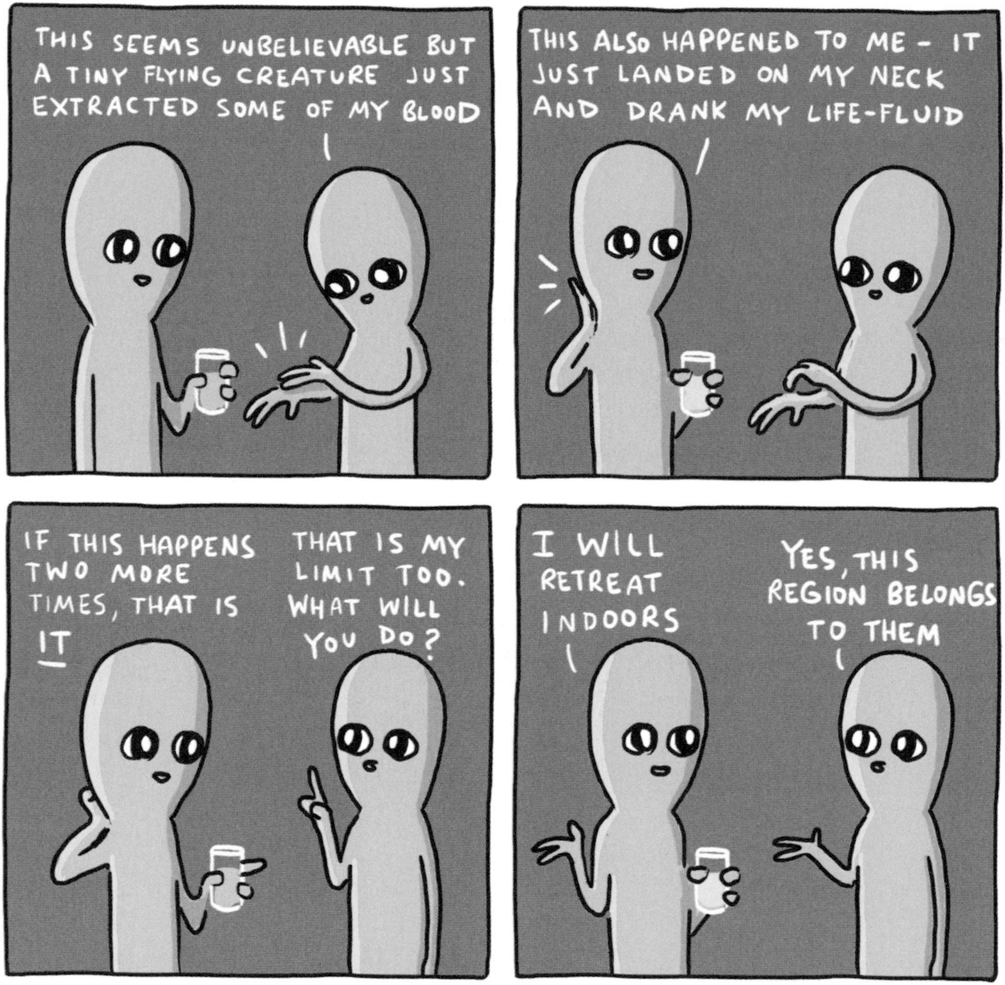
THIS SEEMS UNBELIEVABLE BUT A TINY FLYING CREATURE JUST EXTRACTED SOME OF MY BLOOD
THIS ALSO HAPPENED TO ME - IT JUST LANDED ON MY NECK AND DRANK MY LIFE-FLUID
IF THIS HAPPENS TWO MORE TIMES, THAT IS IT
THAT IS MY LIMIT TOO. WHAT WILL YOU DO?
I WILL RETREAT INDOORS
YES, THIS REGION BELONGS TO THEM

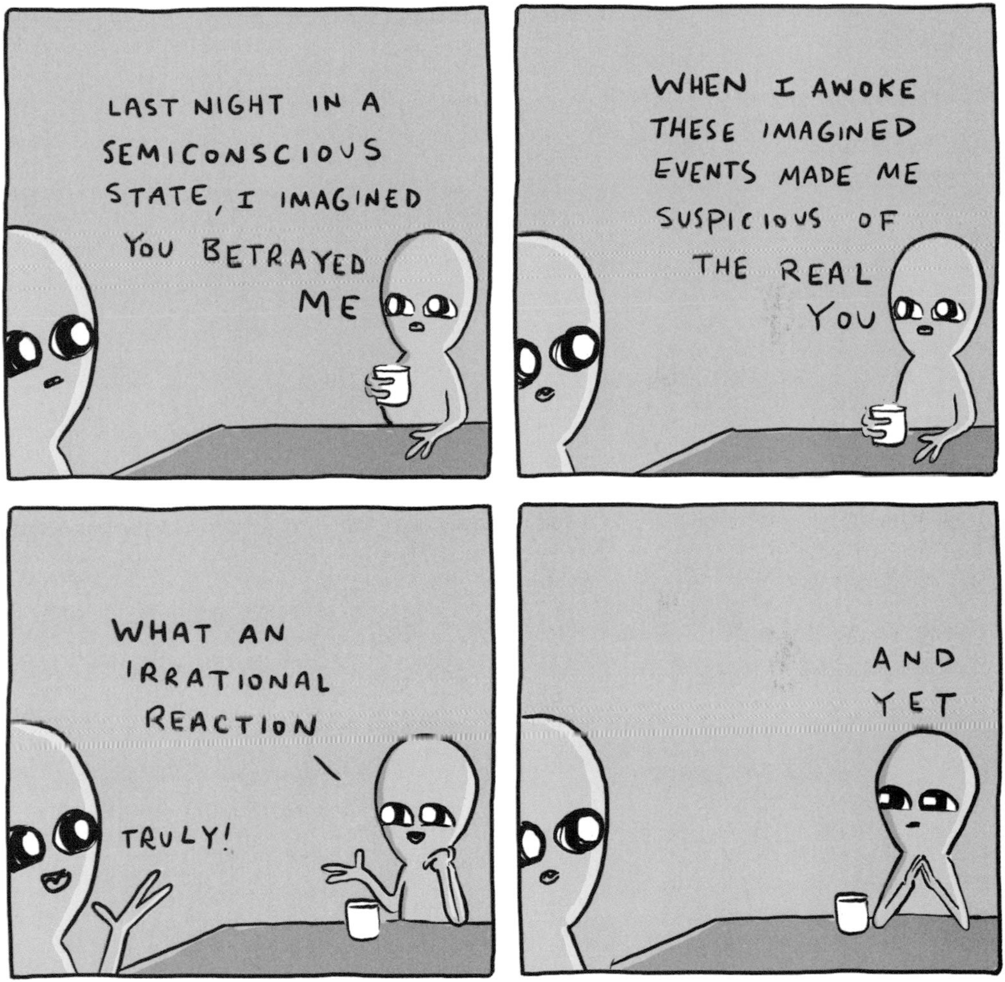
LAST NIGHT IN A SEMICONSCIOUS STATE, I IMAGINED YOU BETRAYED ME
WHEN I AWOKE THESE IMAGINED EVENTS MADE ME SUSPICIOUS OF THE REAL YOU
WHAT AN IRRATIONAL REACTION
TRULY!
AND YET

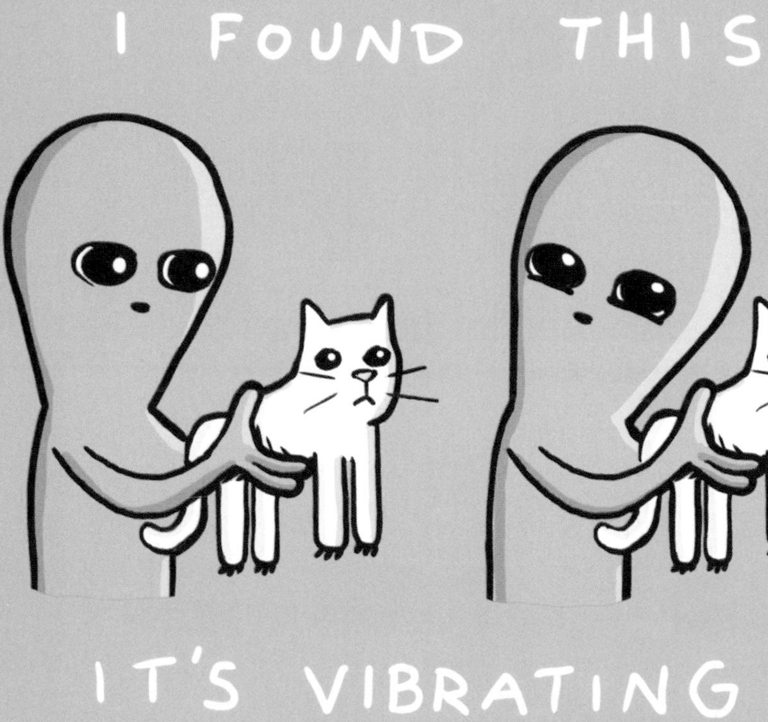
I FOUND THIS
IT'S VIBRATING

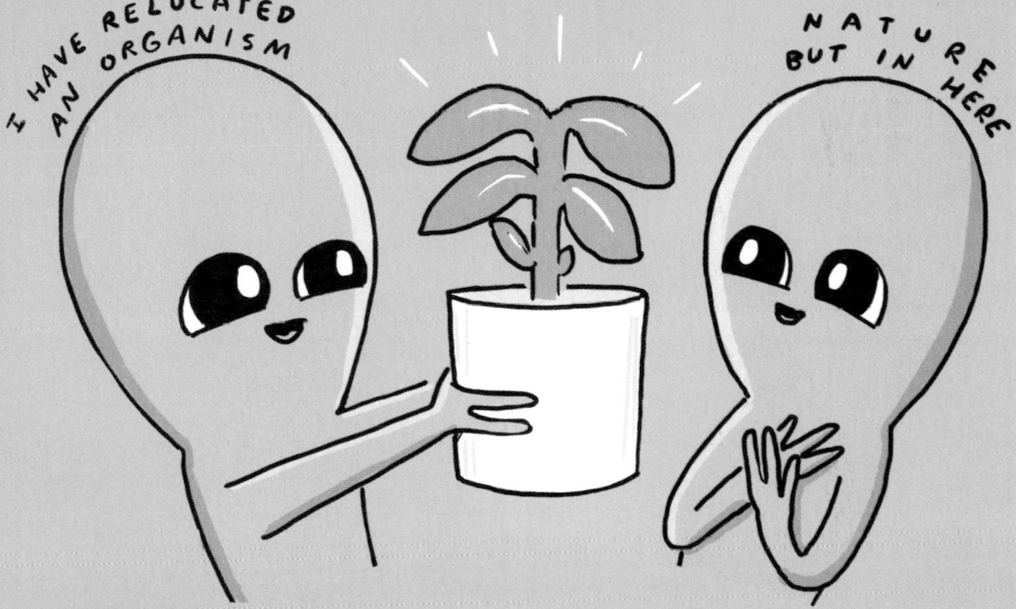
I HAVE RELOCATED AN ORGANISM
NATURE BUT IN HERE

ADULTHOOD

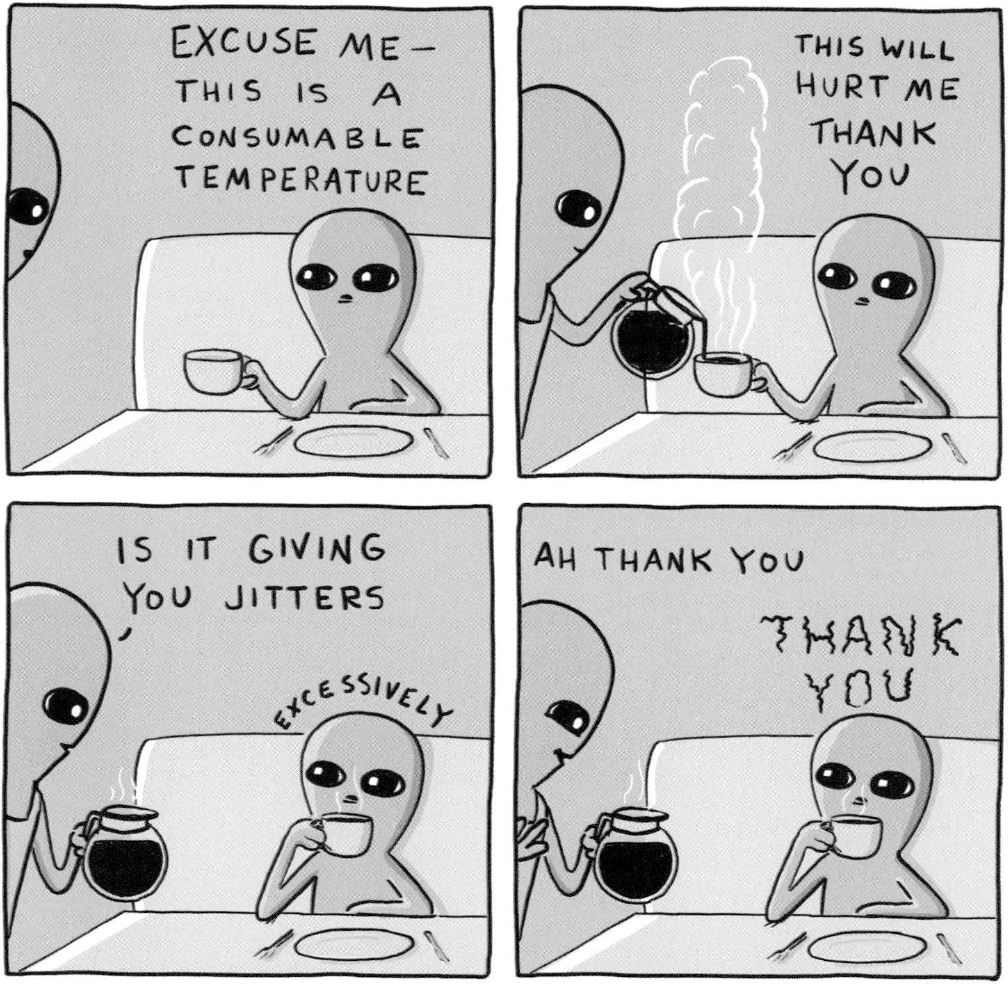
EXCUSE ME—
THIS IS A
CONSUMABLE
TEMPERATURE
THIS WILL
HURT ME
THANK
YOU
IS IT GIVING
YOU JITTERS
EXCESSIVELY
AH THANK YOU
THANK
YOU

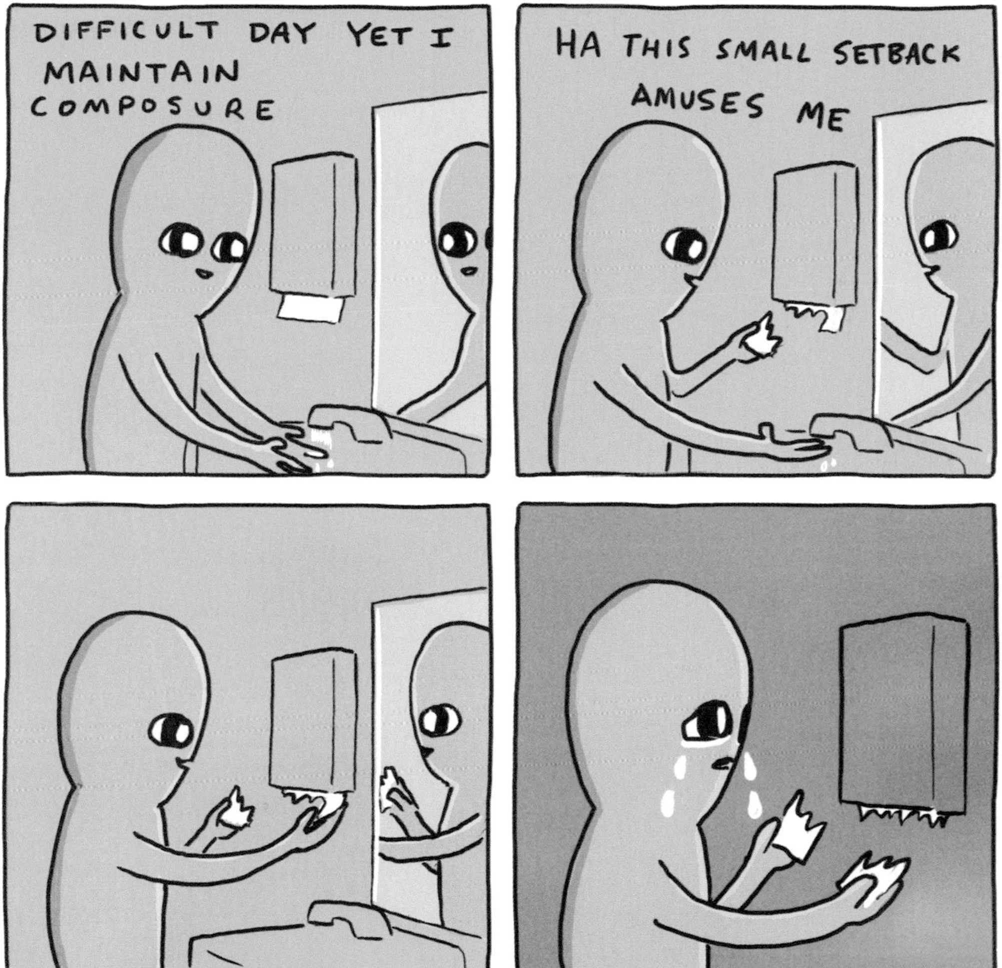
DIFFICULT DAY YET I MAINTAIN COMPOSURE
HA THIS SMALL SETBACK AMUSES ME

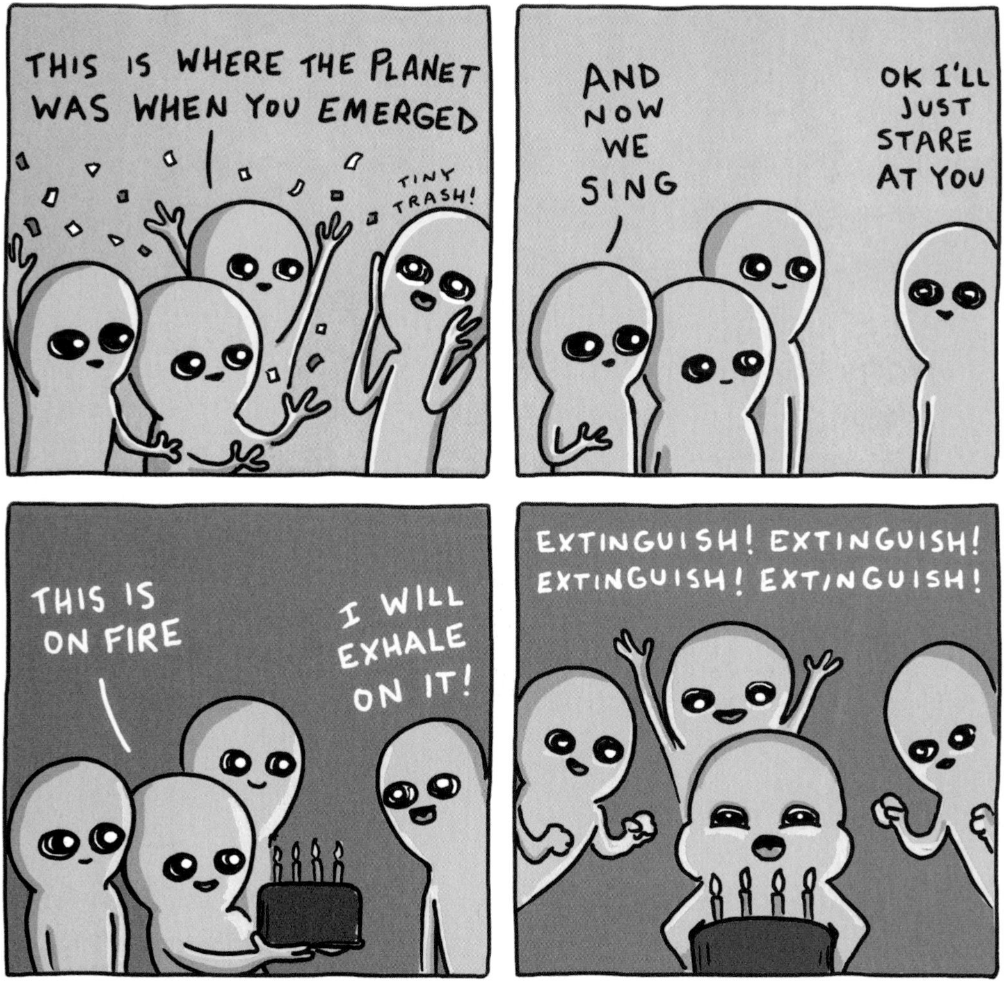

THIS IS WHERE THE PLANET WAS WHEN YOU EMERGED
TINY TRASH!
AND NOW WE SING
OK I'LL JUST STARE AT YOU
THIS IS ON FIRE
I WILL EXHALE ON IT!
EXTINGUISH! EXTINGUISH! EXTINGUISH! EXTINGUISH!

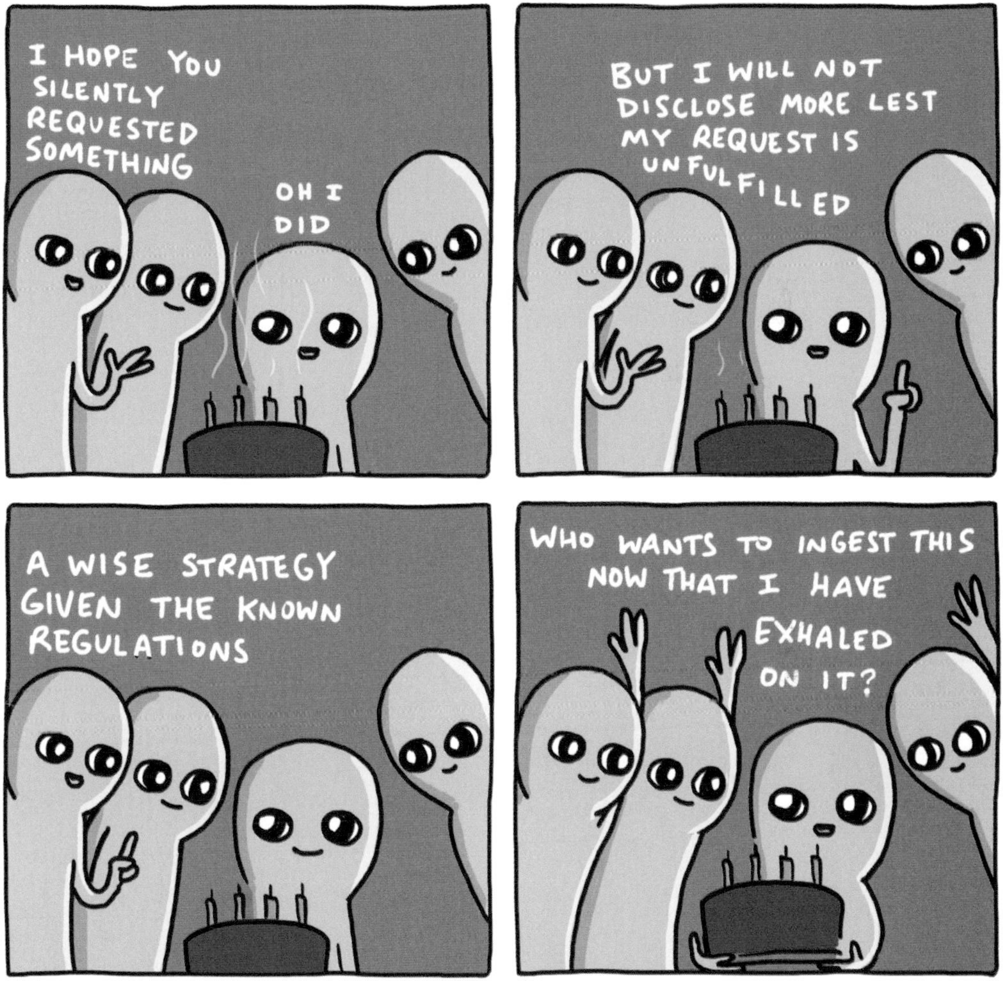
I HOPE YOU SILENTLY REQUESTED SOMETHING
OH I DID
BUT I WILL NOT DISCLOSE MORE LEST MY REQUEST IS UNFULFILLED
A WISE STRATEGY GIVEN THE KNOWN REGULATIONS
WHO WANTS TO INGEST THIS NOW THAT I HAVE EXHALED ON IT?

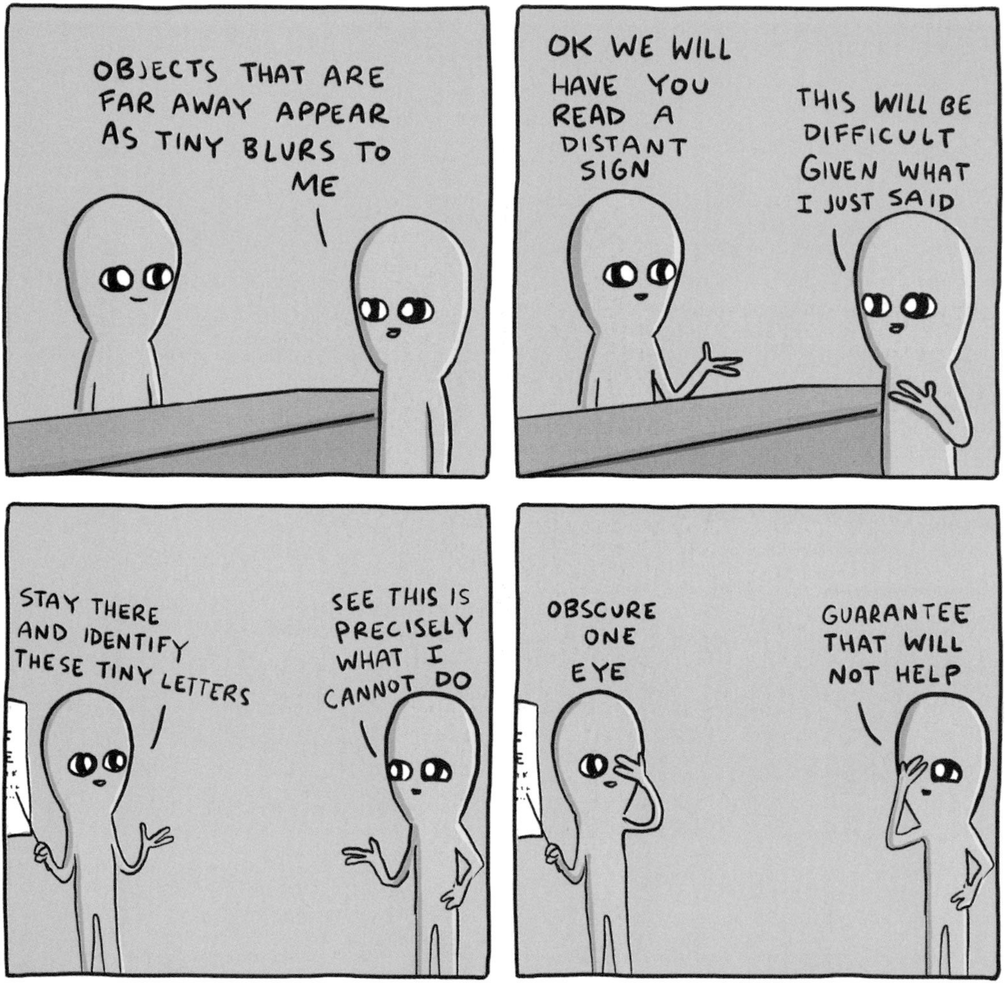
OBJECTS THAT ARE FAR AWAY APPEAR AS TINY BLURS TO ME
OK WE WILL HAVE YOU READ A DISTANT SIGN
THIS WILL BE DIFFICULT GIVEN WHAT I JUST SAID
STAY THERE AND IDENTIFY THESE TINY LETTERS
SEE THIS IS PRECISELY WHAT I CANNOT DO
OBSCURE ONE EYE
GUARANTEE THAT WILL NOT HELP

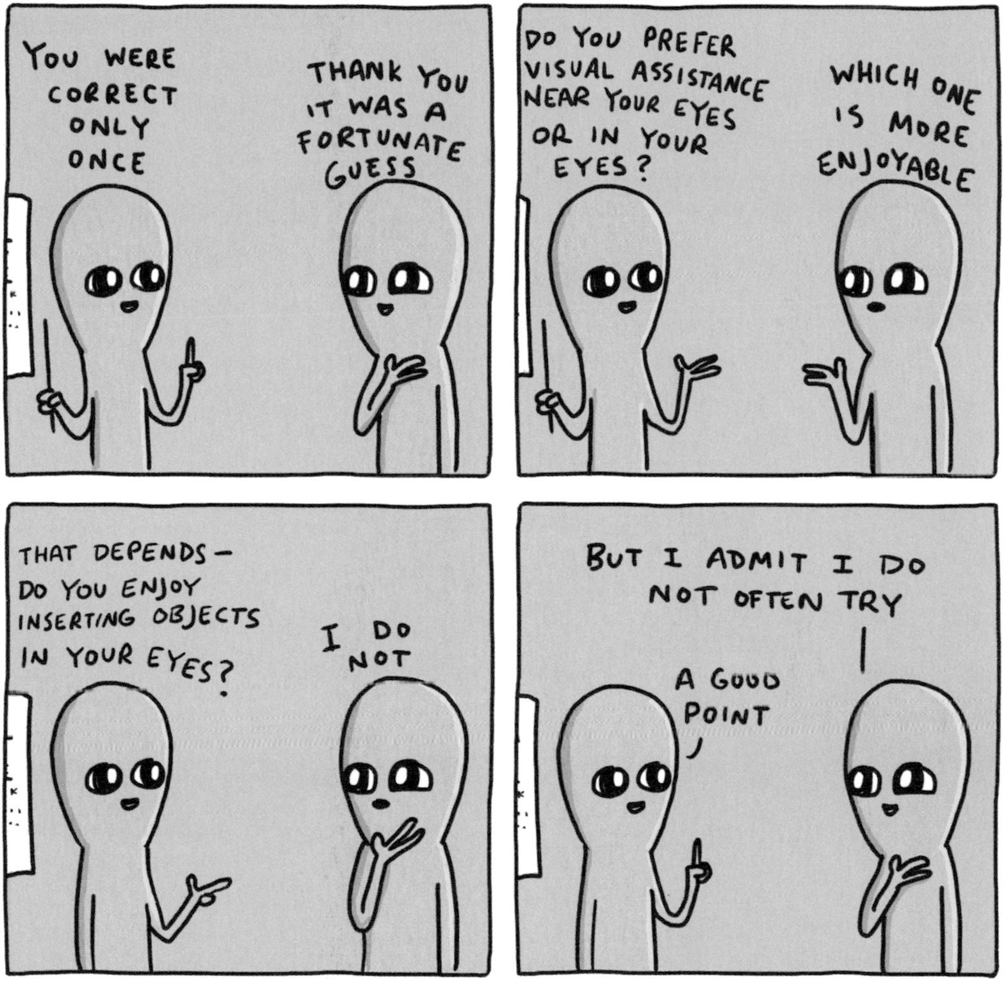

YOU WERE CORRECT ONLY ONCE
THANK YOU IT WAS A FORTUNATE GUESS
DO YOU PREFER VISUAL ASSISTANCE NEAR YOUR EYES OR IN YOUR EYES?
WHICH ONE IS MORE ENJOYABLE
THAT DEPENDS- DO YOU ENJOY INSERTING OBJECTS IN YOUR EYES?
I DO NOT
A GOOD POINT
BUT I ADMIT I DO NOT OFTEN TRY

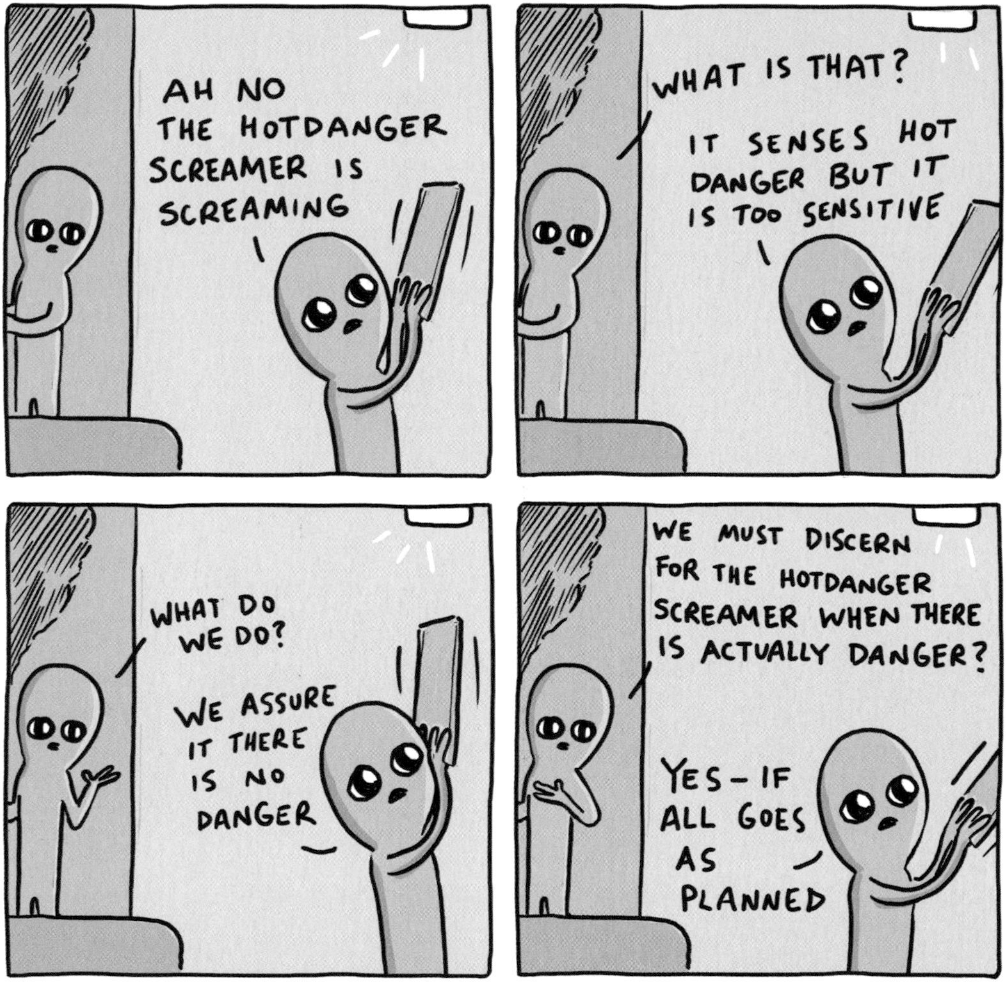
AH NO
THE HOTDANGER
SCREAMER IS
SCREAMING
WHAT IS THAT?
IT SENSES HOT
DANGER BUT IT
IS TOO SENSITIVE
WHAT DO
WE DO?
WE ASSURE
IT THERE
IS NO
DANGER
WE MUST DISCERN
FOR THE HOTDANGER
SCREAMER WHEN THERE
IS ACTUALLY DANGER?
YES - IF
ALL GOES
AS
PLANNED

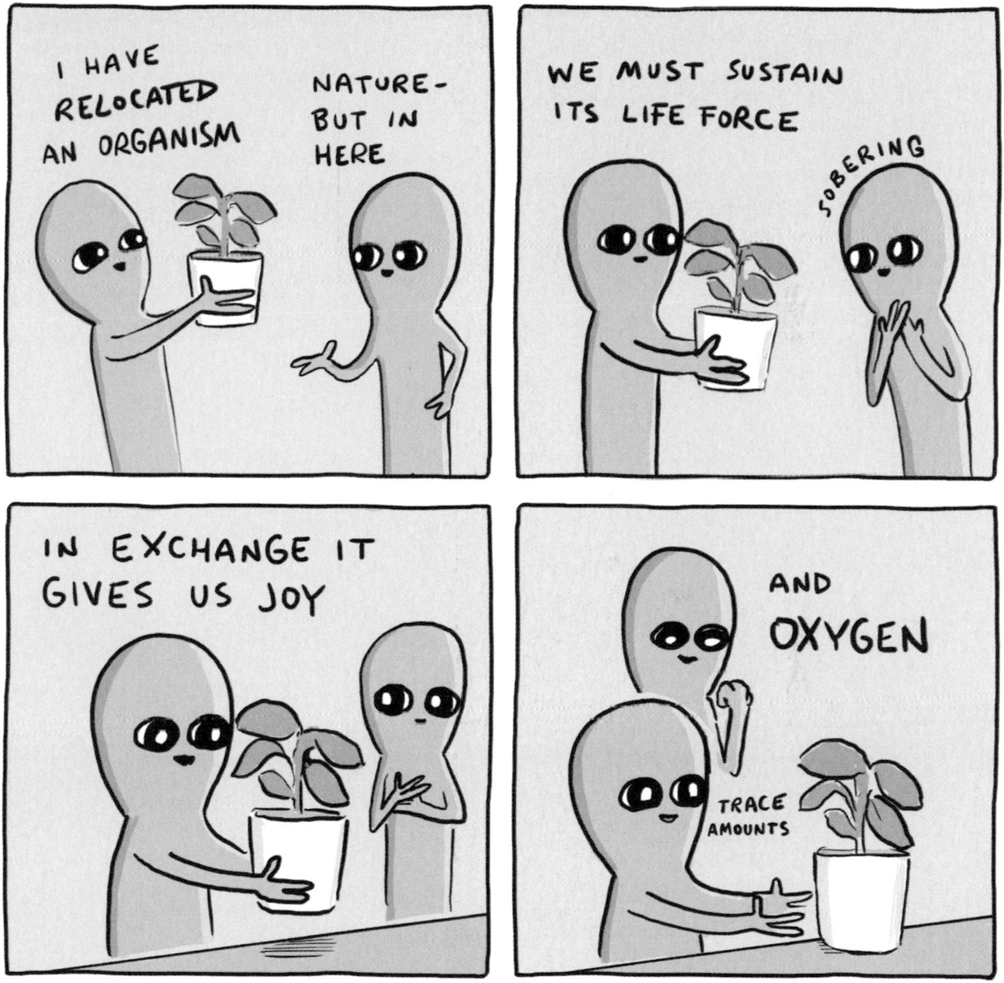
I HAVE RELOCATED AN ORGANISM
NATURE- BUT IN HERE
WE MUST SUSTAIN ITS LIFE FORCE
SOBERING
IN EXCHANGE IT GIVES US JOY
AND
OXYGEN
TRACE AMOUNTS

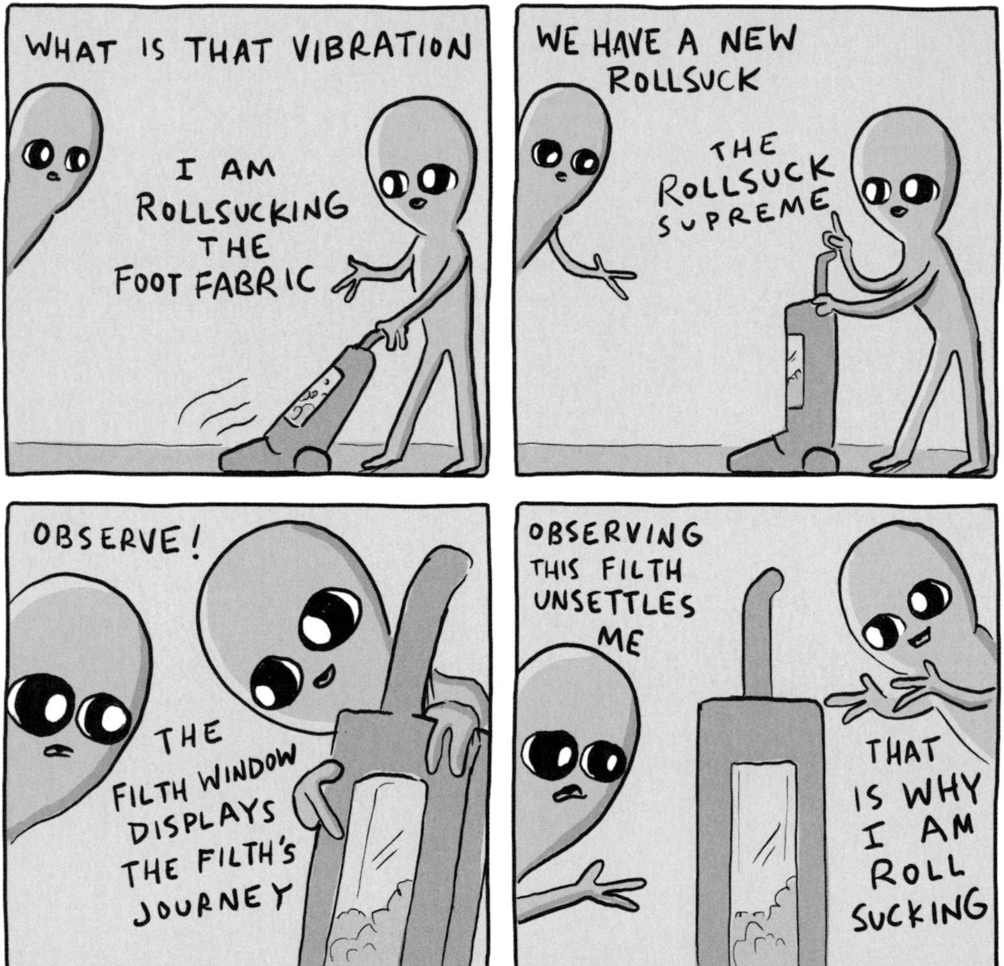
WHAT IS THAT VIBRATION
I AM ROLLSUCKING THE FOOT FABRIC
WE HAVE A NEW ROLLSUCK
THE ROLLSUCK SUPREME
OBSERVE!
THE FILTH WINDOW DISPLAYS THE FILTH'S JOURNEY
OBSERVING THIS FILTH UNSETTLES ME
THAT IS WHY I AM ROLL SUCKING

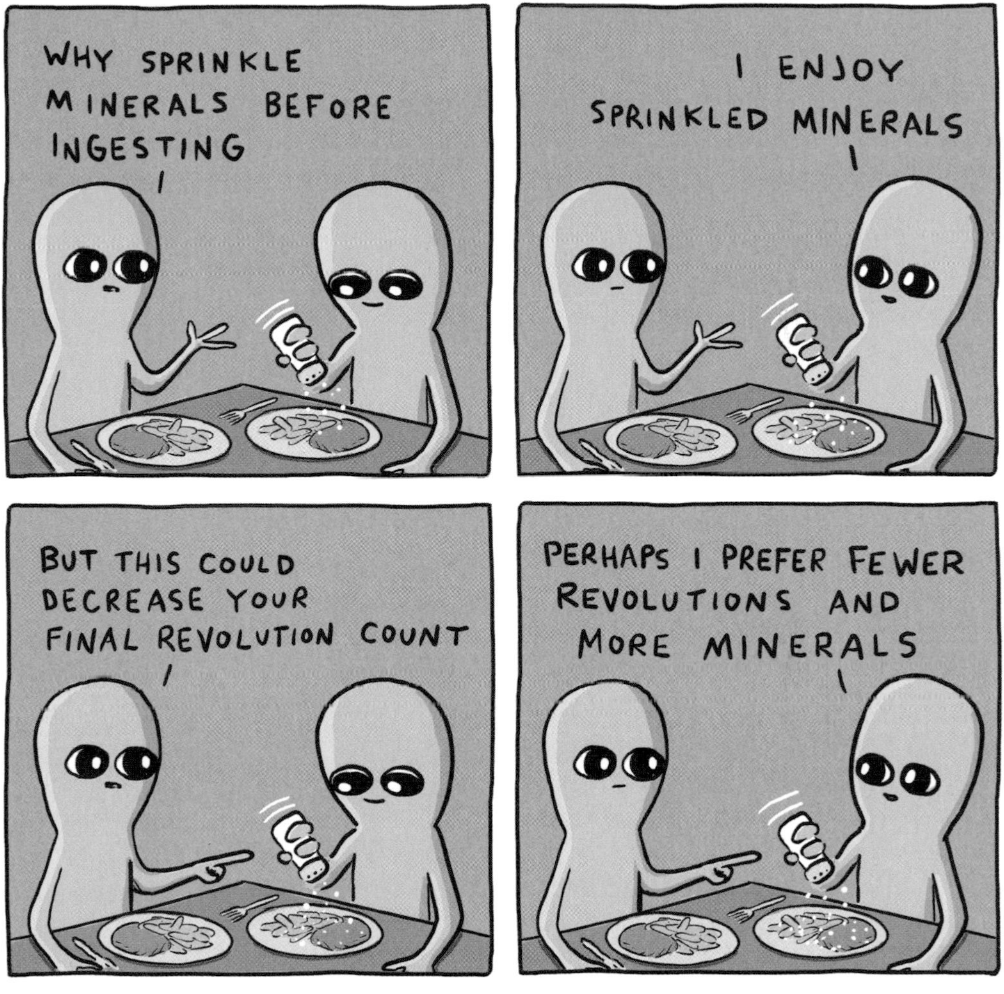
WHY SPRINKLE MINERALS BEFORE INGESTING
I ENJOY SPRINKLED MINERALS
BUT THIS COULD DECREASE YOUR FINAL REVOLUTION COUNT
PERHAPS I PREFER FEWER REVOLUTIONS AND MORE MINERALS

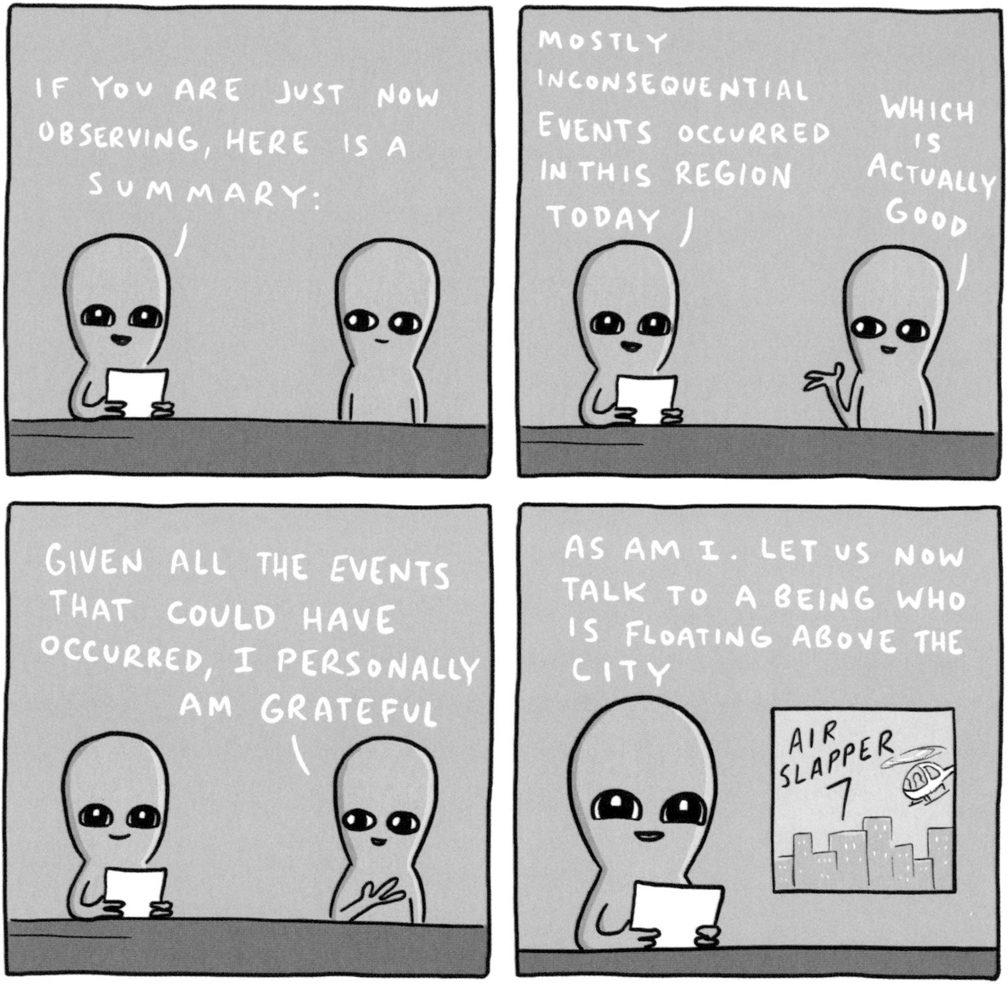
IF YOU ARE JUST NOW OBSERVING, HERE IS A SUMMARY:
MOSTLY INCONSEQUENTIAL EVENTS OCCURRED IN THIS REGION TODAY
WHICH IS ACTUALLY GOOD
GIVEN ALL THE EVENTS THAT COULD HAVE OCCURRED, I PERSONALLY AM GRATEFUL
AS AM I. LET US NOW TALK TO A BEING WHO IS FLOATING ABOVE THE CITY
AIR SLAPPER 7

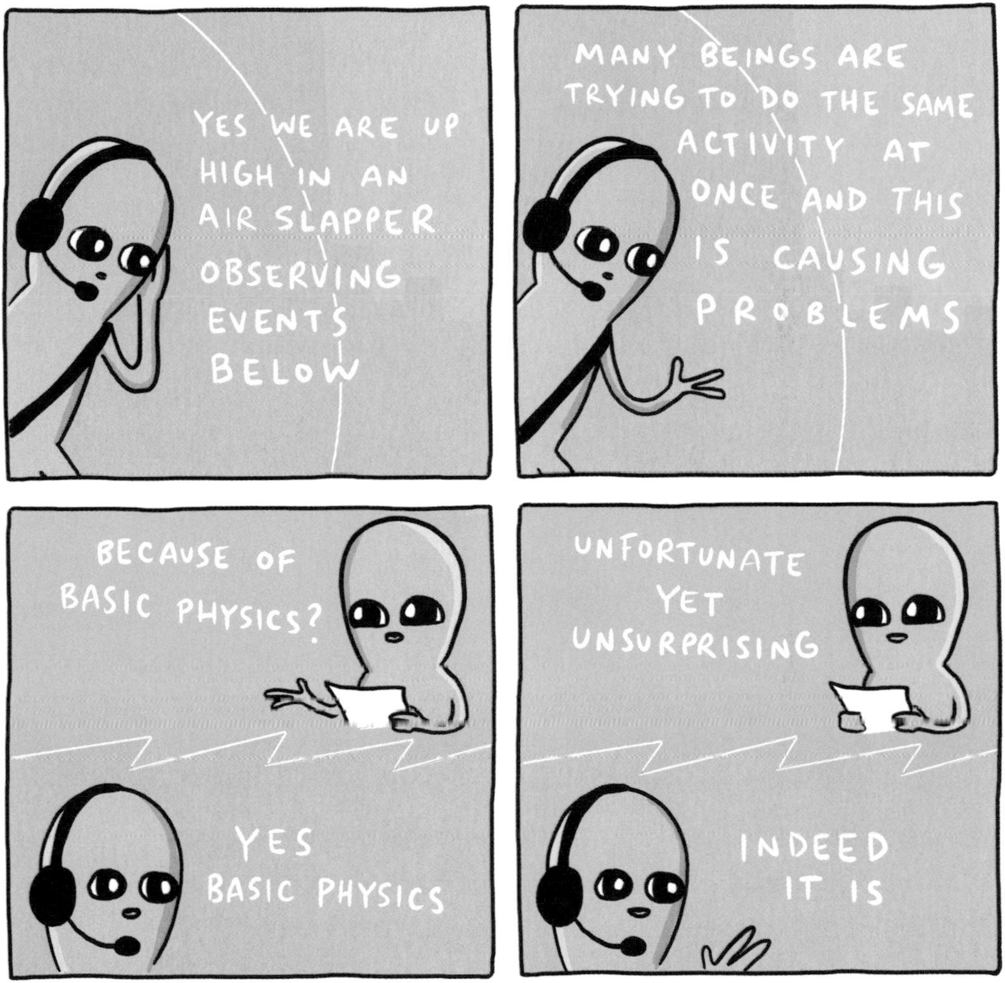
YES WE ARE UP HIGH IN AN AIR SLAPPER OBSERVING EVENTS BELOW
MANY BEINGS ARE TRYING TO DO THE SAME ACTIVITY AT ONCE AND THIS IS CAUSING PROBLEMS
BECAUSE OF BASIC PHYSICS?
YES BASIC PHYSICS
UNFORTUNATE YET UNSURPRISING
INDEED IT IS

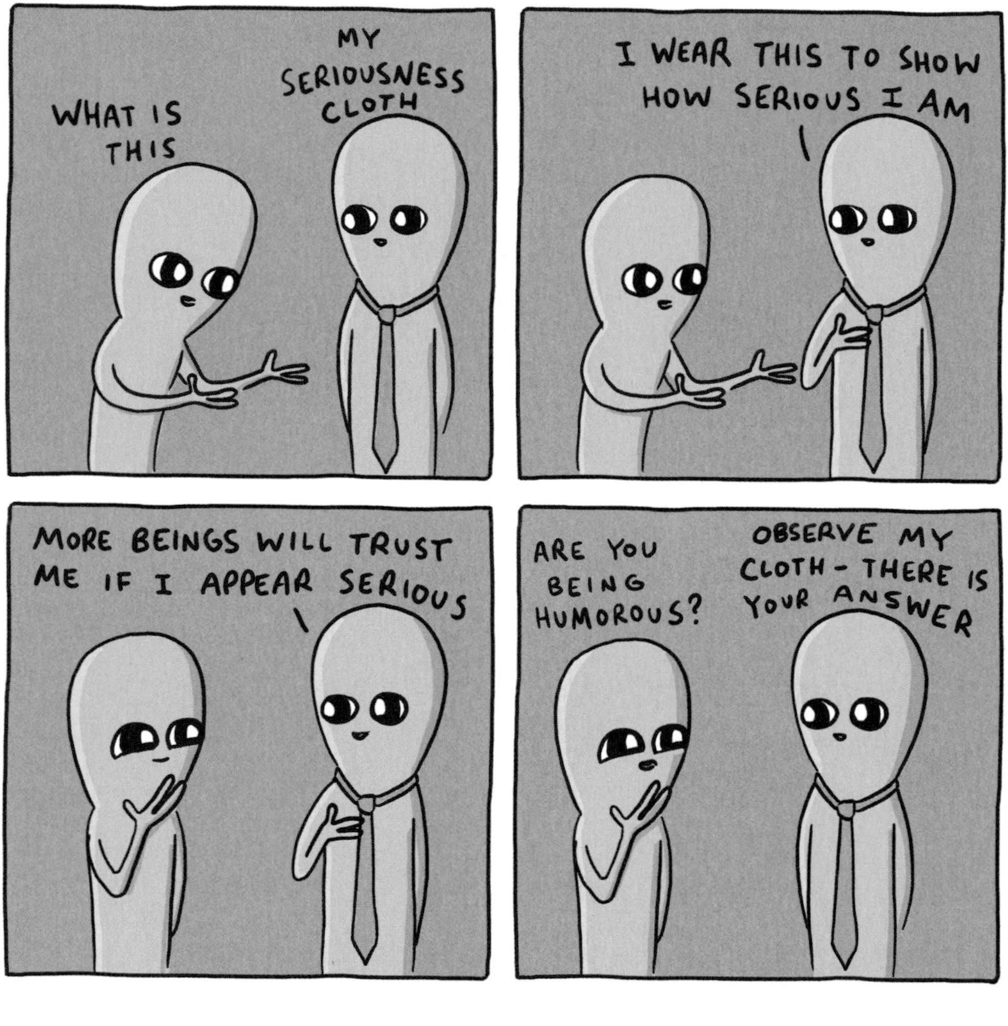
WHAT IS THIS
MY SERIOUSNESS CLOTH
I WEAR THIS TO SHOW HOW SERIOUS I AM
MORE BEINGS WILL TRUST ME IF I APPEAR SERIOUS
ARE YOU BEING HUMOROUS?
OBSERVE MY CLOTH - THERE IS YOUR ANSWER

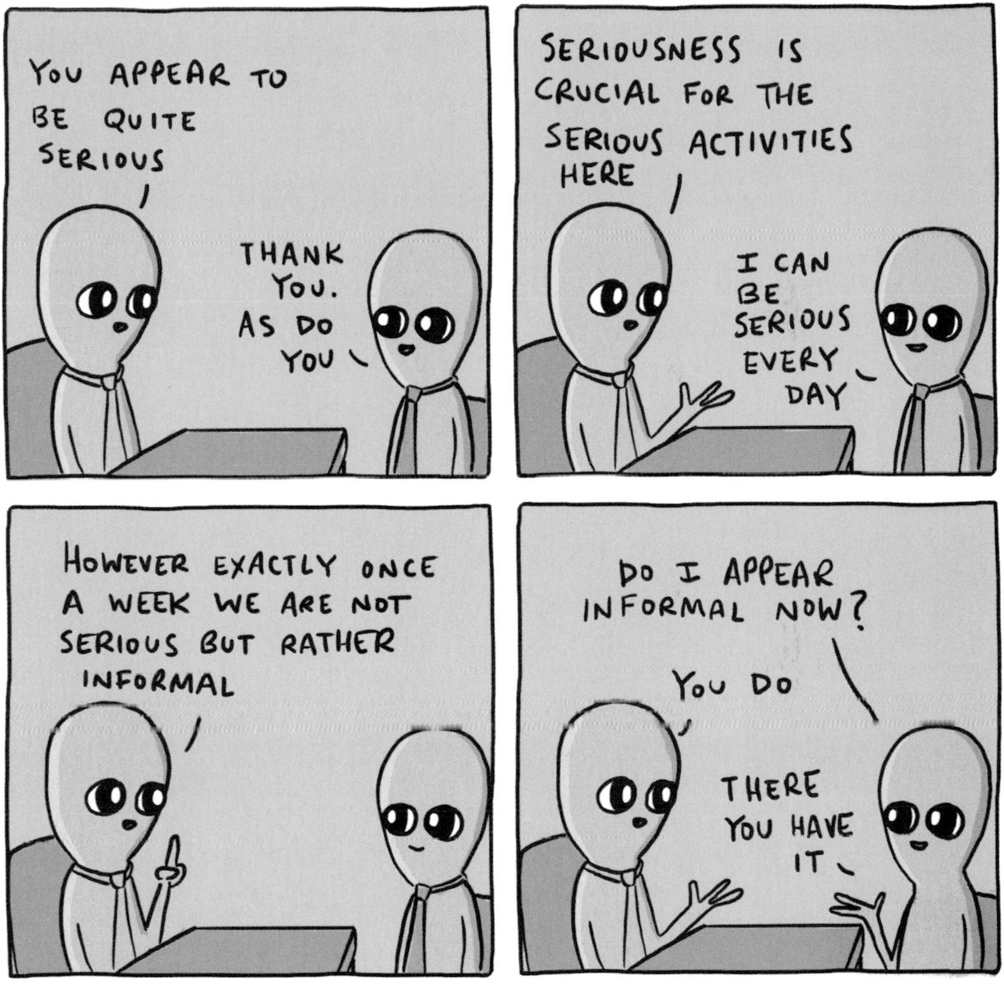
YOU APPEAR TO BE QUITE SERIOUS
THANK YOU. AS DO YOU
SERIOUSNESS IS CRUCIAL FOR THE SERIOUS ACTIVITIES HERE
I CAN BE SERIOUS EVERY DAY
HOWEVER EXACTLY ONCE A WEEK WE ARE NOT SERIOUS BUT RATHER INFORMAL
DO I APPEAR INFORMAL NOW?
YOU DO
THERE YOU HAVE IT

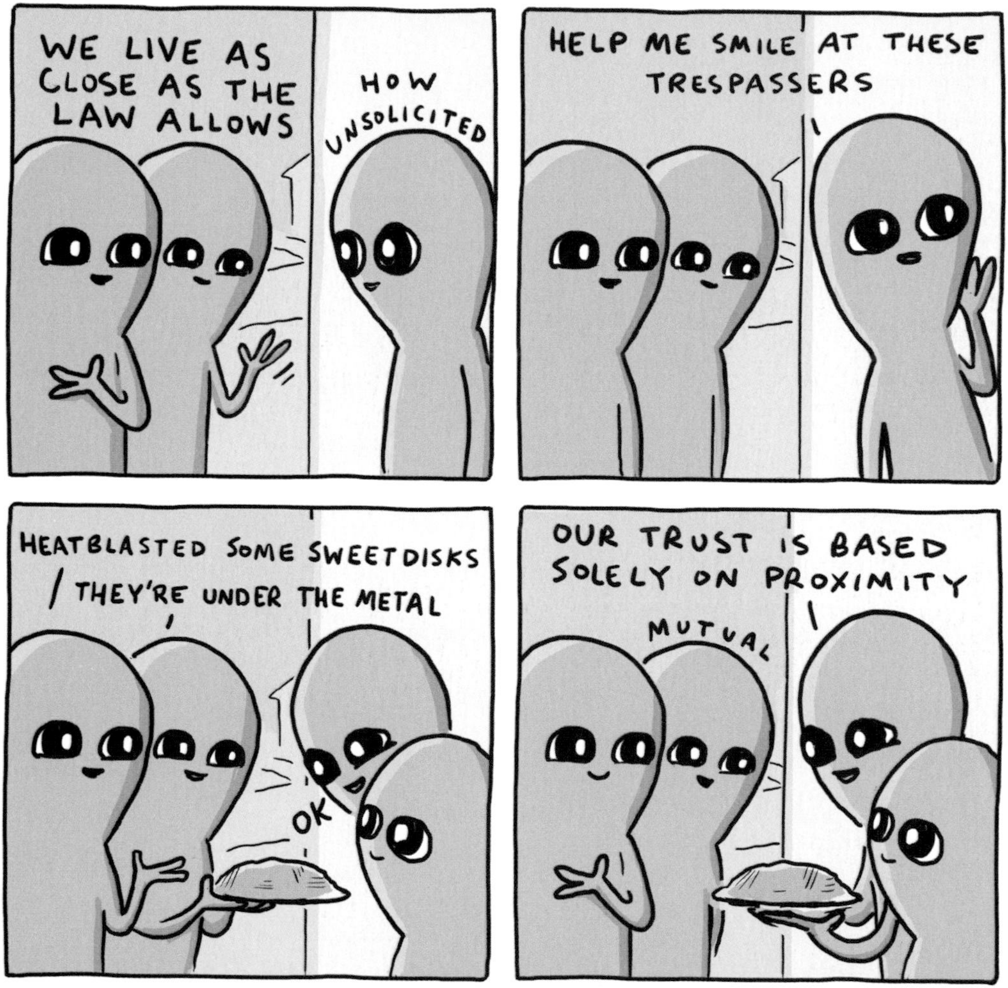
WE LIVE AS CLOSE AS THE LAW ALLOWS
HOW UNSOLICITED
HELP ME SMILE AT THESE TRESPASSERS
HEATBLASTED SOME SWEETDISKS / THEY'RE UNDER THE METAL
OK
OUR TRUST IS BASED SOLELY ON PROXIMITY
MUTUAL

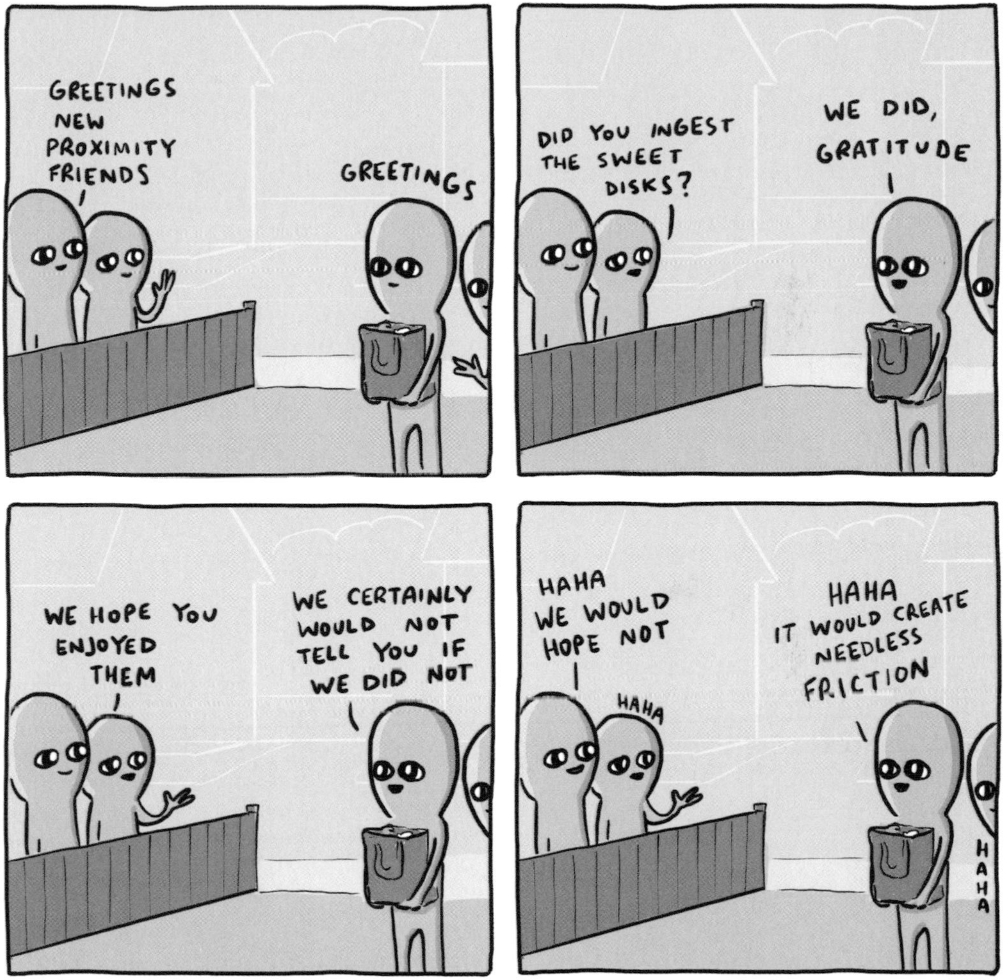
GREETINGS NEW PROXIMITY FRIENDS
GREETINGS
DID YOU INGEST THE SWEET DISKS?
WE DID, GRATITUDE
WE HOPE YOU ENJOYED THEM
WE CERTAINLY WOULD NOT TELL YOU IF WE DID NOT
HAHA WE WOULD HOPE NOT
HAHA
HAHA IT WOULD CREATE NEEDLESS FRICTION
HAHA

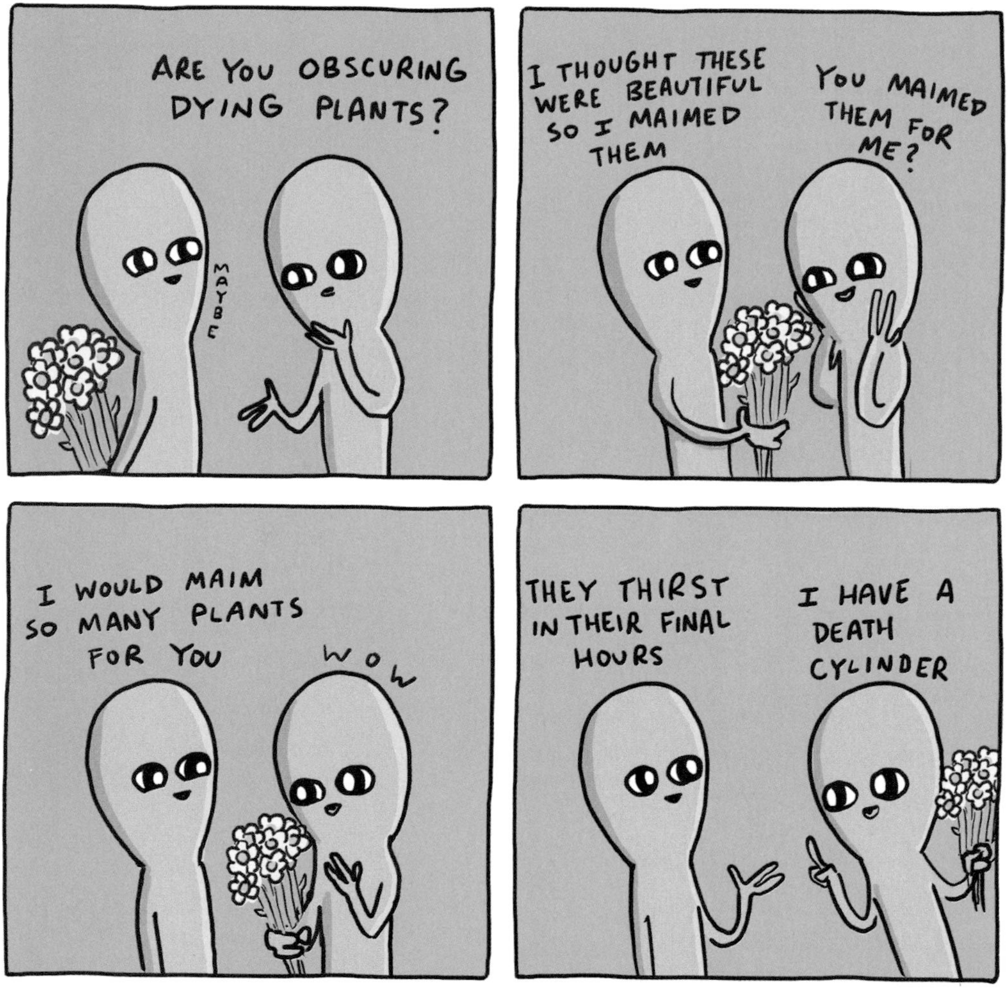
ARE YOU OBSCURING DYING PLANTS?
MAYBE
I THOUGHT THESE WERE BEAUTIFUL SO I MAIMED THEM
YOU MAIMED THEM FOR ME?
I WOULD MAIM SO MANY PLANTS FOR YOU
WOW
THEY THIRST IN THEIR FINAL HOURS
I HAVE A DEATH CYLINDER

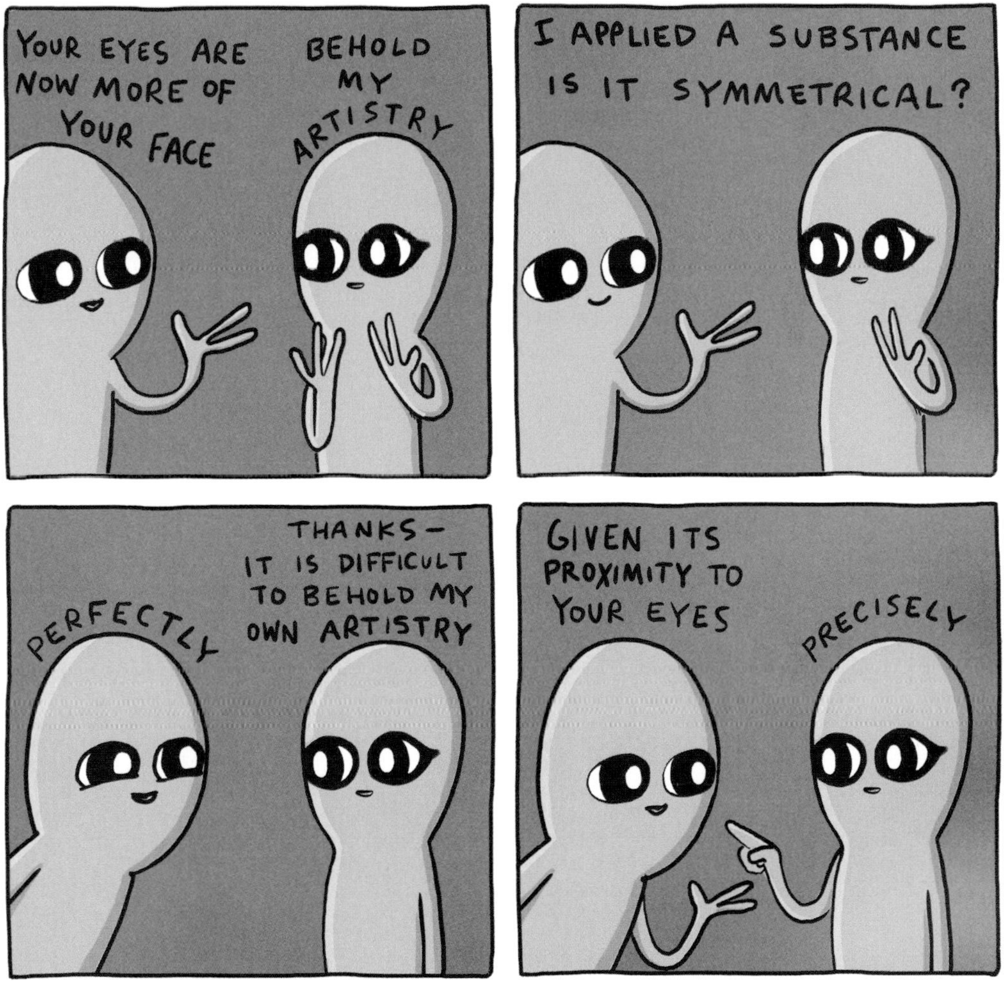

YOUR EYES ARE NOW MORE OF YOUR FACE
BEHOLD MY ARTISTRY
I APPLIED A SUBSTANCE
IS IT SYMMETRICAL?
PERFECTLY
THANKS– IT IS DIFFICULT TO BEHOLD MY OWN ARTISTRY
GIVEN ITS PROXIMITY TO YOUR EYES
PRECISELY

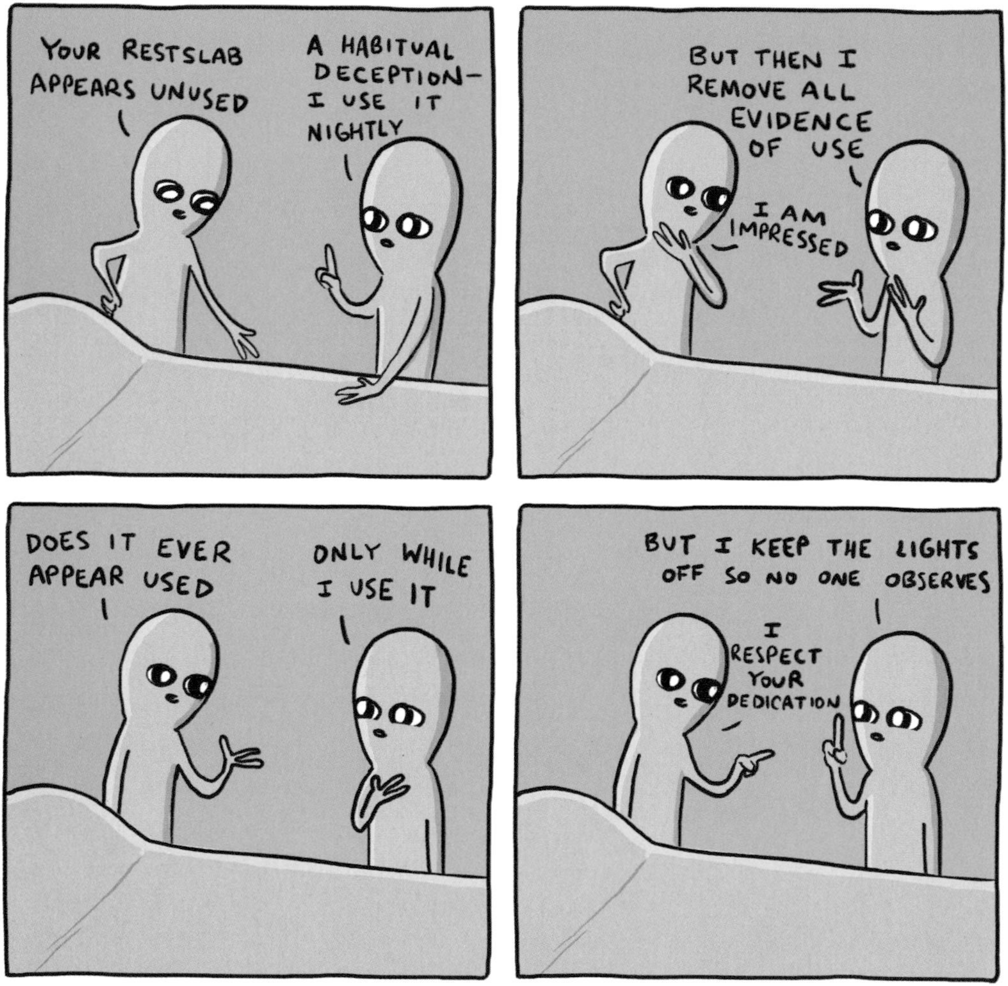
YOUR RESTSLAB APPEARS UNUSED
A HABITUAL DECEPTION— I USE IT NIGHTLY
BUT THEN I REMOVE ALL EVIDENCE OF USE
I AM IMPRESSED
DOES IT EVER APPEAR USED
ONLY WHILE I USE IT
BUT I KEEP THE LIGHTS OFF SO NO ONE OBSERVES
I RESPECT YOUR DEDICATION

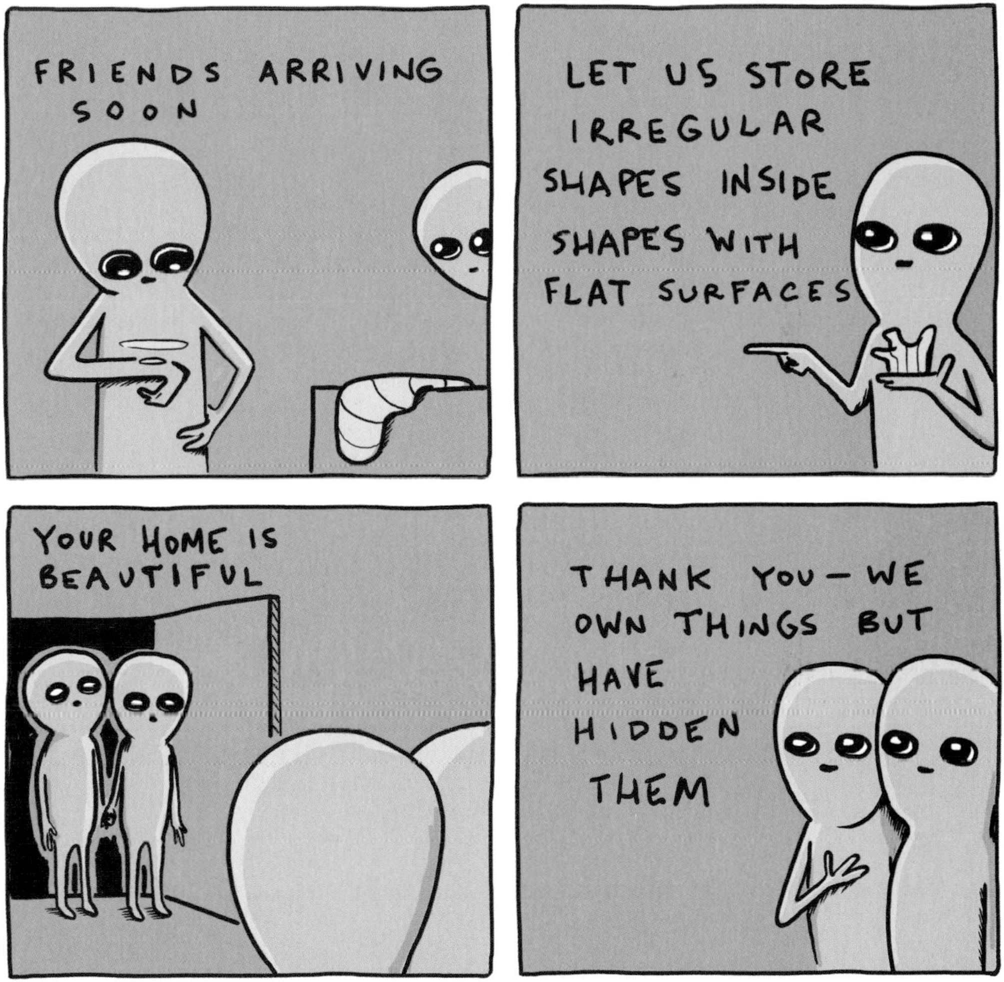
FRIENDS ARRIVING SOON
LET US STORE IRREGULAR SHAPES INSIDE SHAPES WITH FLAT SURFACES
YOUR HOME IS BEAUTIFUL
THANK YOU— WE OWN THINGS BUT HAVE HIDDEN THEM

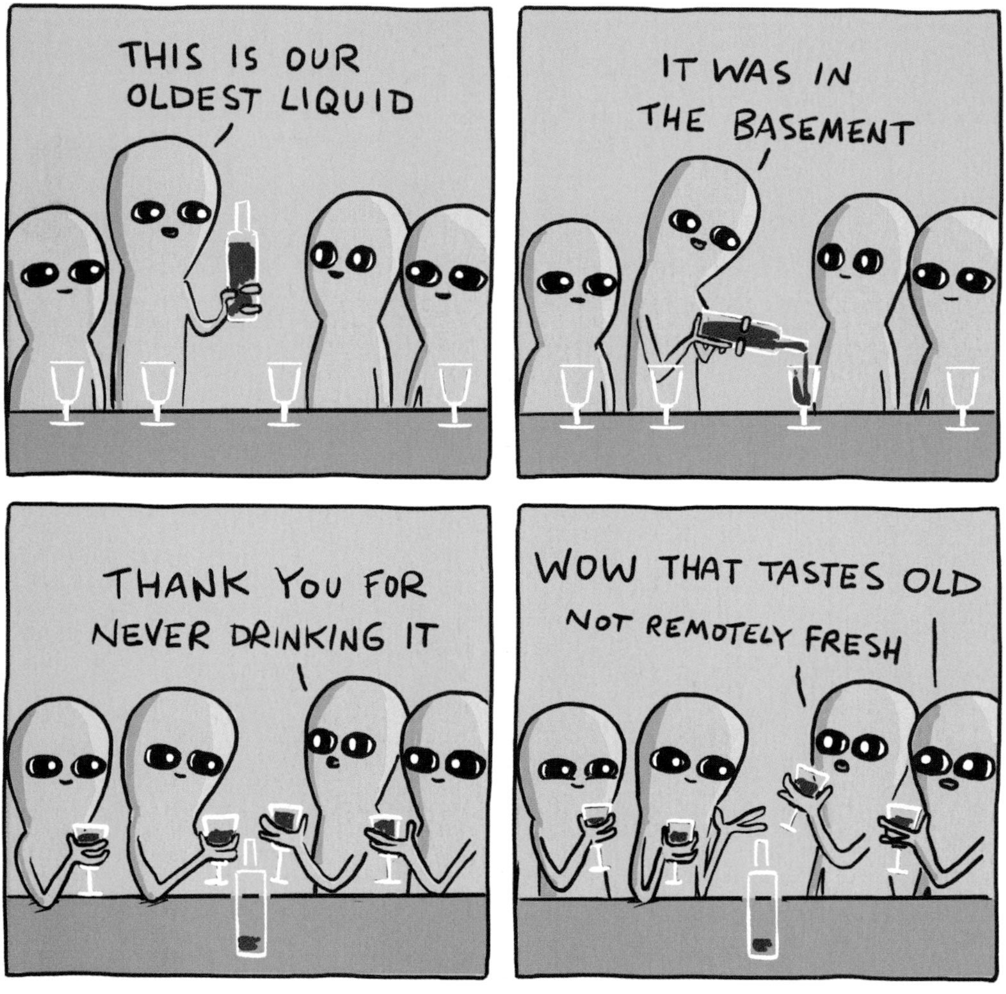
THIS IS OUR OLDEST LIQUID
IT WAS IN THE BASEMENT
THANK YOU FOR NEVER DRINKING IT
WOW THAT TASTES OLD
NOT REMOTELY FRESH

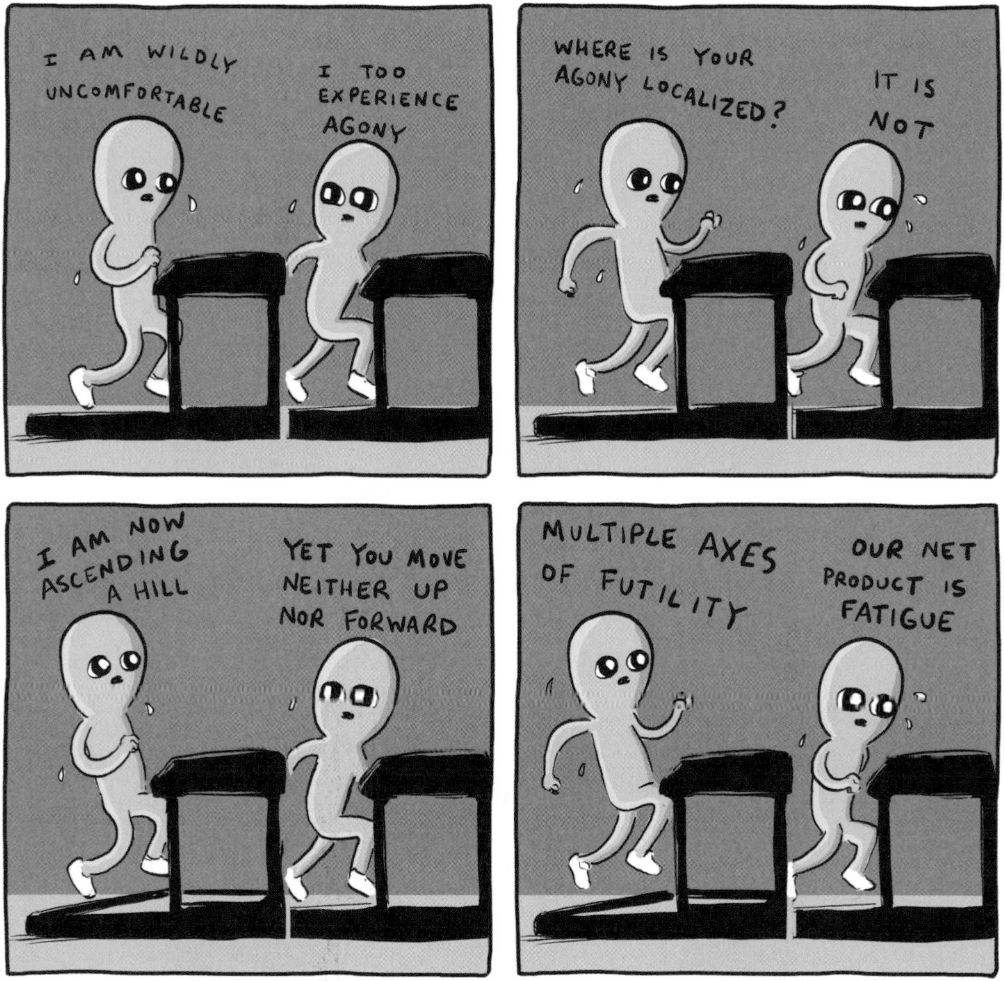
I AM WILDLY UNCOMFORTABLE
I TOO EXPERIENCE AGONY
WHERE IS YOUR AGONY LOCALIZED?
IT IS NOT
I AM NOW ASCENDING A HILL
YET YOU MOVE NEITHER UP NOR FORWARD
MULTIPLE AXES OF FUTILITY
OUR NET PRODUCT IS FATIGUE

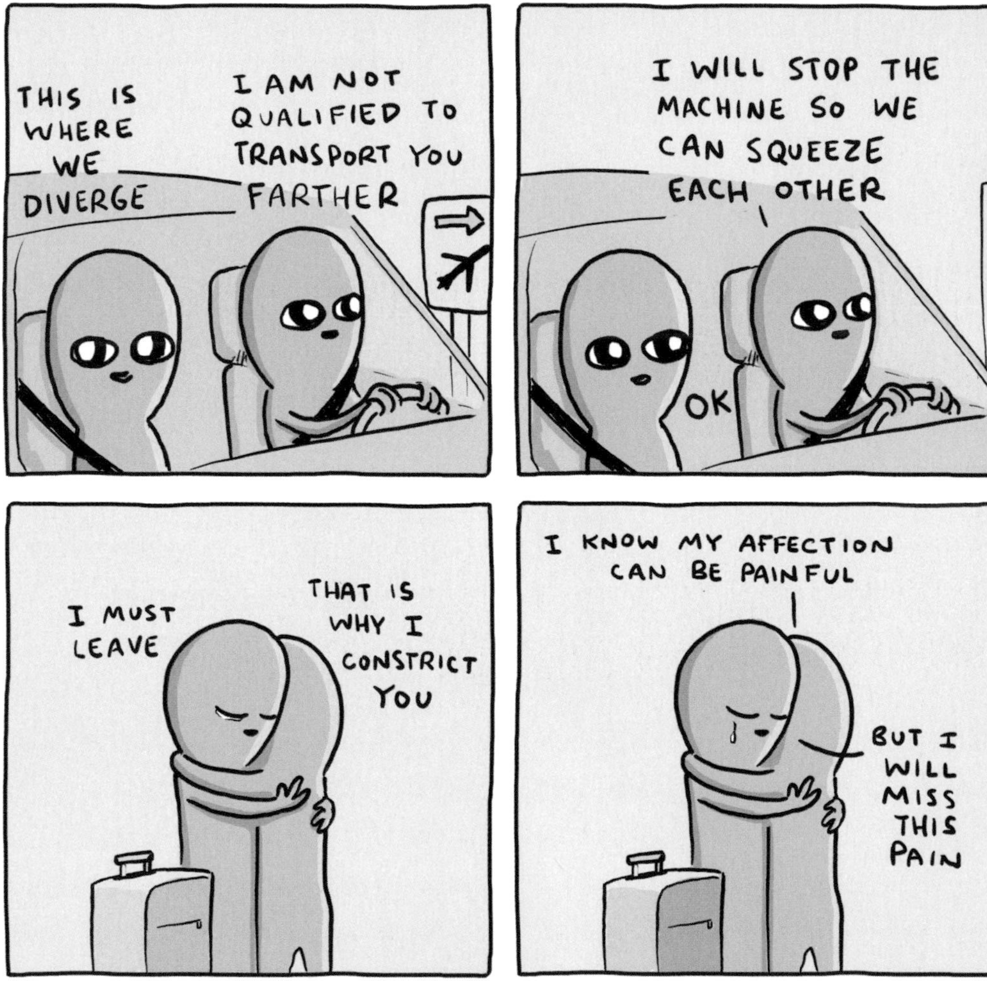
THIS IS WHERE WE DIVERGE
I AM NOT QUALIFIED TO TRANSPORT YOU FARTHER
I WILL STOP THE MACHINE SO WE CAN SQUEEZE EACH OTHER
OK
I MUST LEAVE
THAT IS WHY I CONSTRICT YOU
I KNOW MY AFFECTION CAN BE PAINFUL
BUT I WILL MISS THIS PAIN

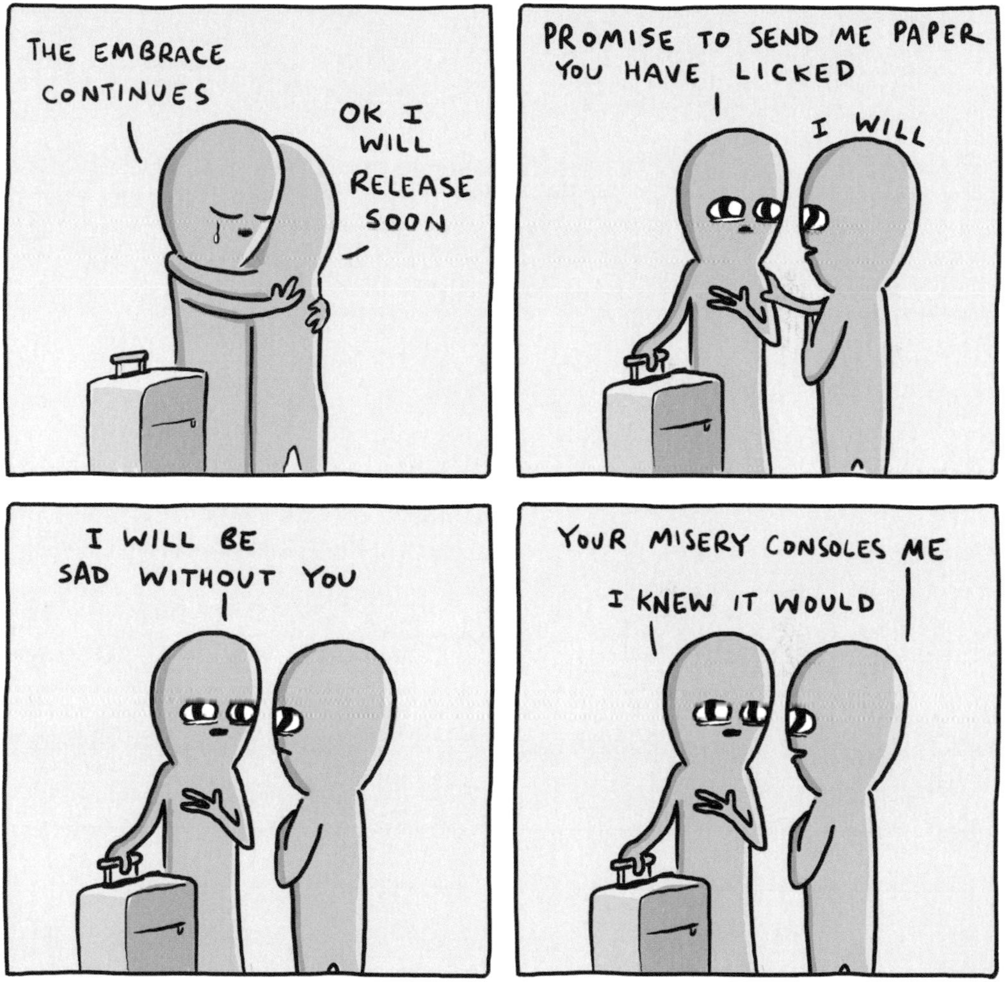
THE EMBRACE CONTINUES
OK I WILL RELEASE SOON
PROMISE TO SEND ME PAPER YOU HAVE LICKED
I WILL
I WILL BE SAD WITHOUT YOU
YOUR MISERY CONSOLES ME
I KNEW IT WOULD

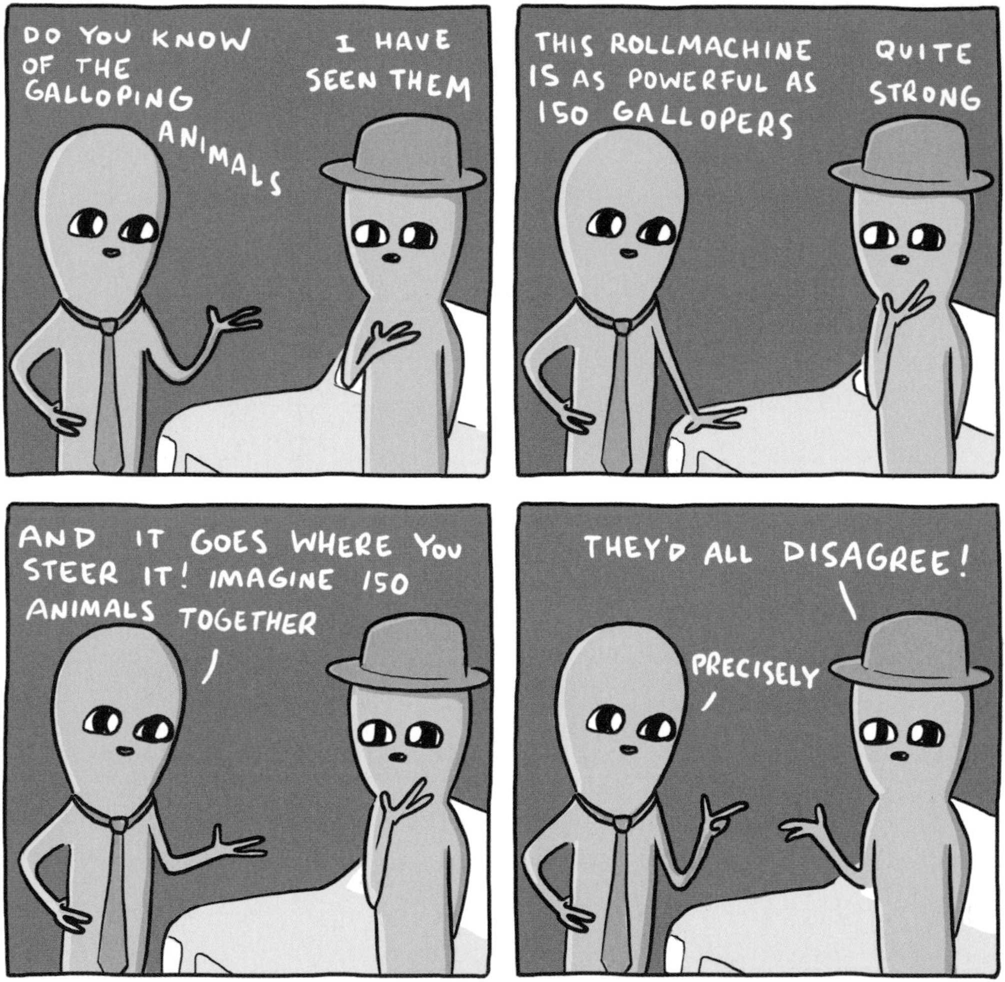
DO YOU KNOW OF THE GALLOPING ANIMALS
I HAVE SEEN THEM
THIS ROLLMACHINE IS AS POWERFUL AS 150 GALLOPERS
QUITE STRONG
AND IT GOES WHERE YOU STEER IT! IMAGINE 150 ANIMALS TOGETHER
THEY'D ALL DISAGREE!
PRECISELY

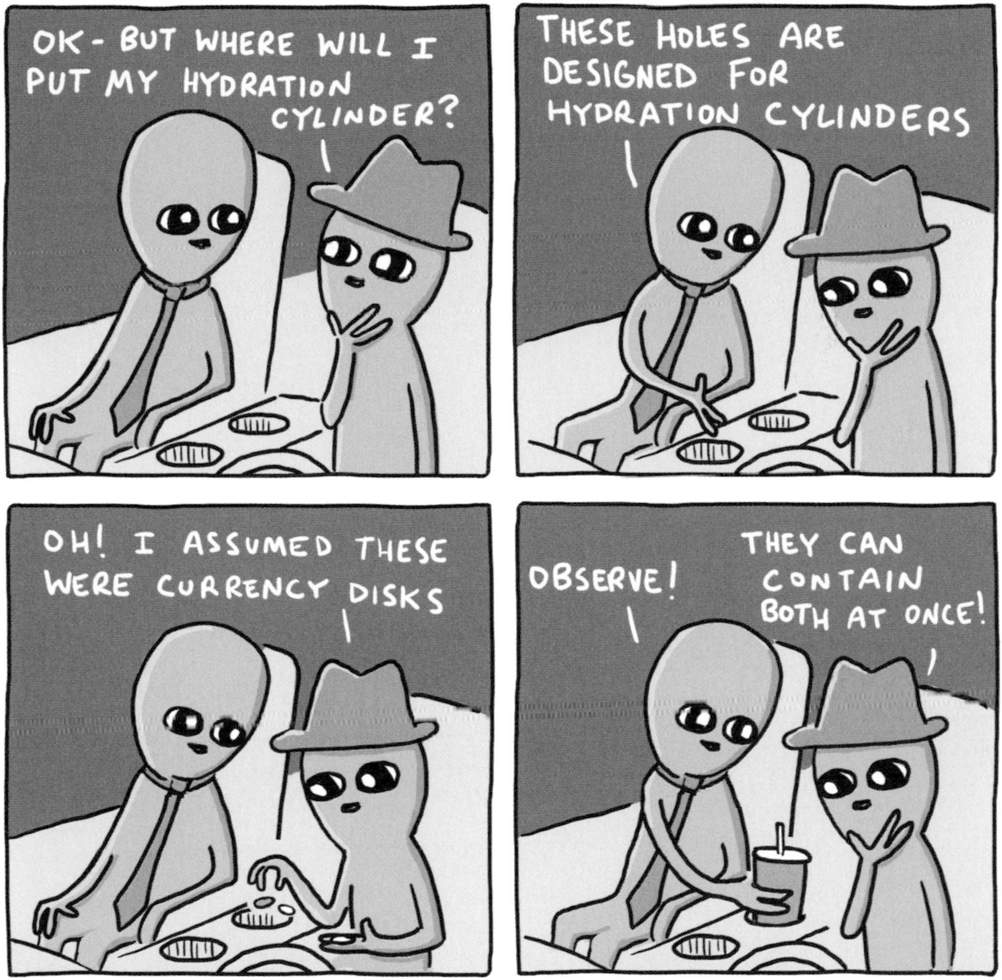
OK - BUT WHERE WILL I PUT MY HYDRATION CYLINDER?
THESE HOLES ARE DESIGNED FOR HYDRATION CYLINDERS
OH! I ASSUMED THESE WERE CURRENCY DISKS
OBSERVE!
THEY CAN CONTAIN BOTH AT ONCE!

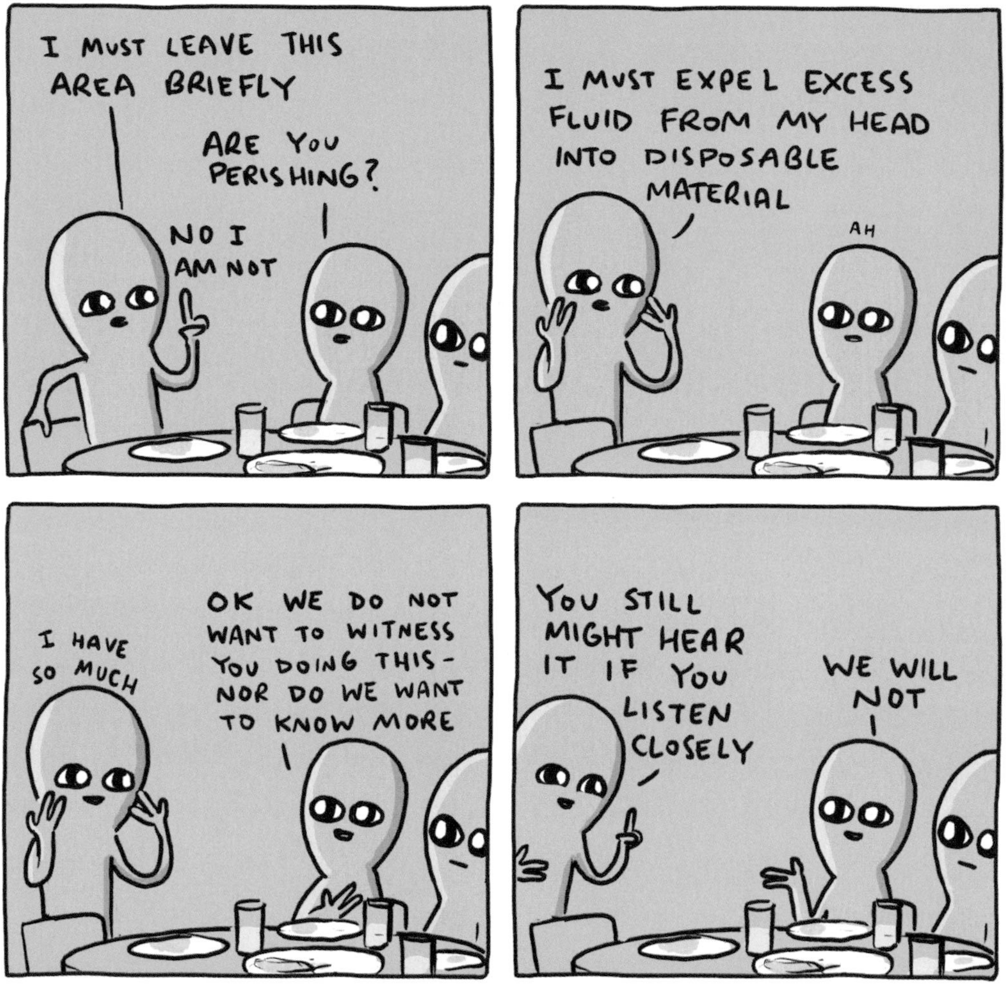
I MUST LEAVE THIS AREA BRIEFLY
ARE YOU PERISHING?
NO I AM NOT
I MUST EXPEL EXCESS FLUID FROM MY HEAD INTO DISPOSABLE MATERIAL
AH
I HAVE SO MUCH
OK WE DO NOT WANT TO WITNESS YOU DOING THIS - NOR DO WE WANT TO KNOW MORE
YOU STILL MIGHT HEAR IT IF YOU LISTEN CLOSELY
WE WILL NOT

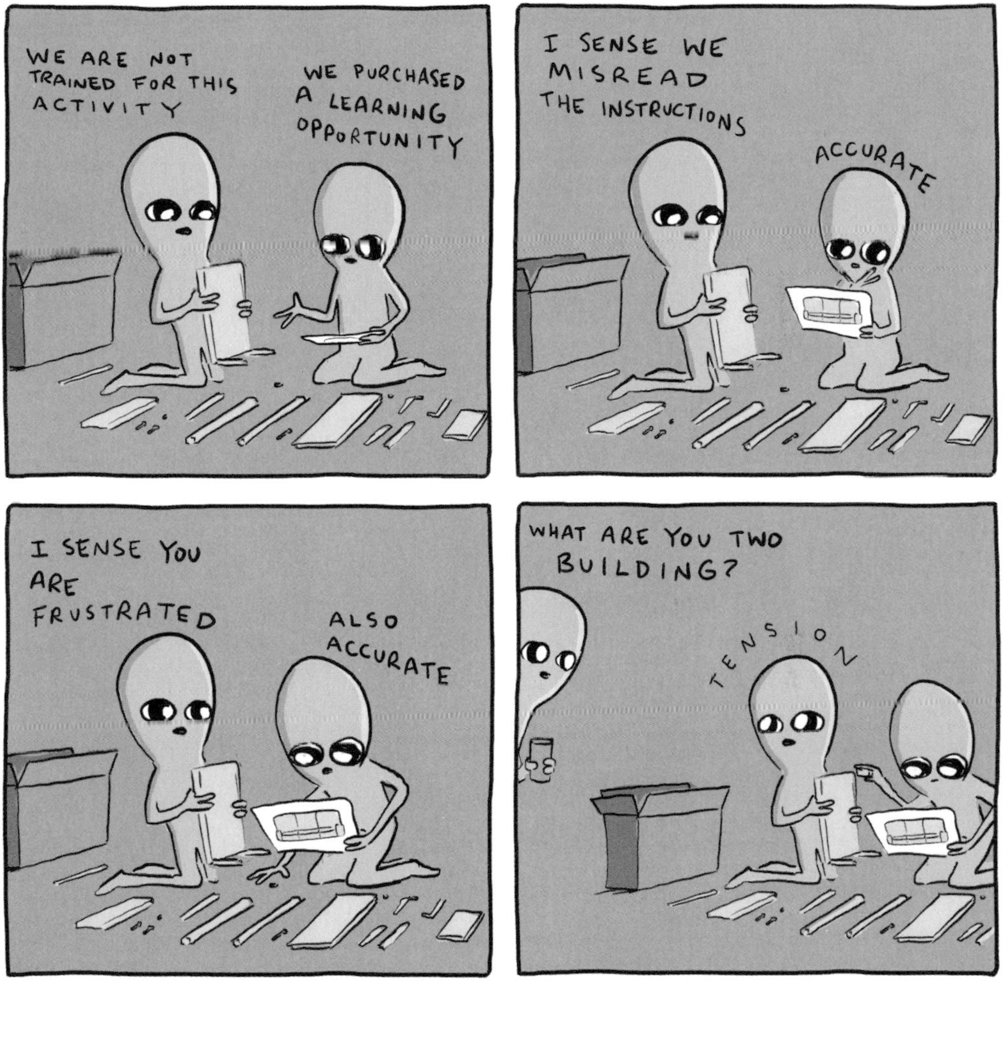
WE ARE NOT TRAINED FOR THIS ACTIVITY
WE PURCHASED A LEARNING OPPORTUNITY
I SENSE WE MISREAD THE INSTRUCTIONS
ACCURATE
I SENSE YOU ARE FRUSTRATED
ALSO ACCURATE
WHAT ARE YOU TWO BUILDING?
TENSION

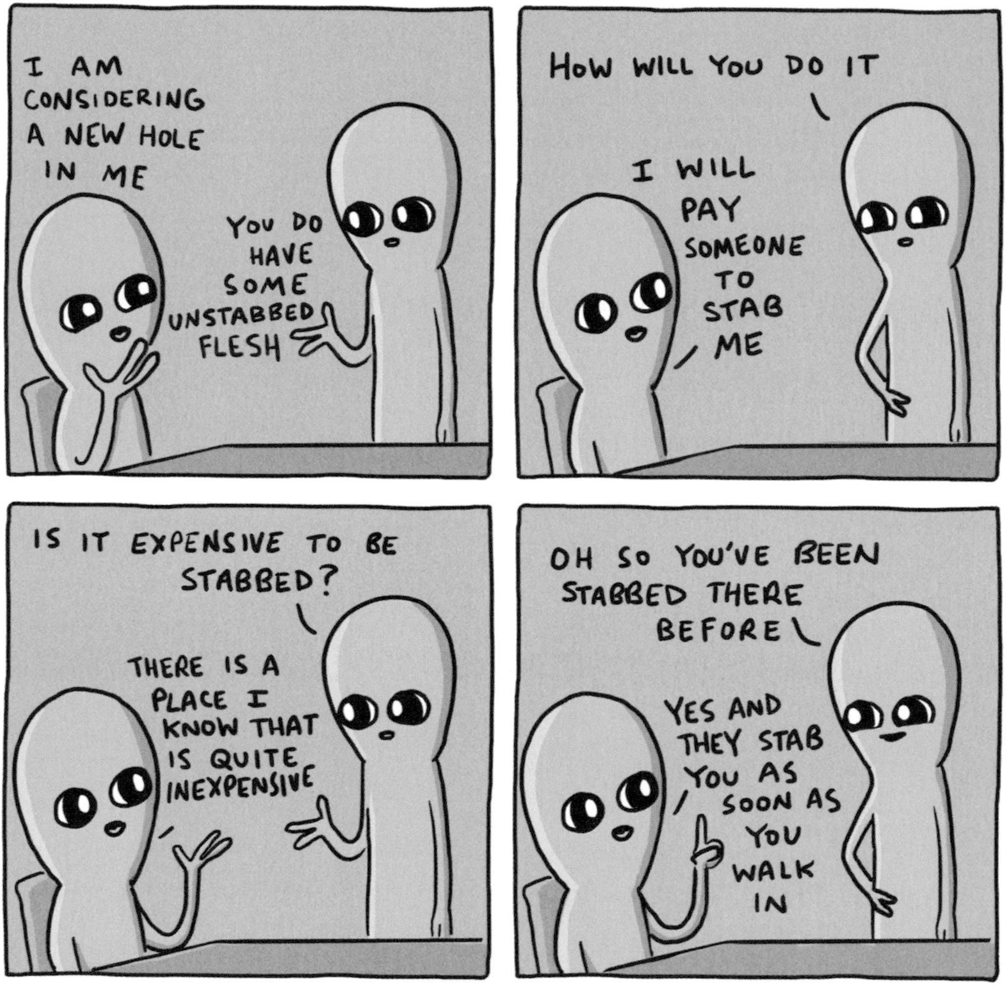
I AM CONSIDERING A NEW HOLE IN ME
YOU DO HAVE SOME UNSTABBED FLESH
HOW WILL YOU DO IT
I WILL PAY SOMEONE TO STAB ME
IS IT EXPENSIVE TO BE STABBED?
THERE IS A PLACE I KNOW THAT IS QUITE INEXPENSIVE
OH SO YOU'VE BEEN STABBED THERE BEFORE
YES AND THEY STAB YOU AS SOON AS YOU WALK IN

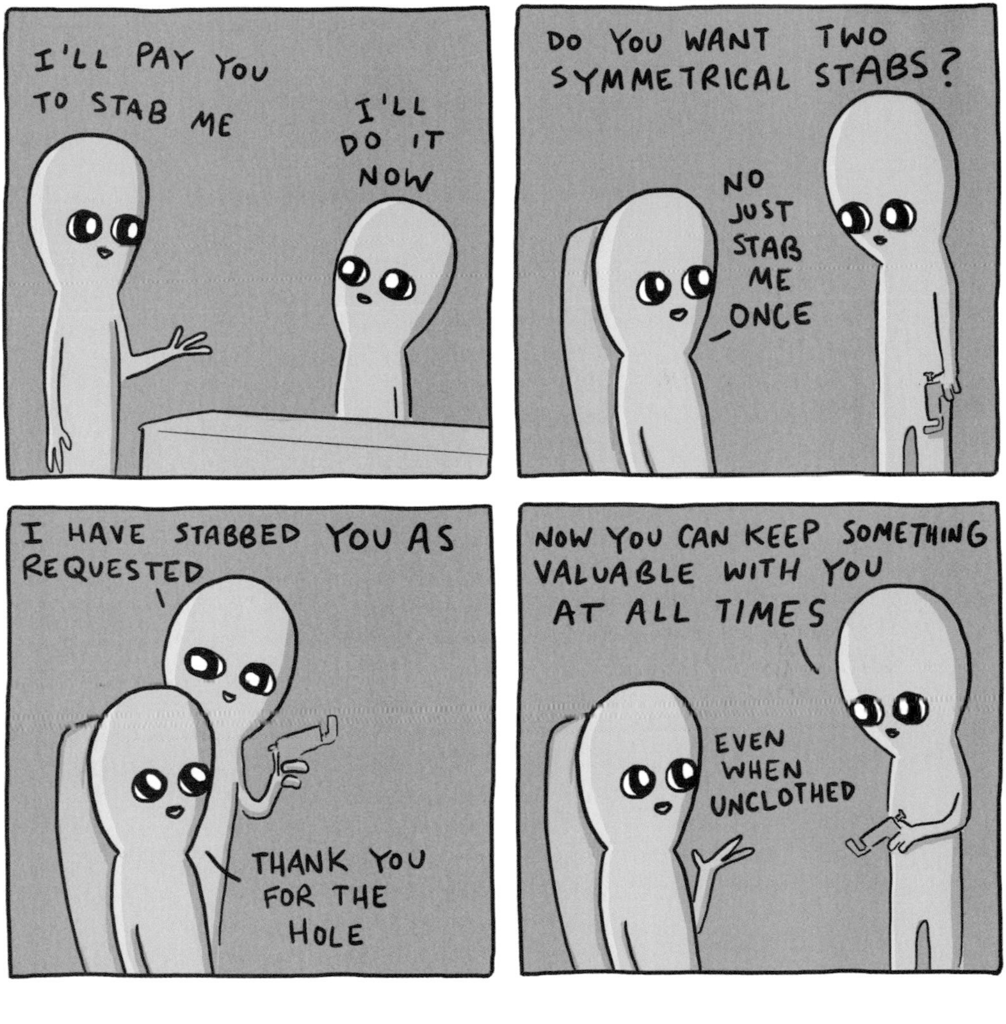
I'LL PAY YOU TO STAB ME
I'LL DO IT NOW
DO YOU WANT TWO SYMMETRICAL STABS?
NO JUST STAB ME ONCE
I HAVE STABBED YOU AS REQUESTED
THANK YOU FOR THE HOLE
NOW YOU CAN KEEP SOMETHING VALUABLE WITH YOU AT ALL TIMES
EVEN WHEN UNCLOTHED

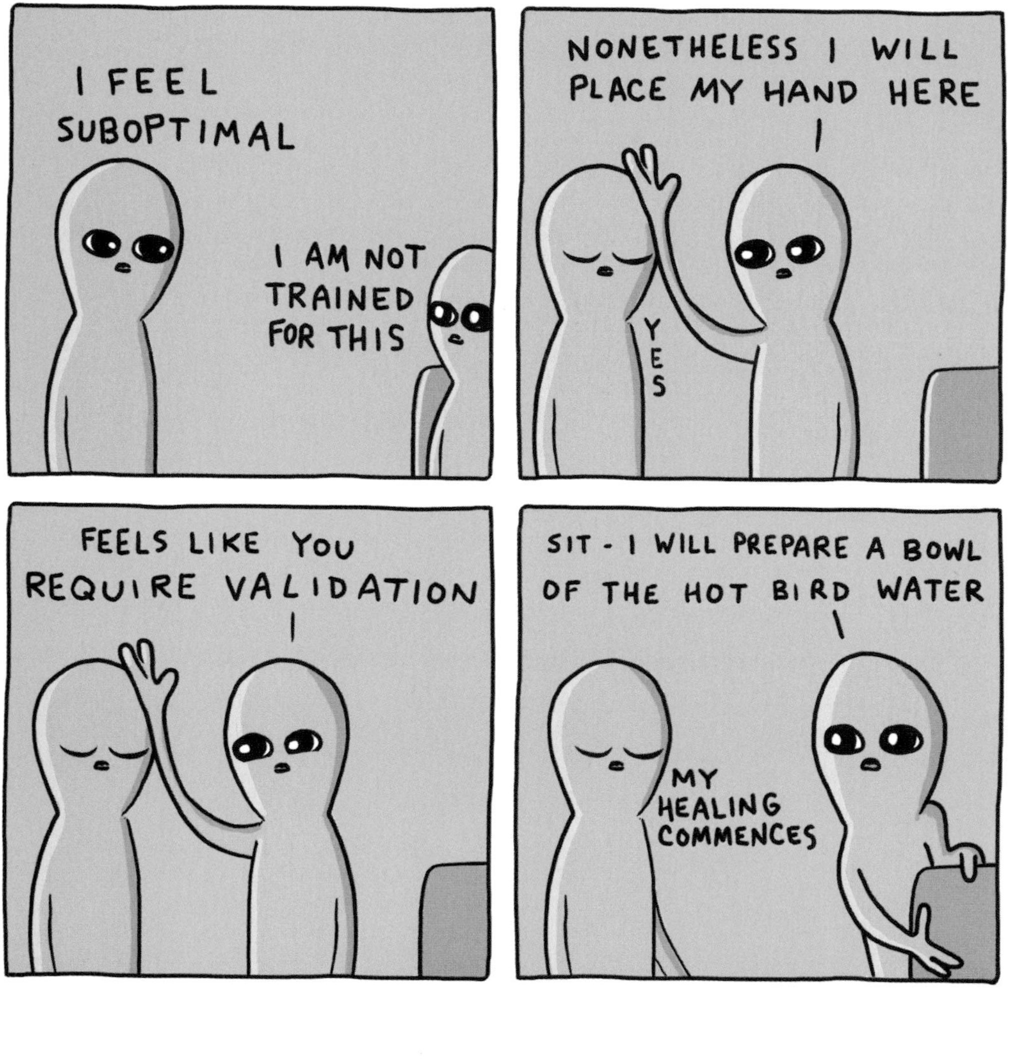
I FEEL
SUBOPTIMAL
I AM NOT
TRAINED
FOR THIS
NONETHELESS I WILL
PLACE MY HAND HERE
YES
FEELS LIKE YOU
REQUIRE VALIDATION
SIT - I WILL PREPARE A BOWL
OF THE HOT BIRD WATER
MY
HEALING
COMMENCES

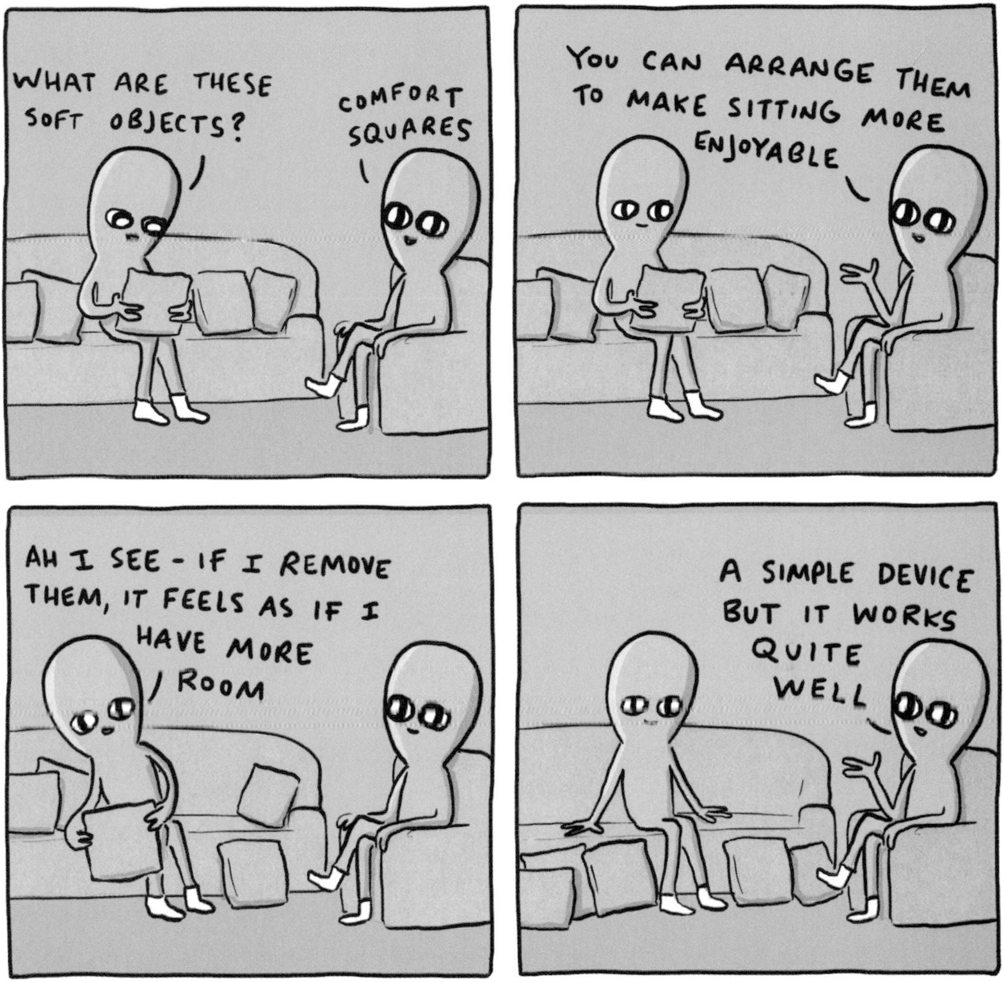
WHAT ARE THESE SOFT OBJECTS?
COMFORT SQUARES
YOU CAN ARRANGE THEM TO MAKE SITTING MORE ENJOYABLE
AH I SEE - IF I REMOVE THEM, IT FEELS AS IF I HAVE MORE ROOM
A SIMPLE DEVICE BUT IT WORKS QUITE WELL

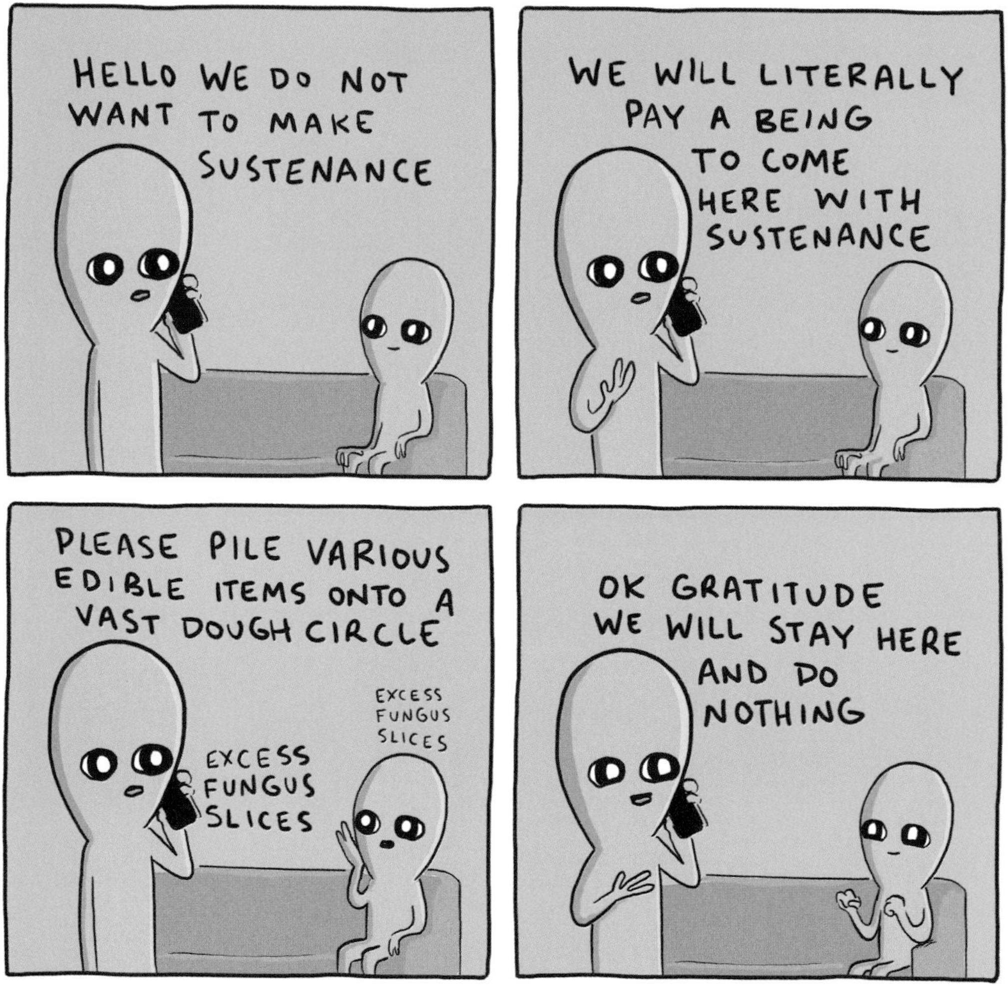
HELLO WE DO NOT WANT TO MAKE SUSTENANCE
WE WILL LITERALLY PAY A BEING TO COME HERE WITH SUSTENANCE
PLEASE PILE VARIOUS EDIBLE ITEMS ONTO A VAST DOUGH CIRCLE
EXCESS FUNGUS SLICES
EXCESS FUNGUS SLICES
OK GRATITUDE WE WILL STAY HERE AND DO NOTHING

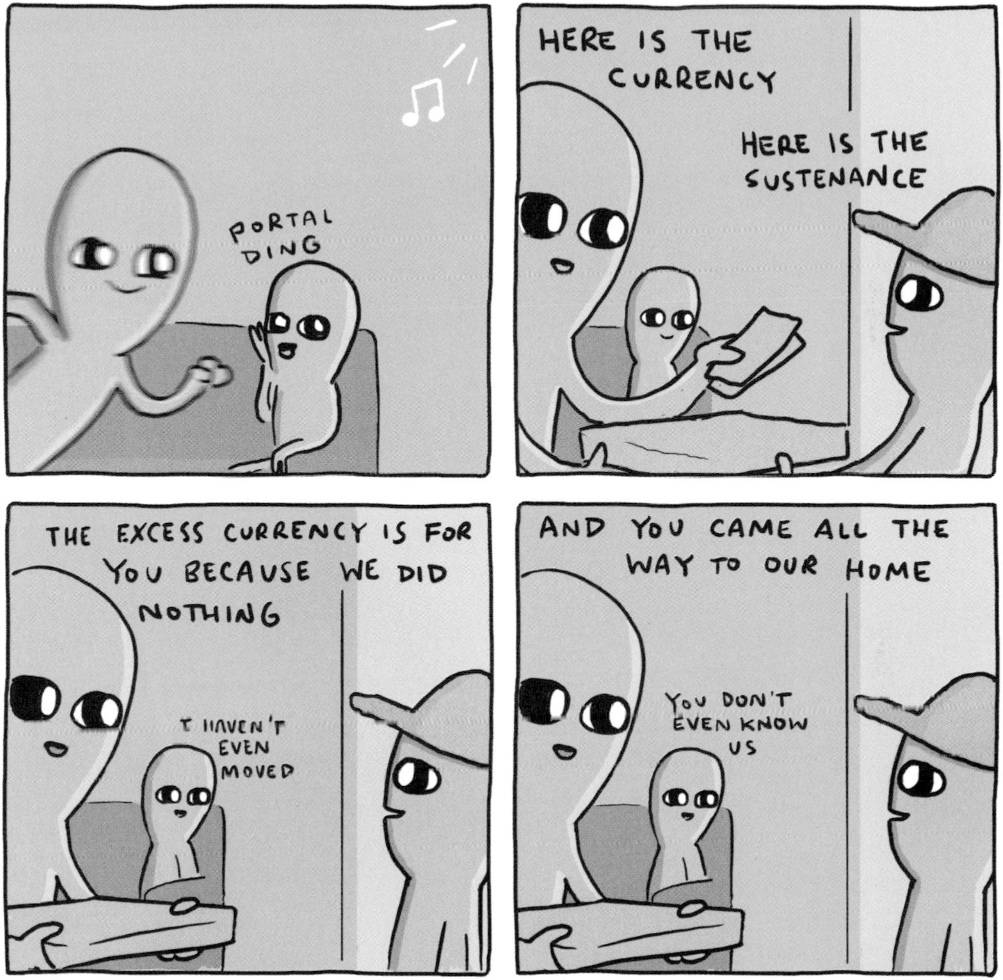
PORTAL DING
HERE IS THE CURRENCY
HERE IS THE SUSTENANCE
THE EXCESS CURRENCY IS FOR YOU BECAUSE WE DID NOTHING
I HAVEN'T EVEN MOVED
AND YOU CAME ALL THE WAY TO OUR HOME
YOU DON'T EVEN KNOW US

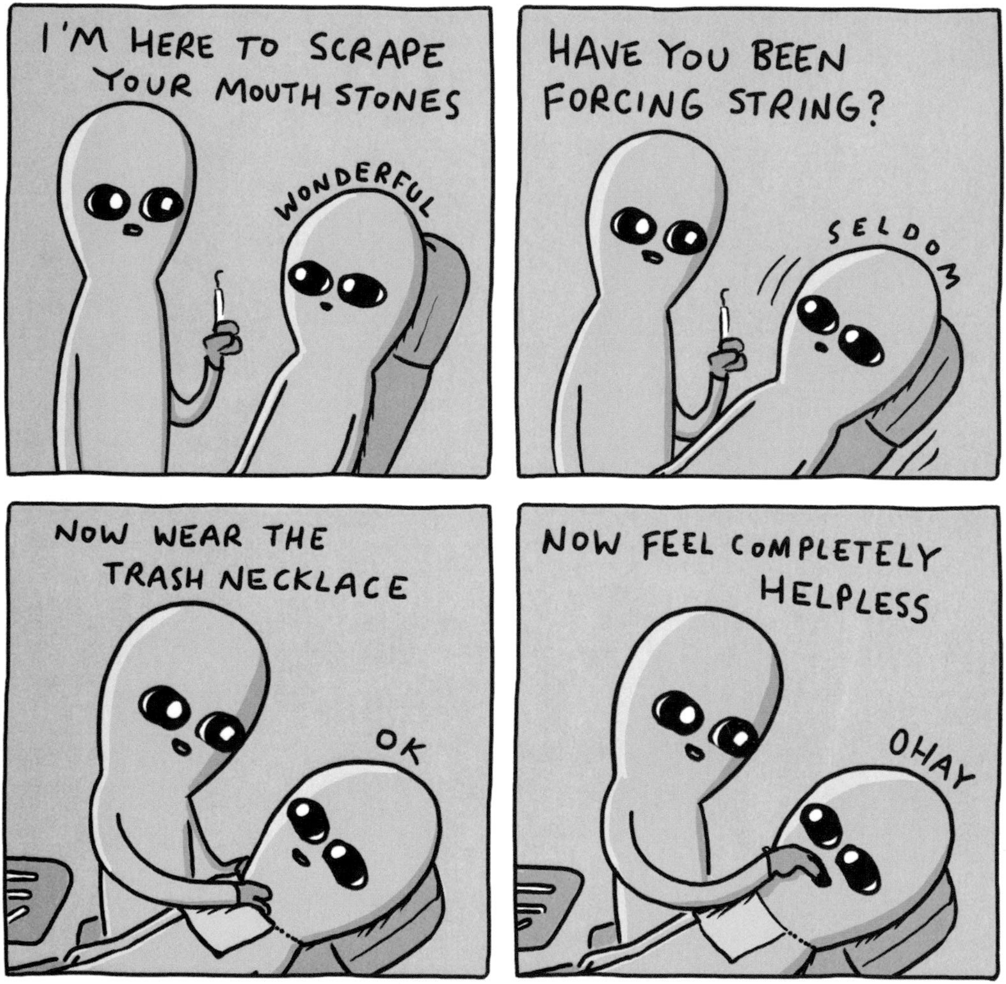
I'M HERE TO SCRAPE YOUR MOUTH STONES
WONDERFUL
HAVE YOU BEEN FORCING STRING?
SELDOM
NOW WEAR THE TRASH NECKLACE
OK
NOW FEEL COMPLETELY HELPLESS
OHAY

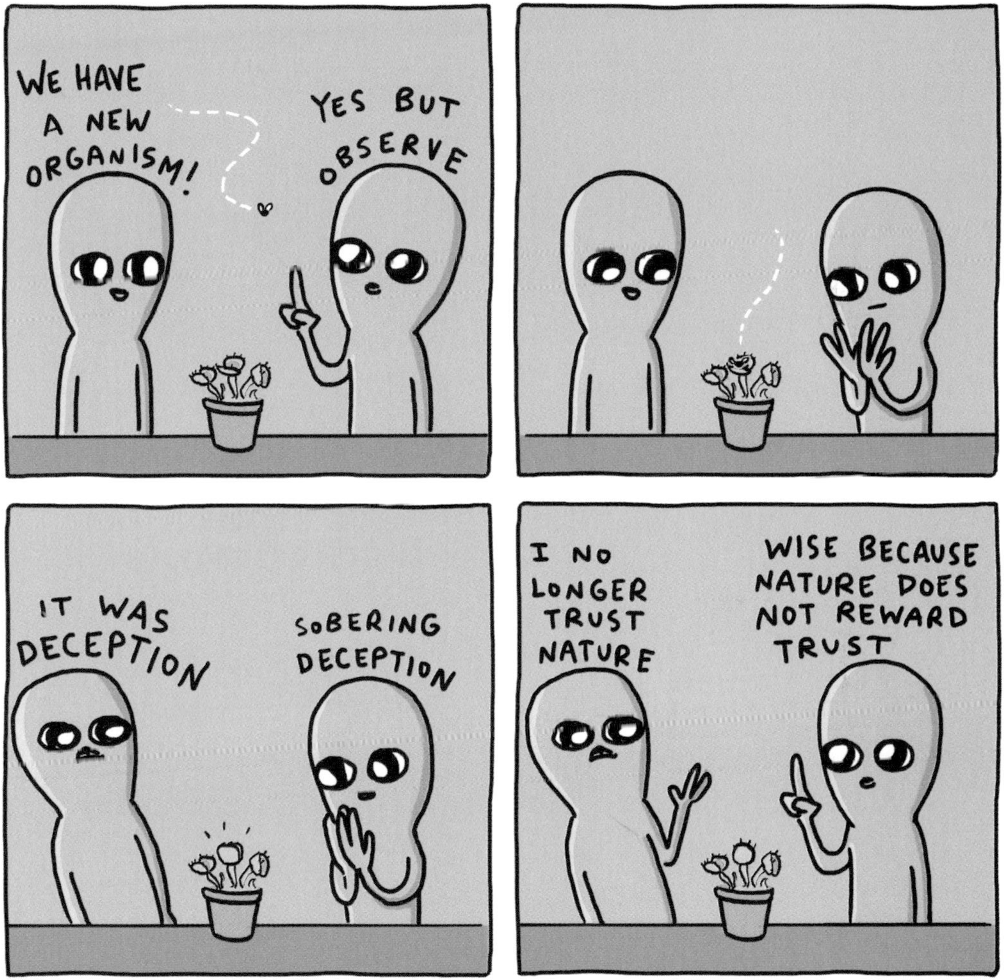
WE HAVE A NEW ORGANISM!
YES BUT OBSERVE
IT WAS DECEPTION
SOBERING DECEPTION
I NO LONGER TRUST NATURE
WISE BECAUSE NATURE DOES NOT REWARD TRUST

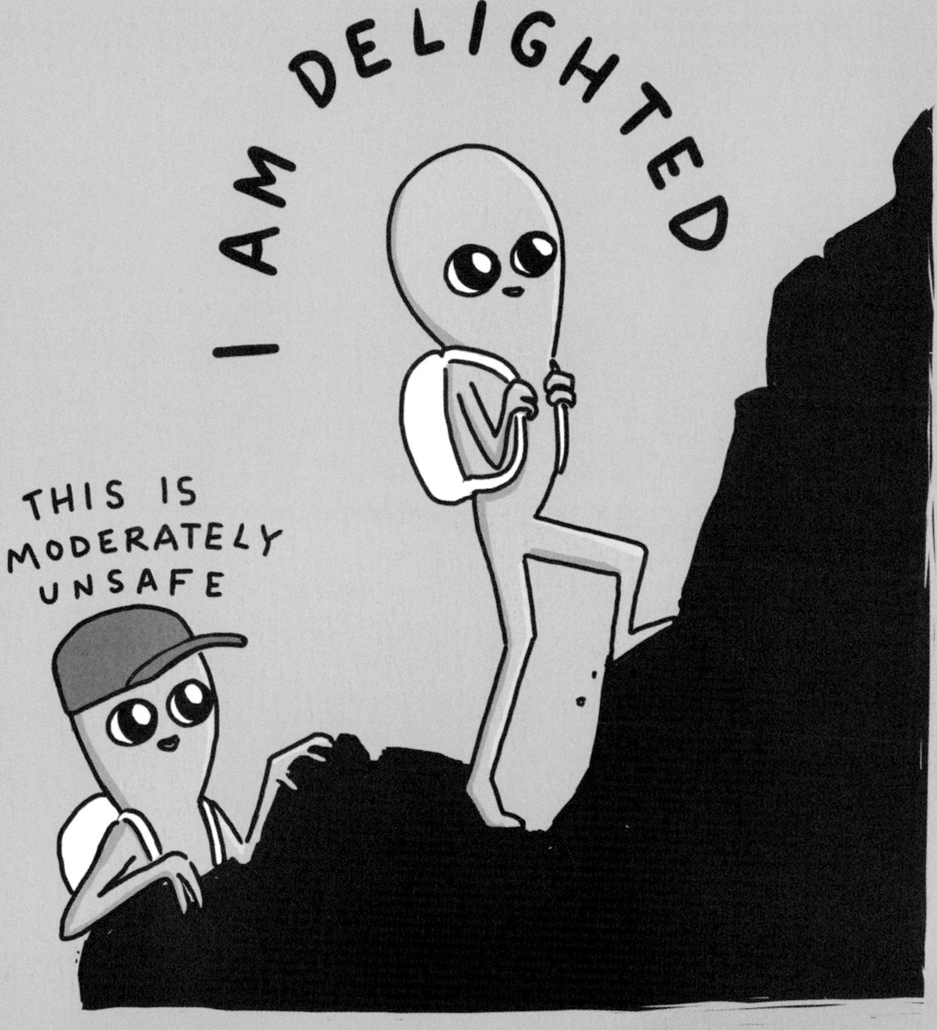
I AM DELIGHTED
THIS IS MODERATELY UNSAFE

RECREATION

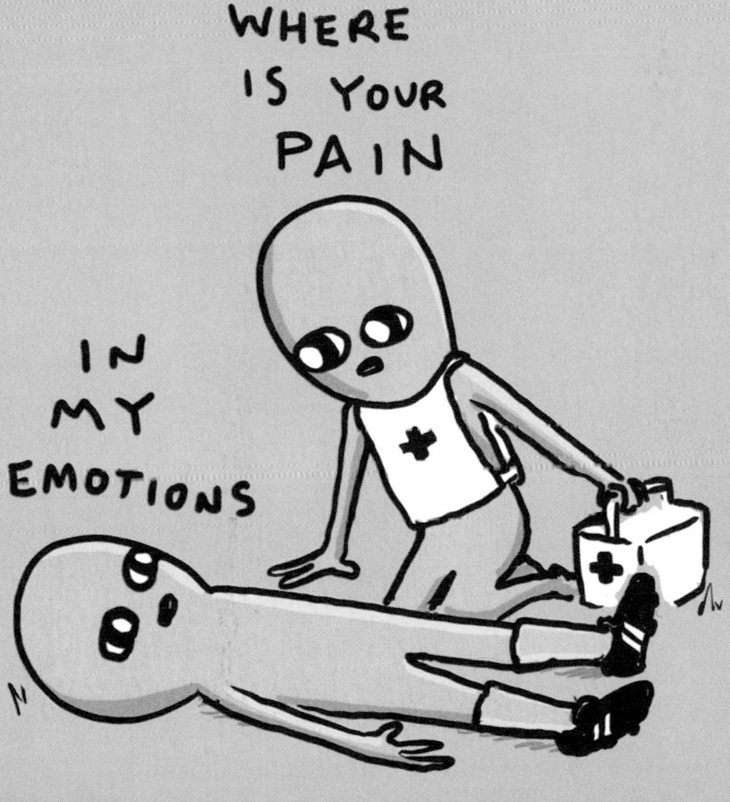

WHERE IS YOUR PAIN
IN MY EMOTIONS

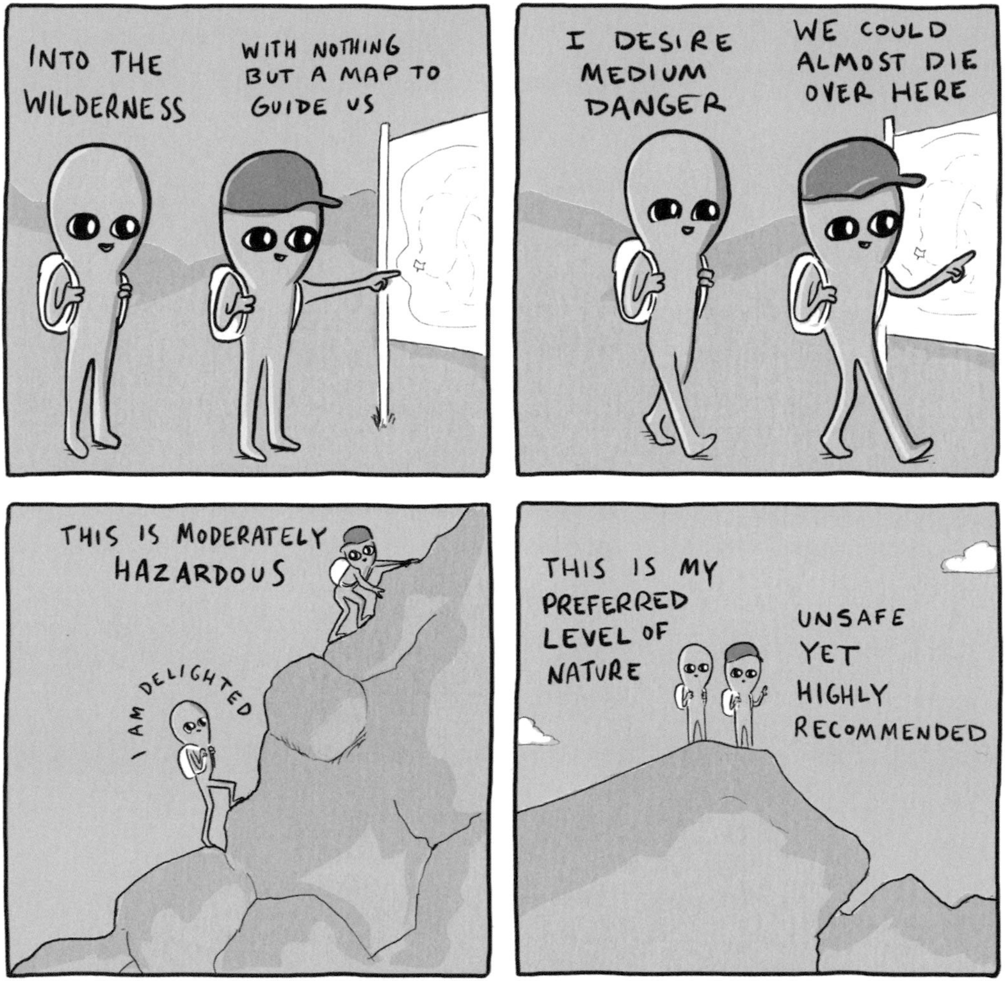
INTO THE WILDERNESS
WITH NOTHING BUT A MAP TO GUIDE US
I DESIRE MEDIUM DANGER
WE COULD ALMOST DIE OVER HERE
THIS IS MODERATELY HAZARDOUS
I AM DELIGHTED
THIS IS MY PREFERRED LEVEL OF NATURE
UNSAFE YET HIGHLY RECOMMENDED

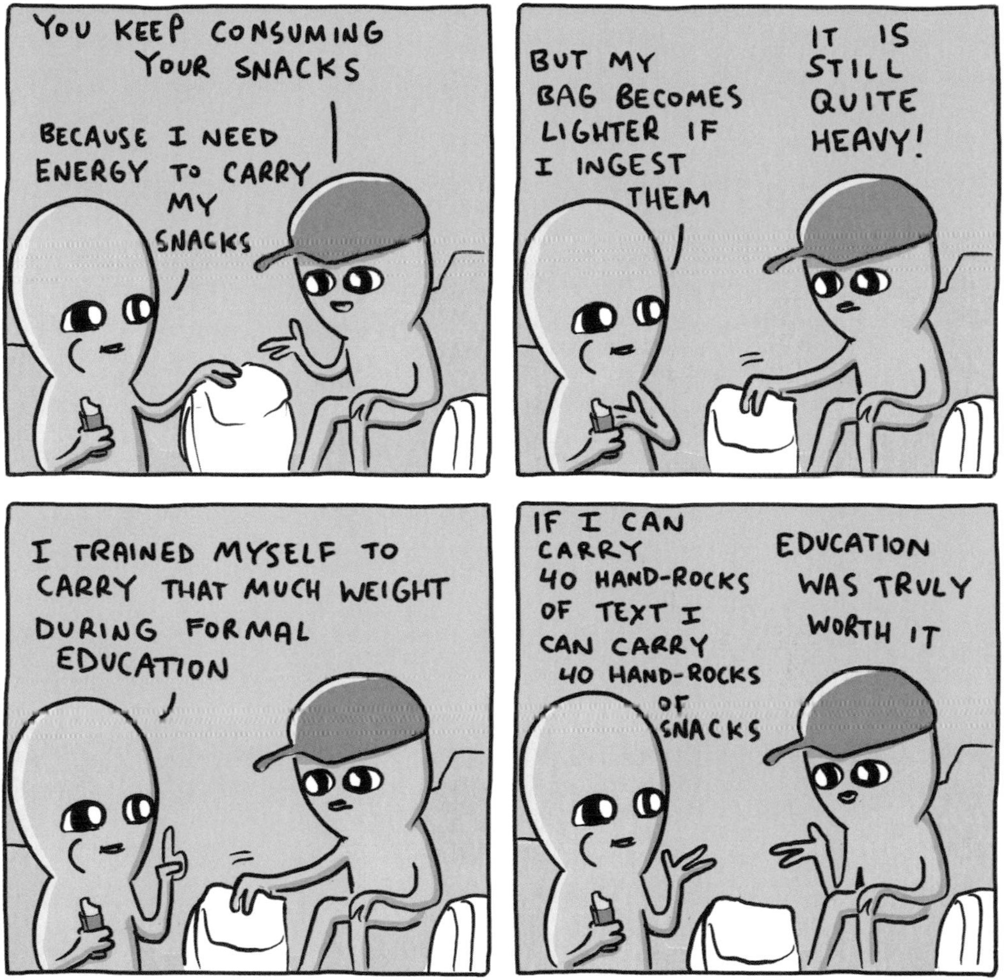
YOU KEEP CONSUMING YOUR SNACKS
BECAUSE I NEED ENERGY TO CARRY MY SNACKS
BUT MY BAG BECOMES LIGHTER IF I INGEST THEM
IT IS STILL QUITE HEAVY!
I TRAINED MYSELF TO CARRY THAT MUCH WEIGHT DURING FORMAL EDUCATION
IF I CAN CARRY 40 HAND-ROCKS OF TEXT I CAN CARRY 40 HAND-ROCKS OF SNACKS
EDUCATION WAS TRULY WORTH IT

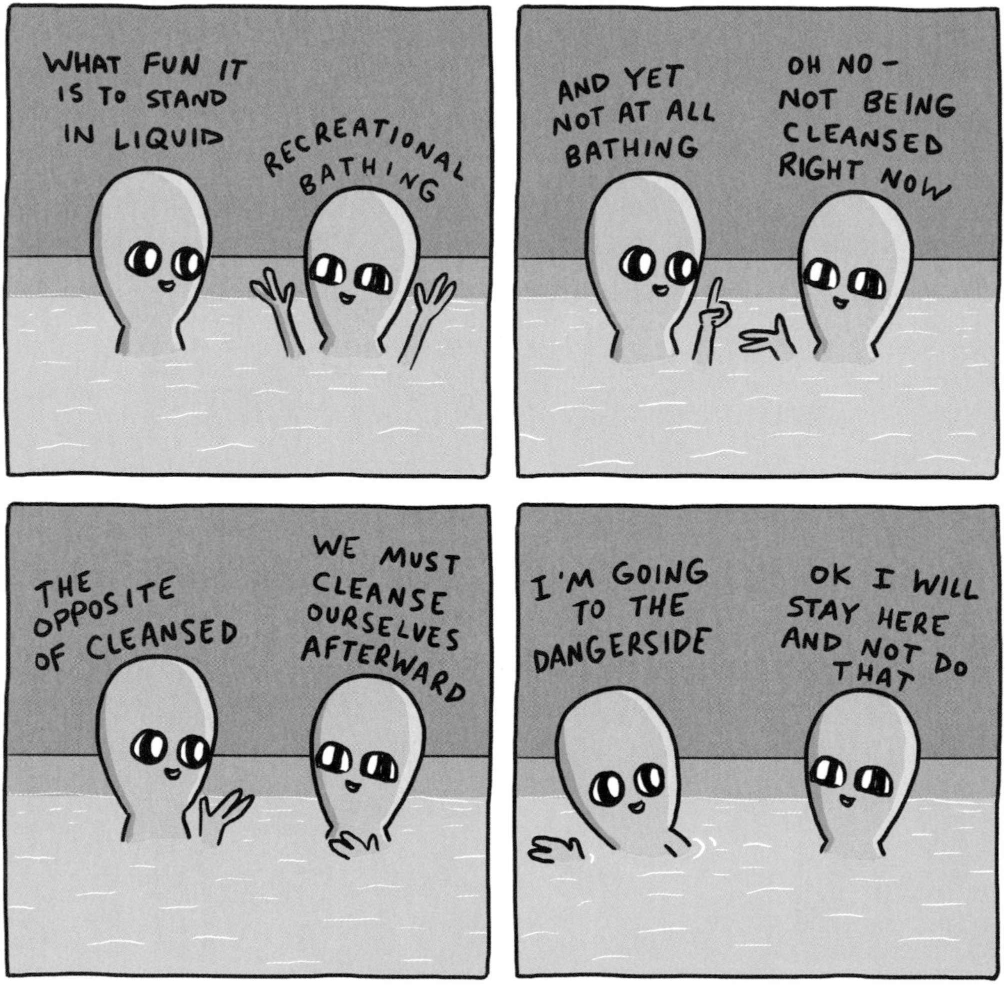
WHAT FUN IT IS TO STAND IN LIQUID
RECREATIONAL BATHING
AND YET NOT AT ALL BATHING
OH NO - NOT BEING CLEANSED RIGHT NOW
THE OPPOSITE OF CLEANSED
WE MUST CLEANSE OURSELVES AFTERWARD
I'M GOING TO THE DANGERSIDE
OK I WILL STAY HERE AND NOT DO THAT

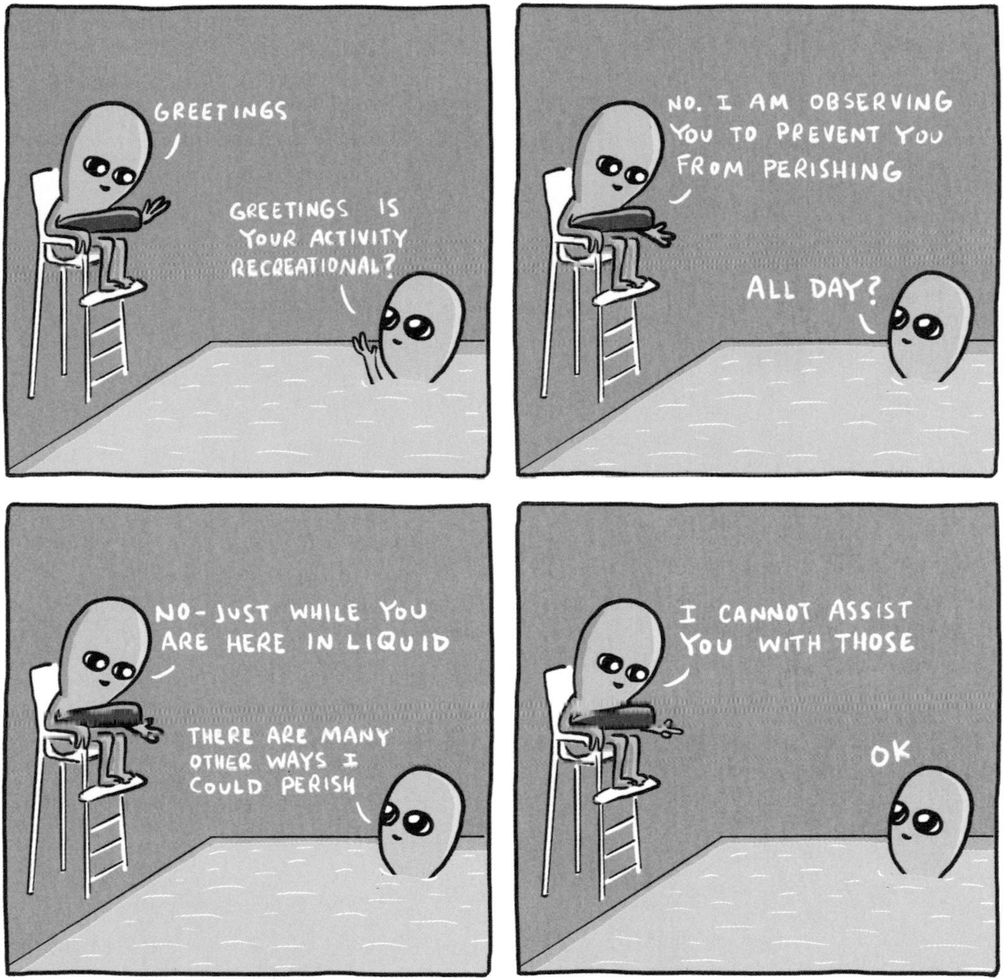
GREETINGS
GREETINGS IS YOUR ACTIVITY RECREATIONAL?
NO. I AM OBSERVING YOU TO PREVENT YOU FROM PERISHING
ALL DAY?
NO- JUST WHILE YOU ARE HERE IN LIQUID
THERE ARE MANY OTHER WAYS I COULD PERISH
I CANNOT ASSIST YOU WITH THOSE
OK

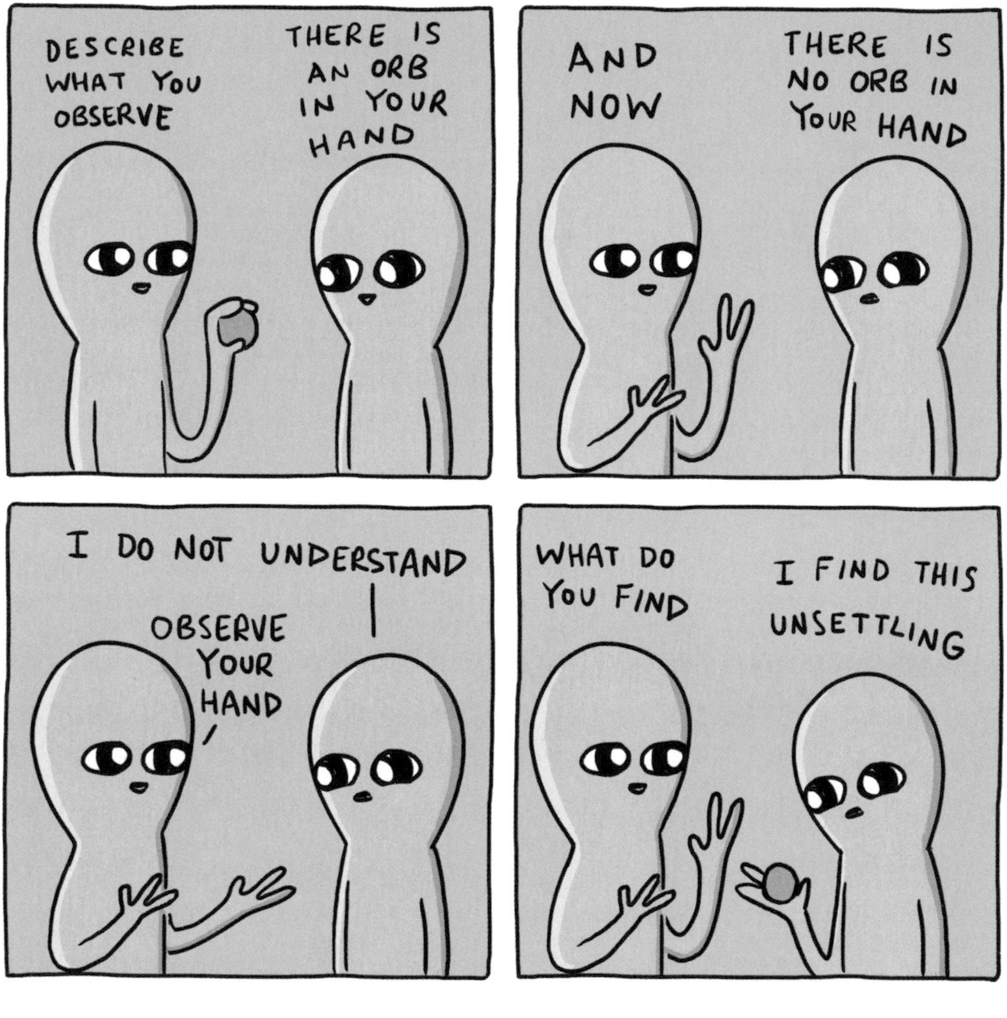
DESCRIBE WHAT YOU OBSERVE
THERE IS AN ORB IN YOUR HAND
AND NOW
THERE IS NO ORB IN YOUR HAND
I DO NOT UNDERSTAND
OBSERVE YOUR HAND
WHAT DO YOU FIND
I FIND THIS UNSETTLING

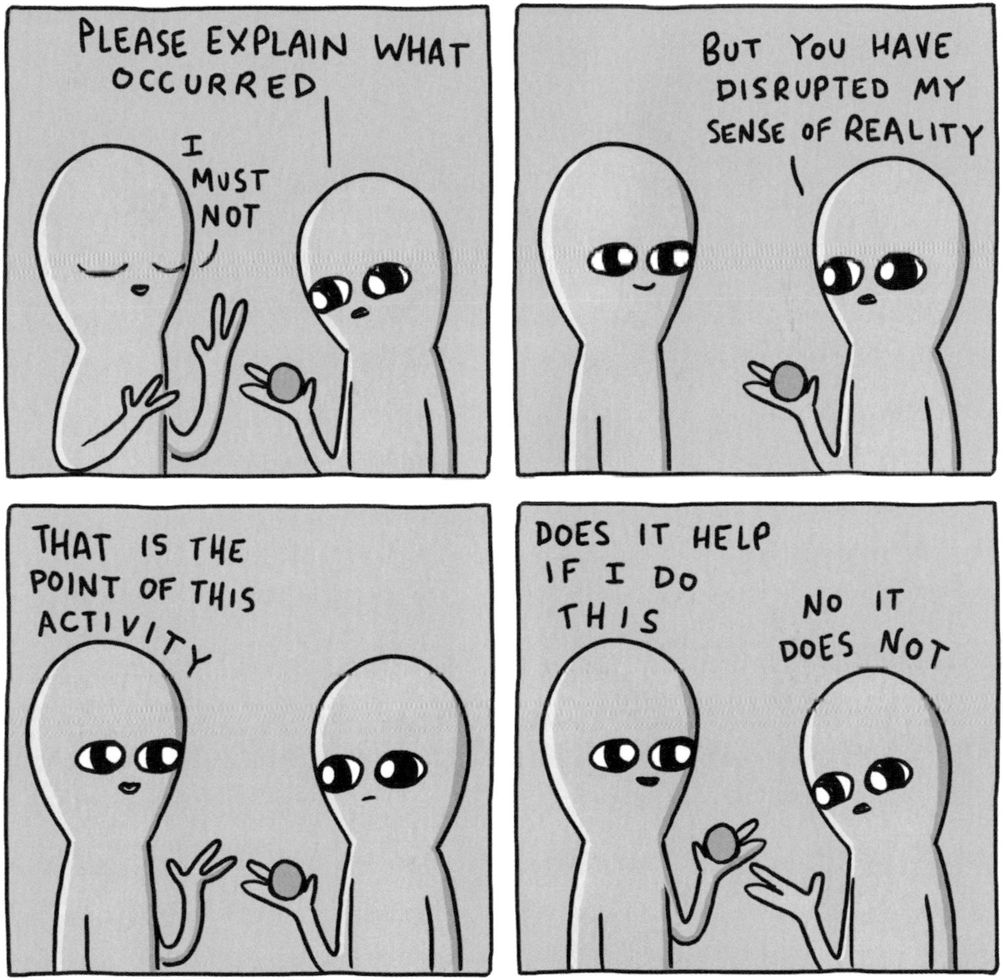
PLEASE EXPLAIN WHAT OCCURRED
I MUST NOT
BUT YOU HAVE DISRUPTED MY SENSE OF REALITY
THAT IS THE POINT OF THIS ACTIVITY
DOES IT HELP IF I DO THIS
NO IT DOES NOT

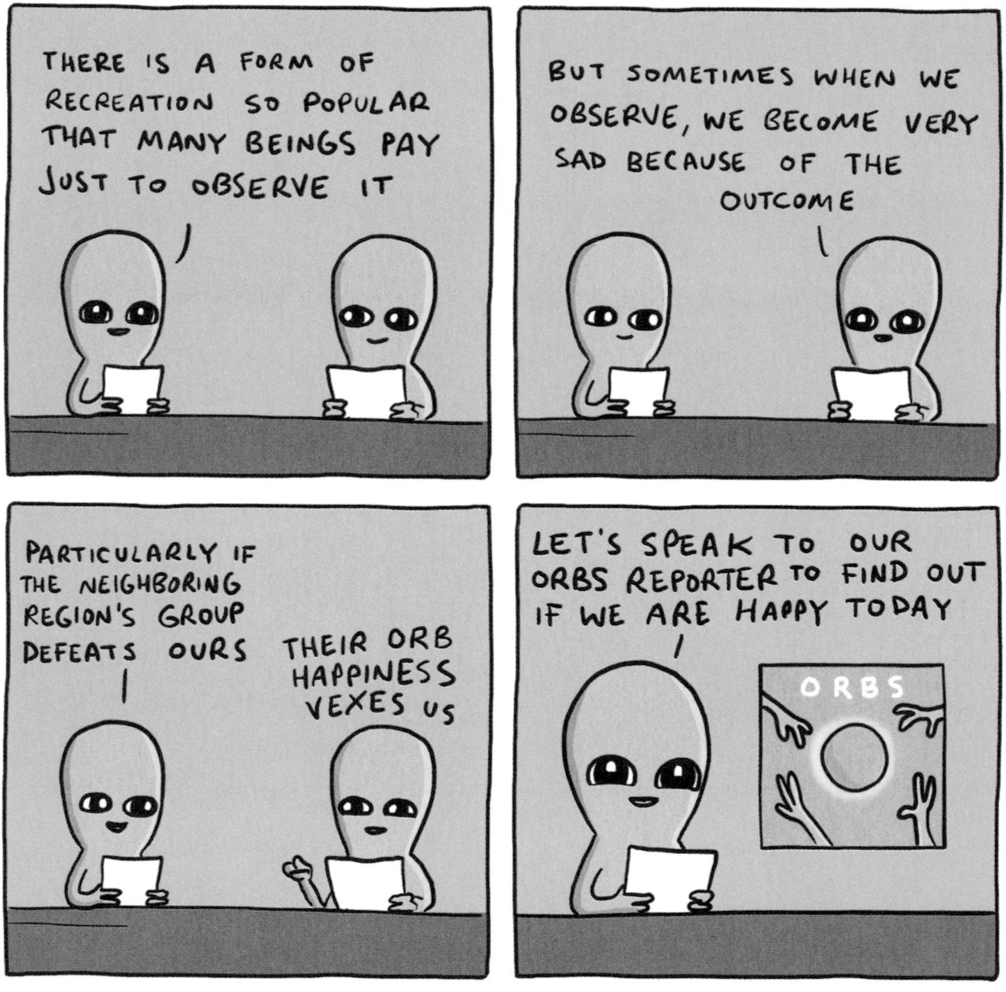
THERE IS A FORM OF RECREATION SO POPULAR THAT MANY BEINGS PAY JUST TO OBSERVE IT
BUT SOMETIMES WHEN WE OBSERVE, WE BECOME VERY SAD BECAUSE OF THE OUTCOME
PARTICULARLY IF THE NEIGHBORING REGION'S GROUP DEFEATS OURS
THEIR ORB HAPPINESS VEXES US
LET'S SPEAK TO OUR ORBS REPORTER TO FIND OUT IF WE ARE HAPPY TODAY
ORBS

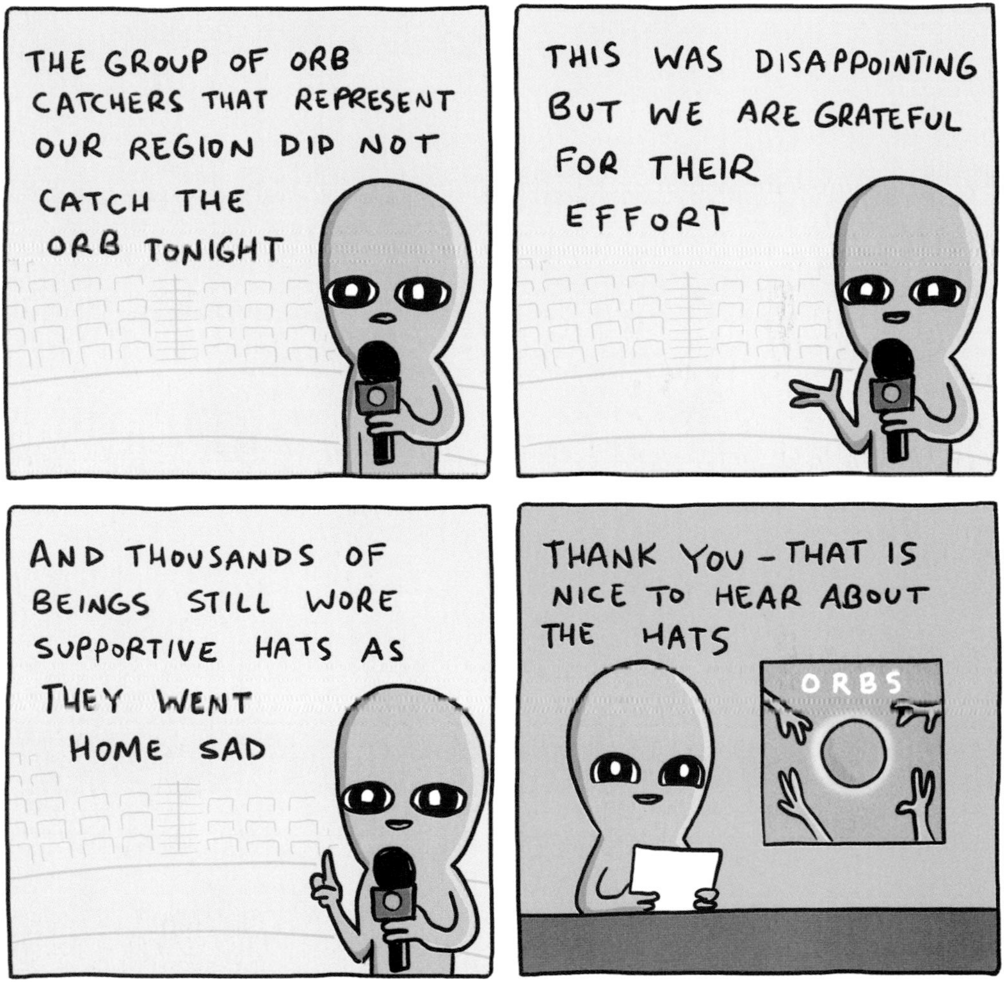
THE GROUP OF ORB CATCHERS THAT REPRESENT OUR REGION DID NOT CATCH THE ORB TONIGHT
THIS WAS DISAPPOINTING BUT WE ARE GRATEFUL FOR THEIR EFFORT
AND THOUSANDS OF BEINGS STILL WORE SUPPORTIVE HATS AS THEY WENT HOME SAD
THANK YOU - THAT IS NICE TO HEAR ABOUT THE HATS
ORBS

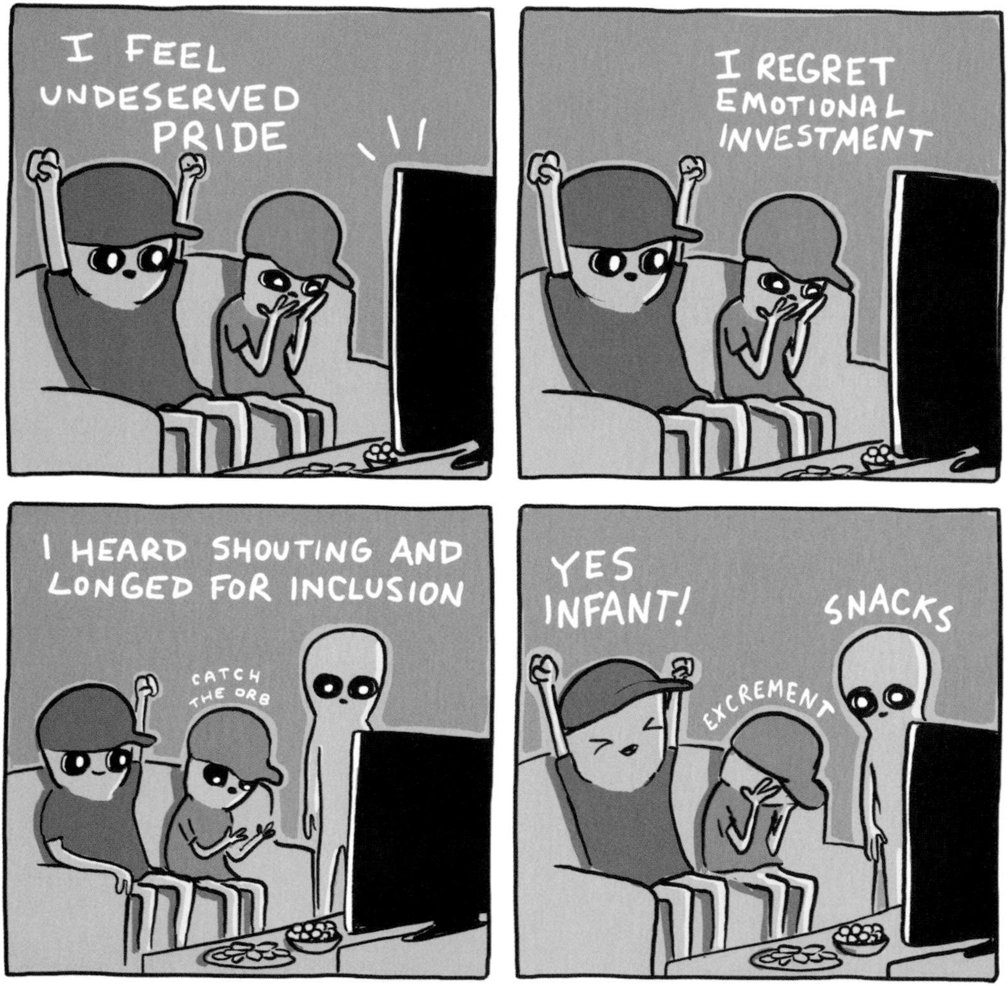

I FEEL UNDESERVED PRIDE
I REGRET EMOTIONAL INVESTMENT
I HEARD SHOUTING AND LONGED FOR INCLUSION
CATCH THE ORB
YES INFANT!
EXCREMENT
SNACKS

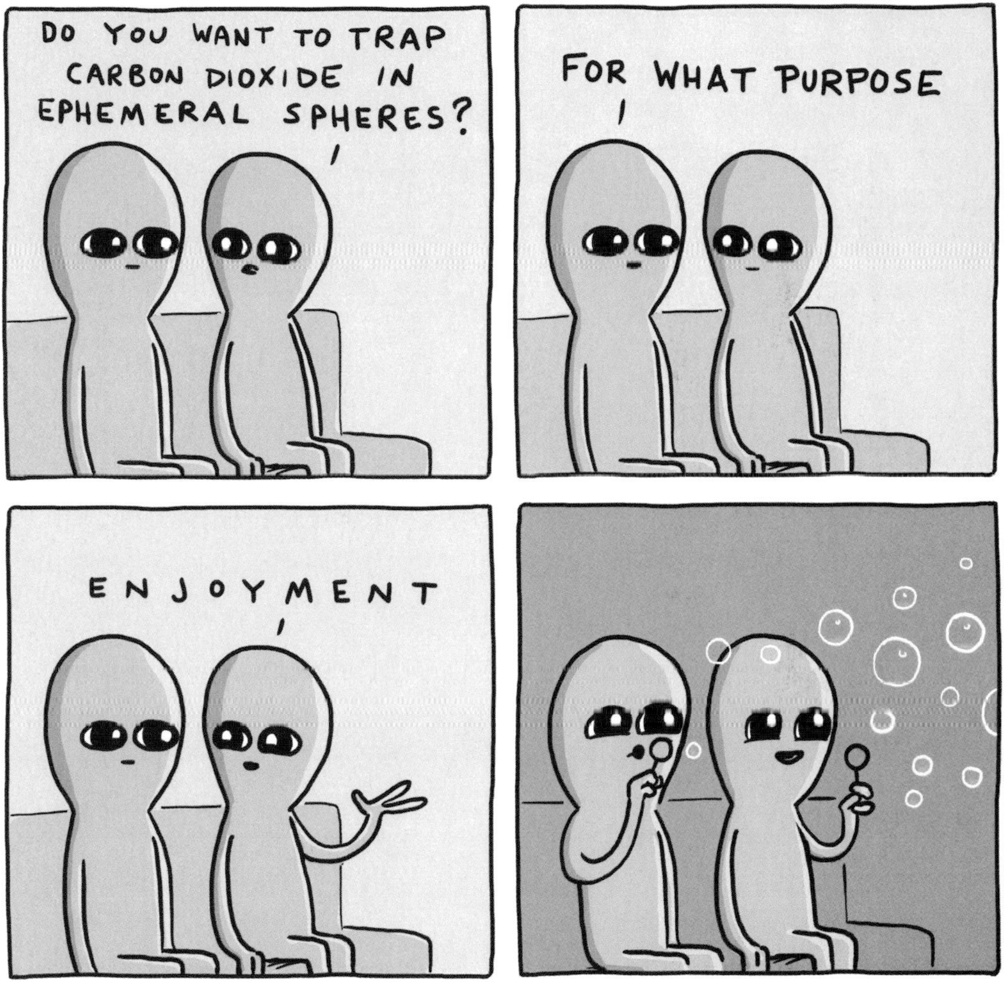
DO YOU WANT TO TRAP CARBON DIOXIDE IN EPHEMERAL SPHERES?
FOR WHAT PURPOSE
ENJOYMENT

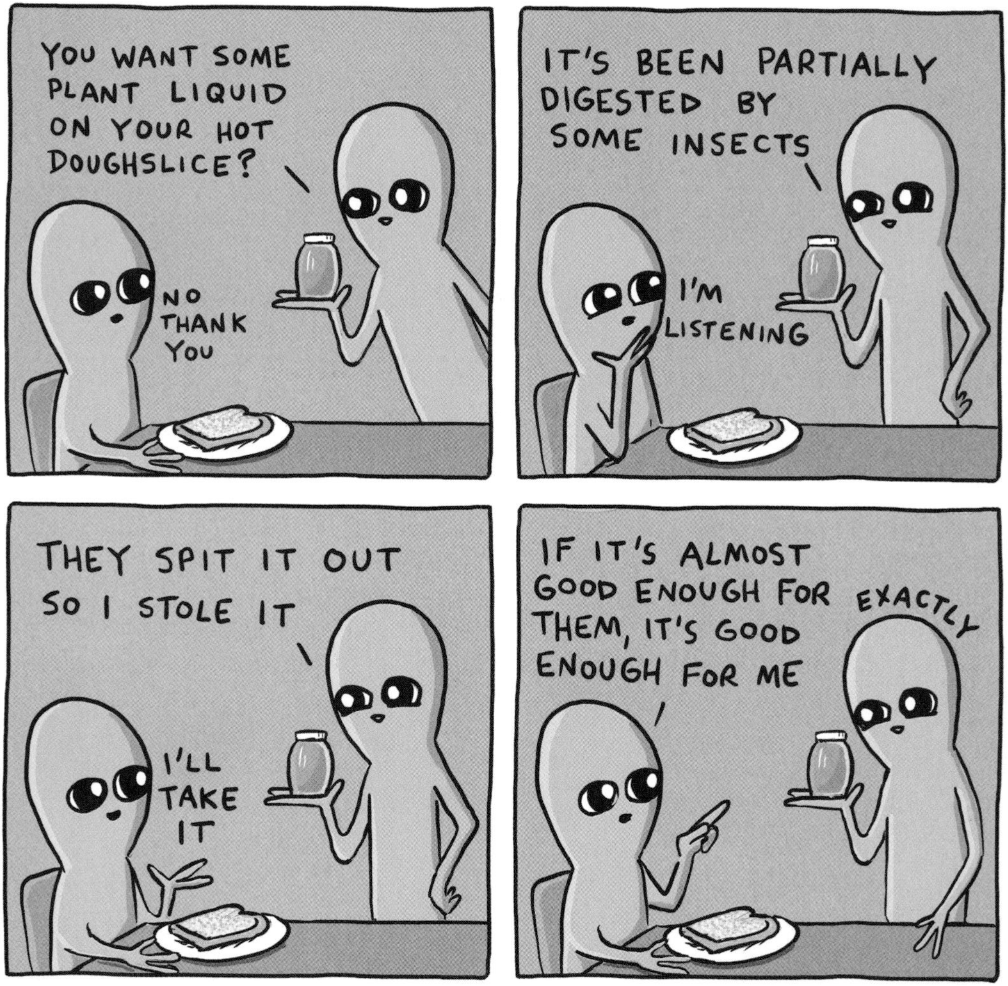
YOU WANT SOME PLANT LIQUID ON YOUR HOT DOUGHSLICE?
NO THANK YOU
IT'S BEEN PARTIALLY DIGESTED BY SOME INSECTS
I'M LISTENING
THEY SPIT IT OUT SO I STOLE IT
I'LL TAKE IT
IF IT'S ALMOST GOOD ENOUGH FOR THEM, IT'S GOOD ENOUGH FOR ME
EXACTLY

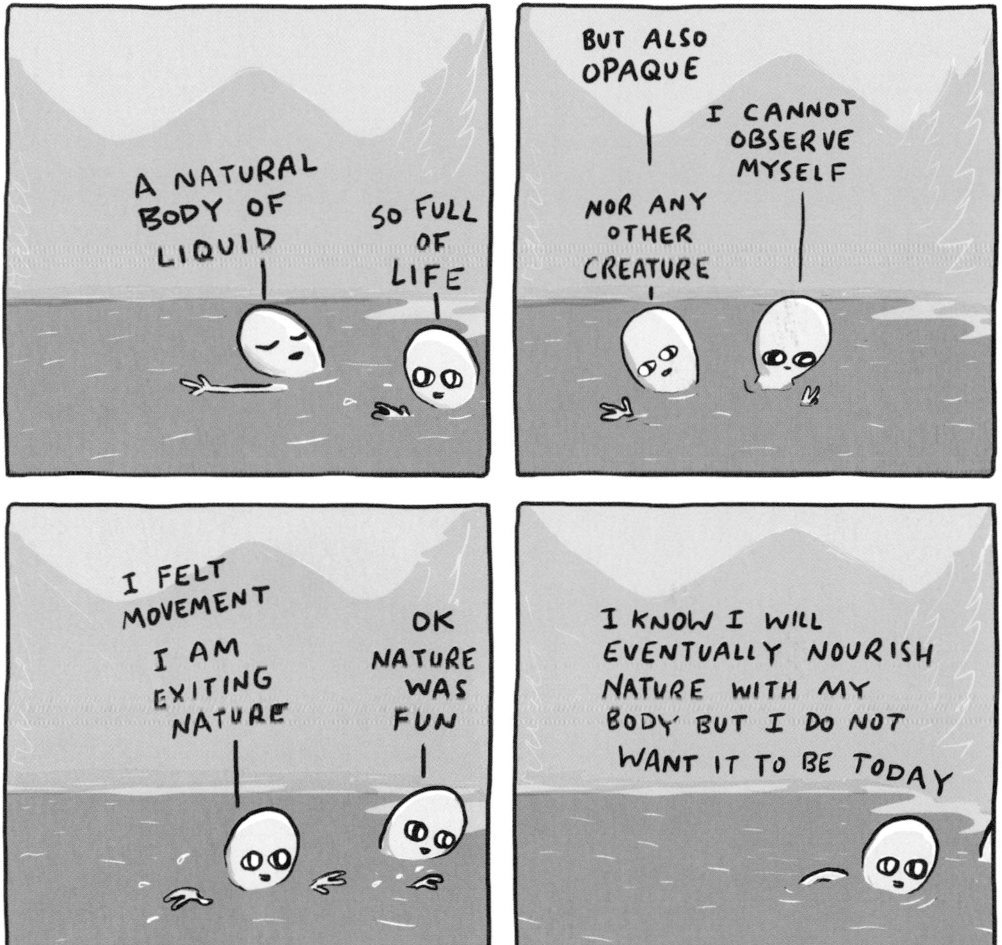
A NATURAL BODY OF LIQUID
SO FULL OF LIFE
BUT ALSO OPAQUE
I CANNOT OBSERVE MYSELF
NOR ANY OTHER CREATURE
I FELT MOVEMENT
I AM EXITING NATURE
OK NATURE WAS FUN
I KNOW I WILL EVENTUALLY NOURISH NATURE WITH MY BODY BUT I DO NOT WANT IT TO BE TODAY

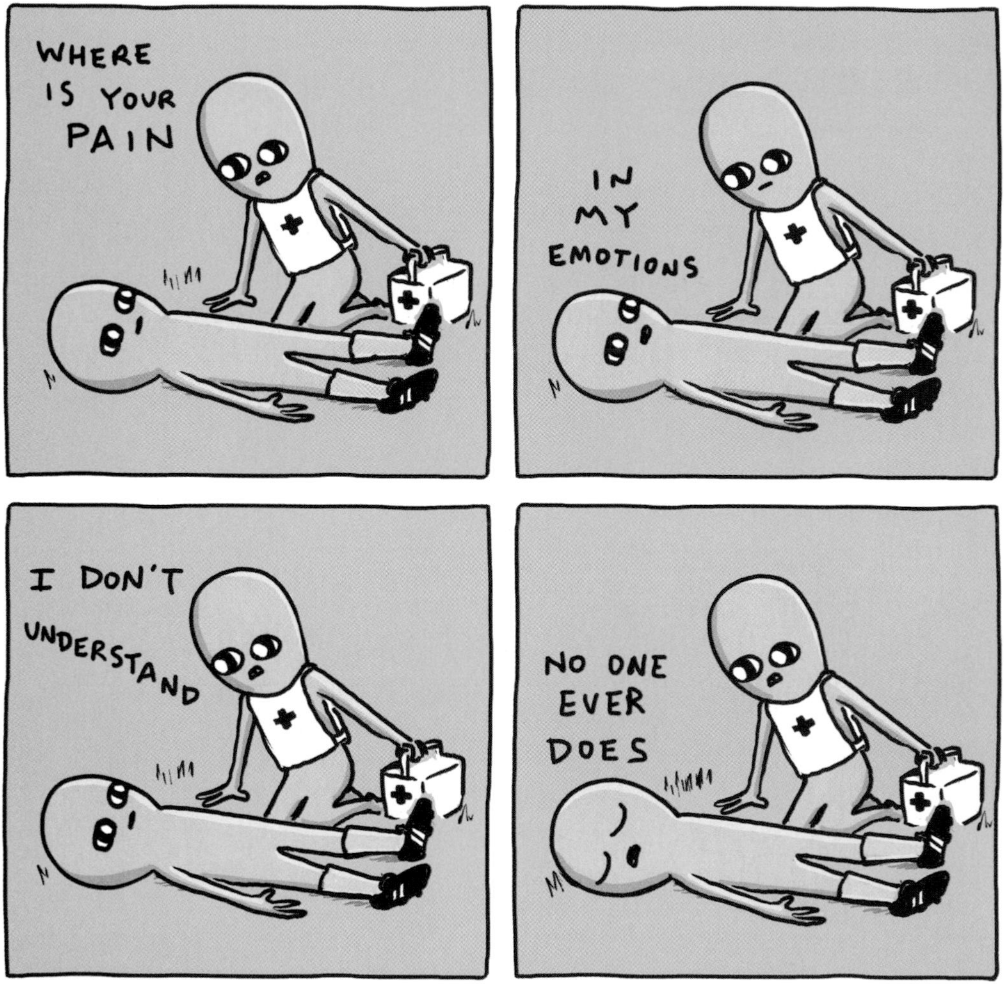
WHERE IS YOUR PAIN
IN MY EMOTIONS
I DON'T UNDERSTAND
NO ONE EVER DOES

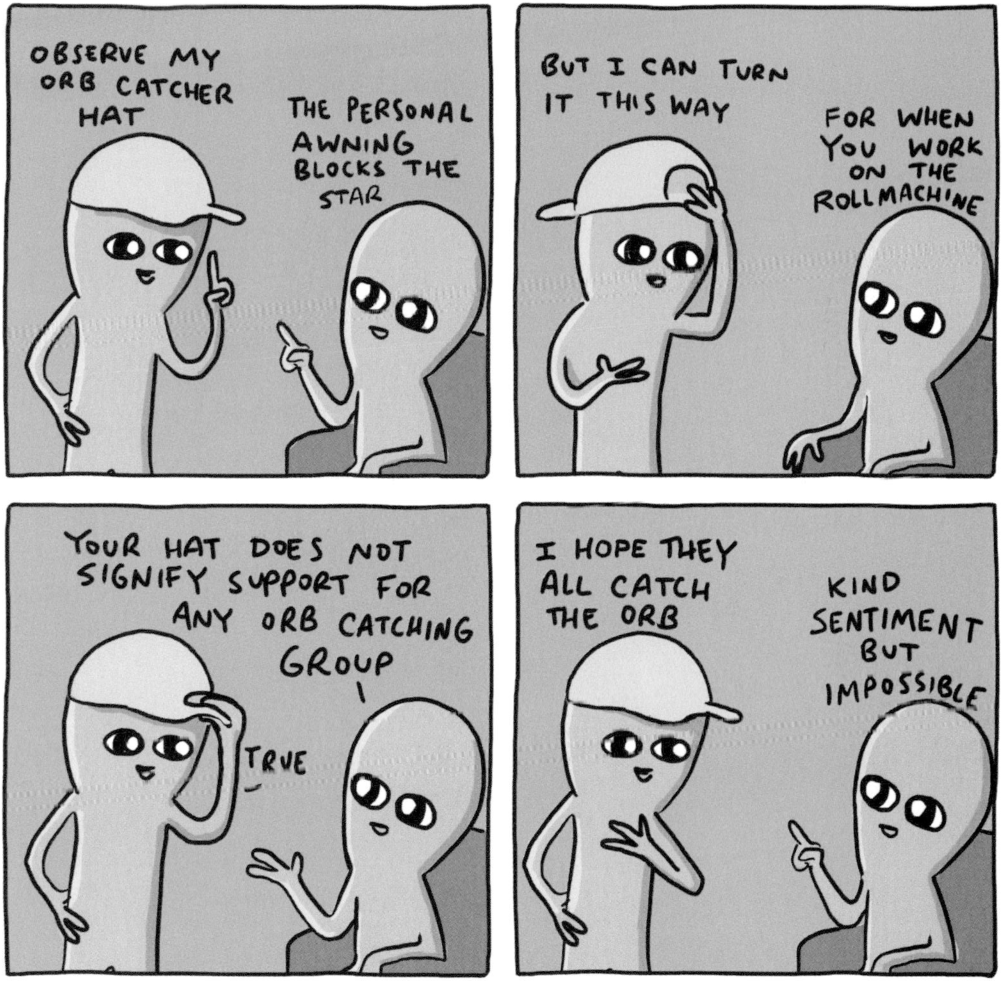
OBSERVE MY ORB CATCHER HAT
THE PERSONAL AWNING BLOCKS THE STAR
BUT I CAN TURN IT THIS WAY
FOR WHEN YOU WORK ON THE ROLLMACHINE
YOUR HAT DOES NOT SIGNIFY SUPPORT FOR ANY ORB CATCHING GROUP
TRUE
I HOPE THEY ALL CATCH THE ORB
KIND SENTIMENT BUT IMPOSSIBLE

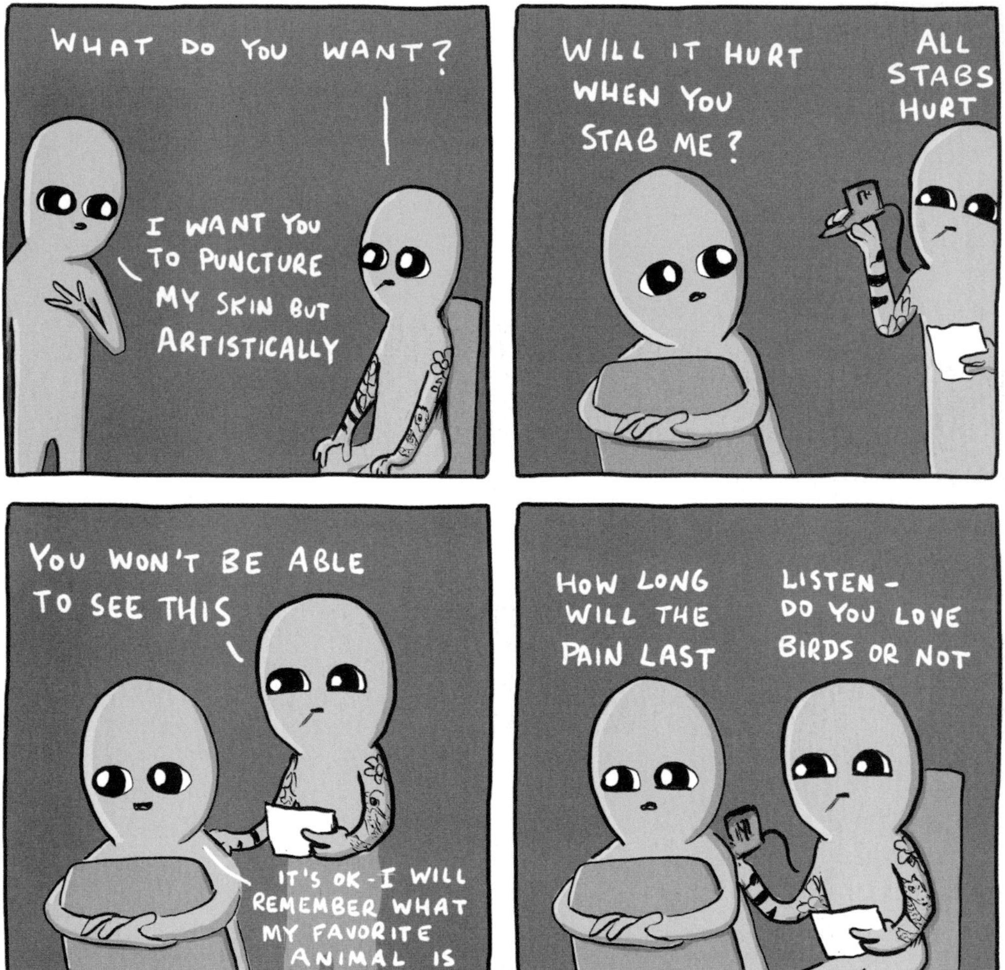
WHAT DO YOU WANT?
I WANT YOU TO PUNCTURE MY SKIN BUT ARTISTICALLY
WILL IT HURT WHEN YOU STAB ME?
ALL STABS HURT
YOU WON'T BE ABLE TO SEE THIS
IT'S OK - I WILL REMEMBER WHAT MY FAVORITE ANIMAL IS
HOW LONG WILL THE PAIN LAST
LISTEN - DO YOU LOVE BIRDS OR NOT

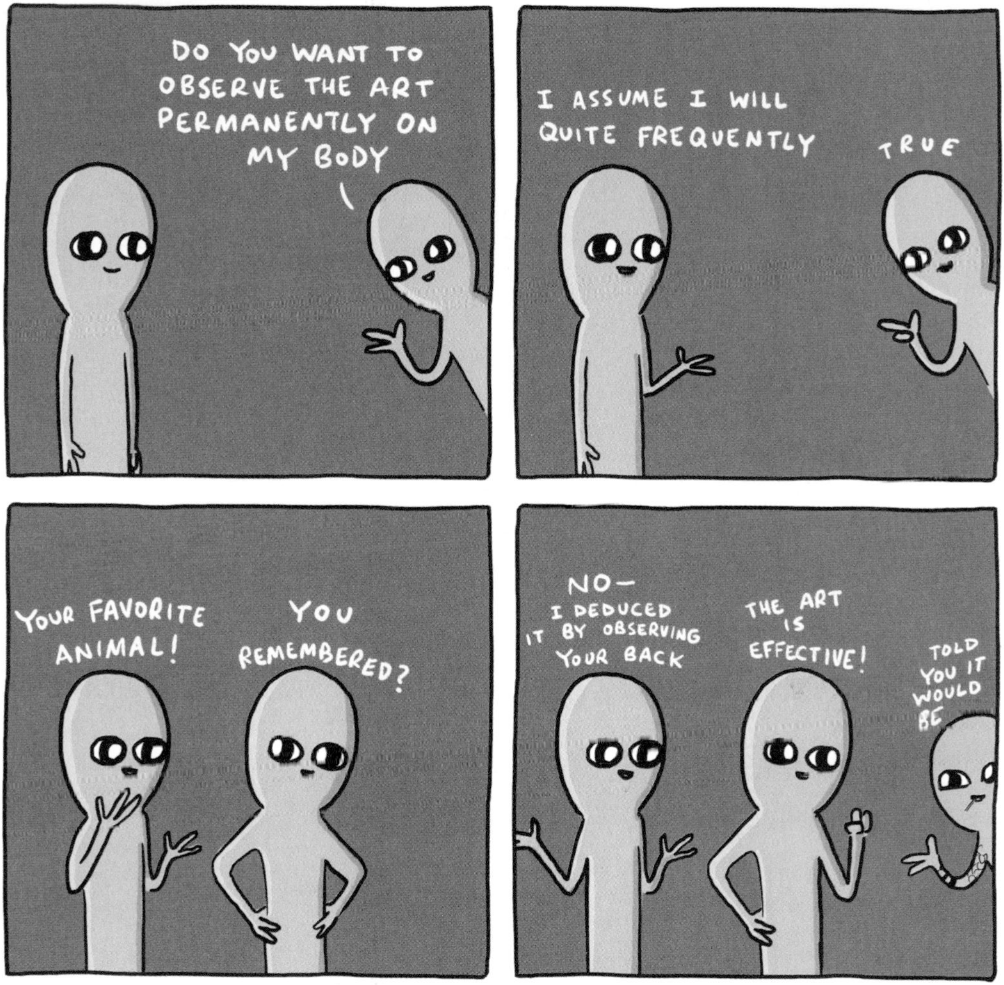
DO YOU WANT TO OBSERVE THE ART PERMANENTLY ON MY BODY
I ASSUME I WILL QUITE FREQUENTLY
TRUE
YOUR FAVORITE ANIMAL!
YOU REMEMBERED?
NO—
I DEDUCED IT BY OBSERVING YOUR BACK
THE ART IS EFFECTIVE!
TOLD YOU IT WOULD BE

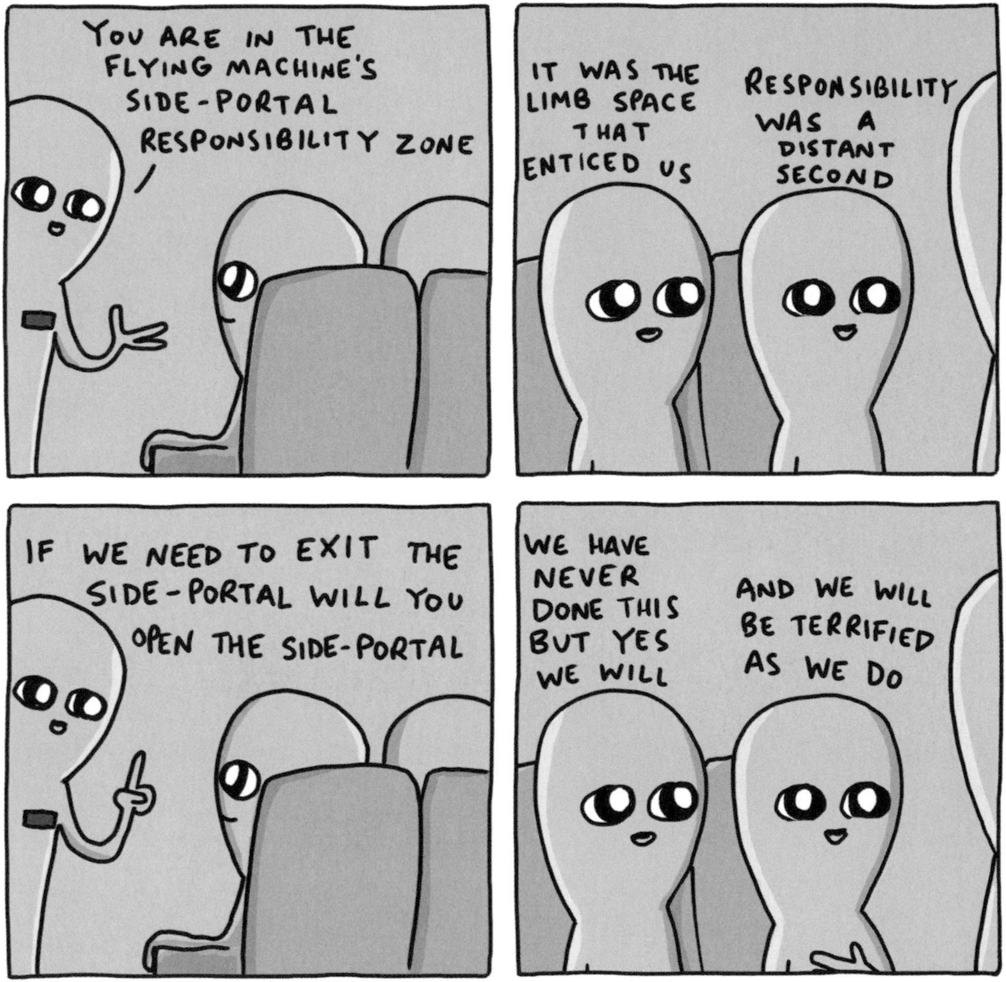
YOU ARE IN THE FLYING MACHINE'S SIDE-PORTAL RESPONSIBILITY ZONE
IT WAS THE LIMB SPACE THAT ENTICED US
RESPONSIBILITY WAS A DISTANT SECOND
IF WE NEED TO EXIT THE SIDE-PORTAL WILL YOU OPEN THE SIDE-PORTAL
WE HAVE NEVER DONE THIS BUT YES WE WILL
AND WE WILL BE TERRIFIED AS WE DO

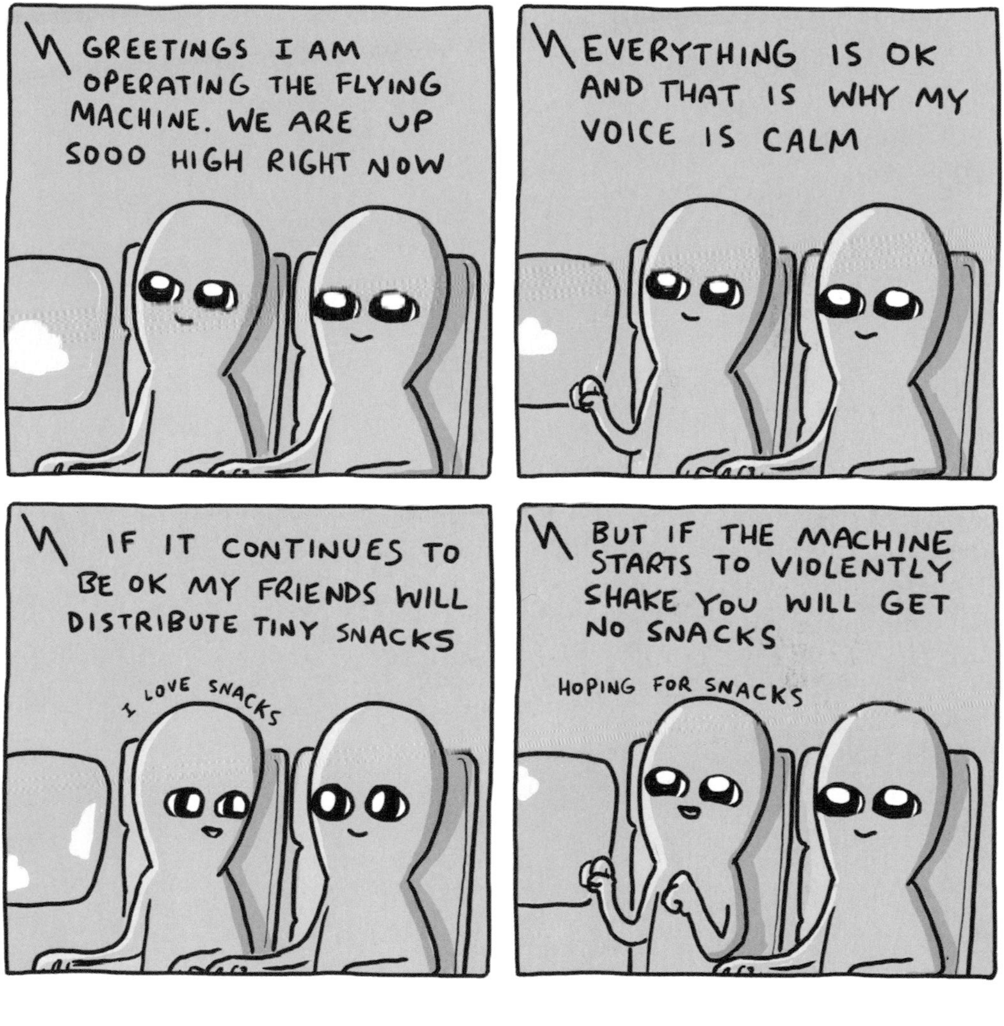
GREETINGS I AM OPERATING THE FLYING MACHINE. WE ARE UP SOOO HIGH RIGHT NOW
EVERYTHING IS OK AND THAT IS WHY MY VOICE IS CALM
IF IT CONTINUES TO BE OK MY FRIENDS WILL DISTRIBUTE TINY SNACKS
I LOVE SNACKS
BUT IF THE MACHINE STARTS TO VIOLENTLY SHAKE YOU WILL GET NO SNACKS
HOPING FOR SNACKS

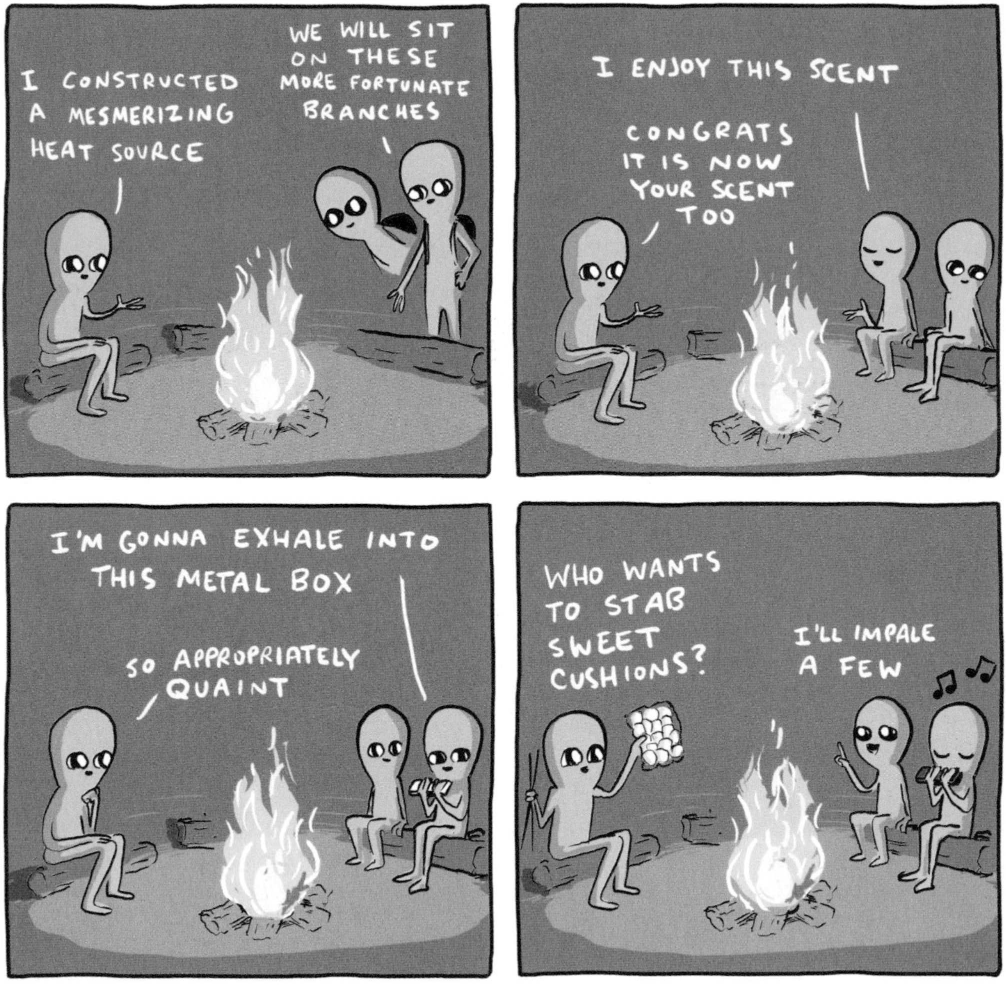
I CONSTRUCTED A MESMERIZING HEAT SOURCE
WE WILL SIT ON THESE MORE FORTUNATE BRANCHES
I ENJOY THIS SCENT
CONGRATS IT IS NOW YOUR SCENT TOO
I'M GONNA EXHALE INTO THIS METAL BOX
SO APPROPRIATELY QUAINT
WHO WANTS TO STAB SWEET CUSHIONS?
I'LL IMPALE A FEW

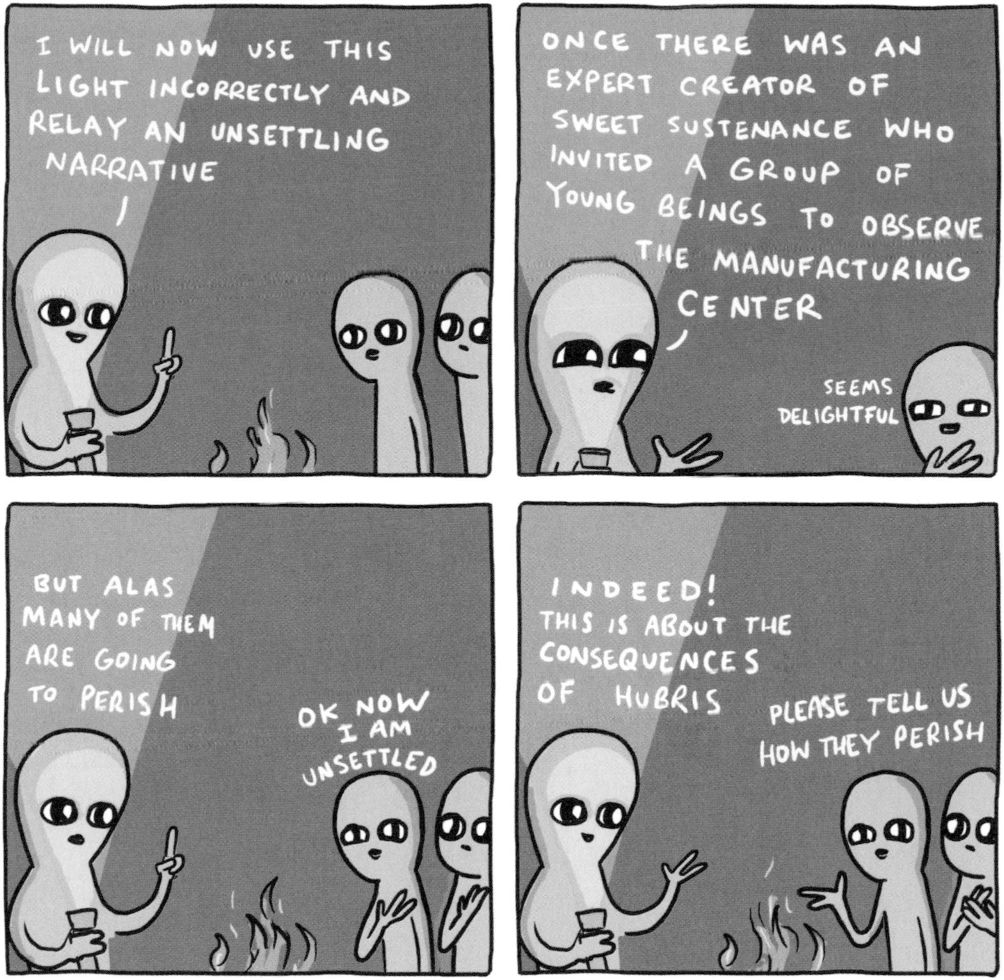

I WILL NOW USE THIS LIGHT INCORRECTLY AND RELAY AN UNSETTLING NARRATIVE
ONCE THERE WAS AN EXPERT CREATOR OF SWEET SUSTENANCE WHO INVITED A GROUP OF YOUNG BEINGS TO OBSERVE THE MANUFACTURING CENTER
SEEMS DELIGHTFUL
BUT ALAS MANY OF THEM ARE GOING TO PERISH
OK NOW I AM UNSETTLED
INDEED! THIS IS ABOUT THE CONSEQUENCES OF HUBRIS
PLEASE TELL US HOW THEY PERISH

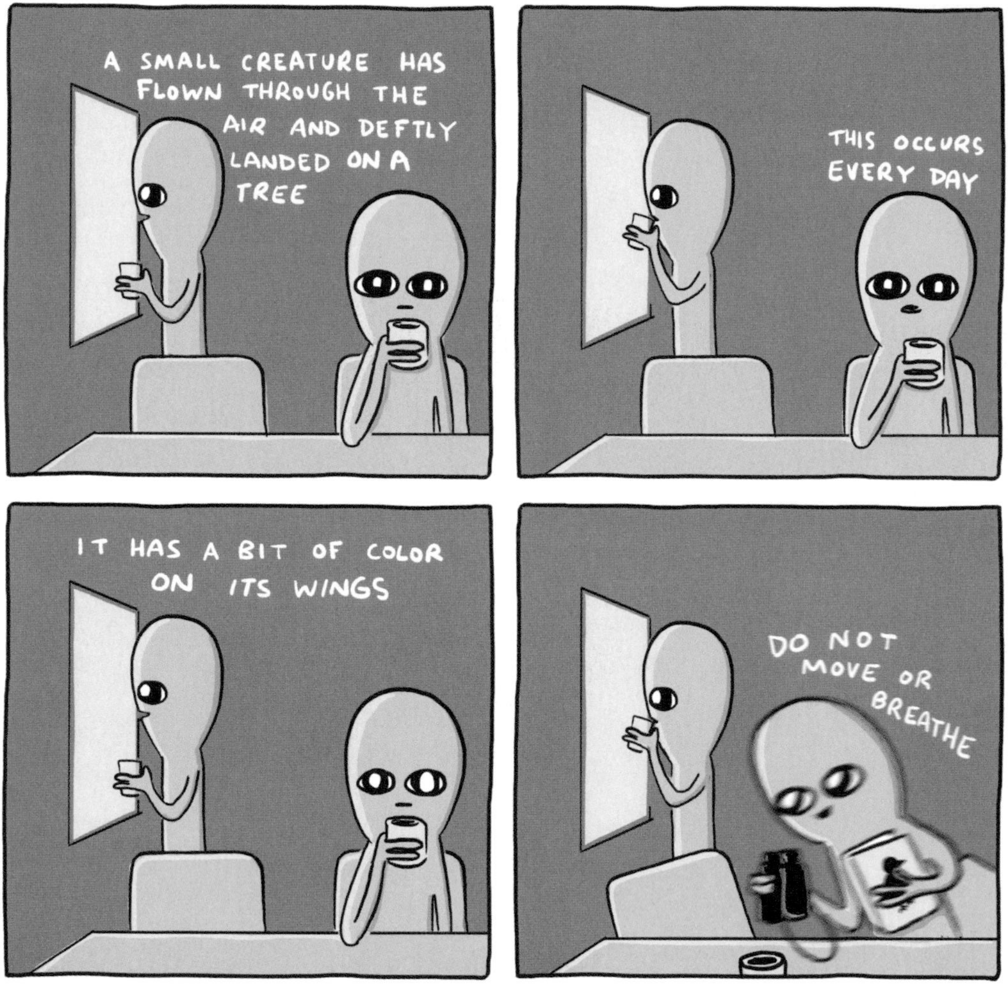

A SMALL CREATURE HAS FLOWN THROUGH THE AIR AND DEFTLY LANDED ON A TREE
THIS OCCURS EVERY DAY
IT HAS A BIT OF COLOR ON ITS WINGS
DO NOT MOVE OR BREATHE

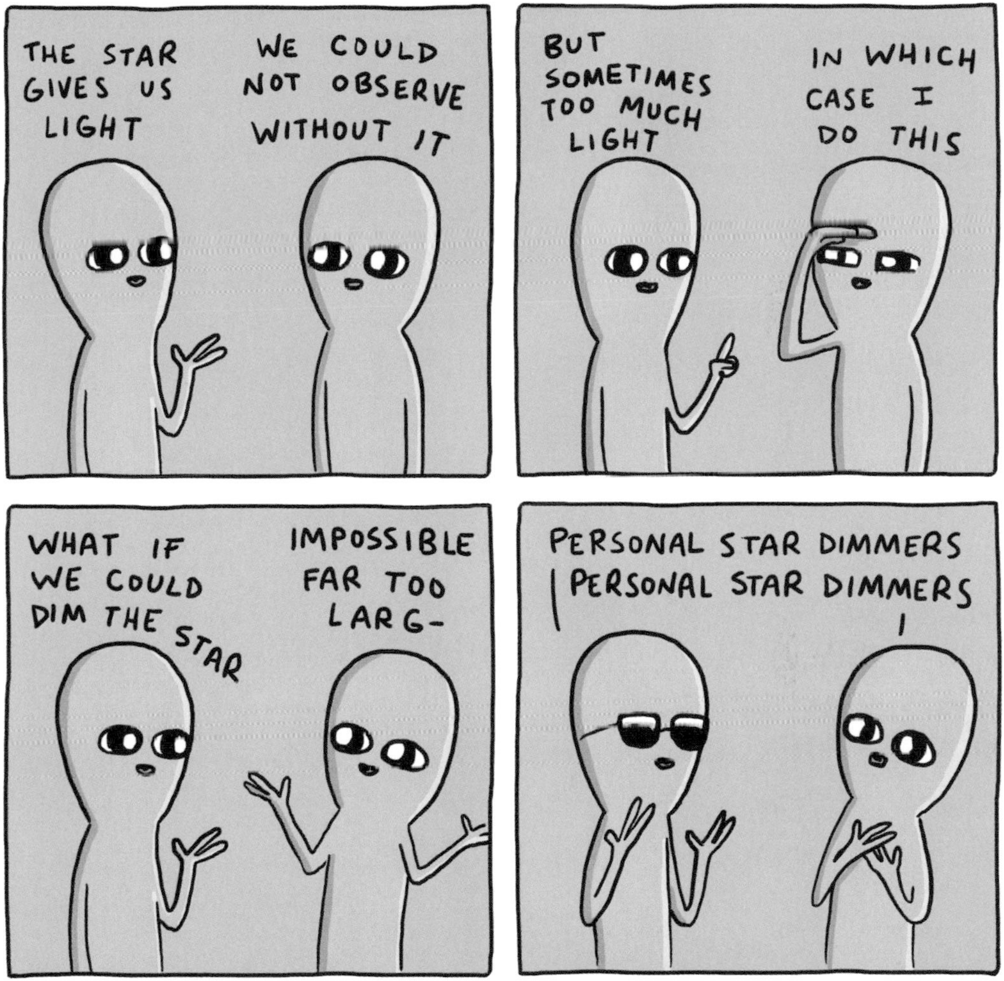
THE STAR GIVES US LIGHT
WE COULD NOT OBSERVE WITHOUT IT
BUT SOMETIMES TOO MUCH LIGHT
IN WHICH CASE I DO THIS
WHAT IF WE COULD DIM THE STAR
IMPOSSIBLE FAR TOO LARG-
PERSONAL STAR DIMMERS
PERSONAL STAR DIMMERS

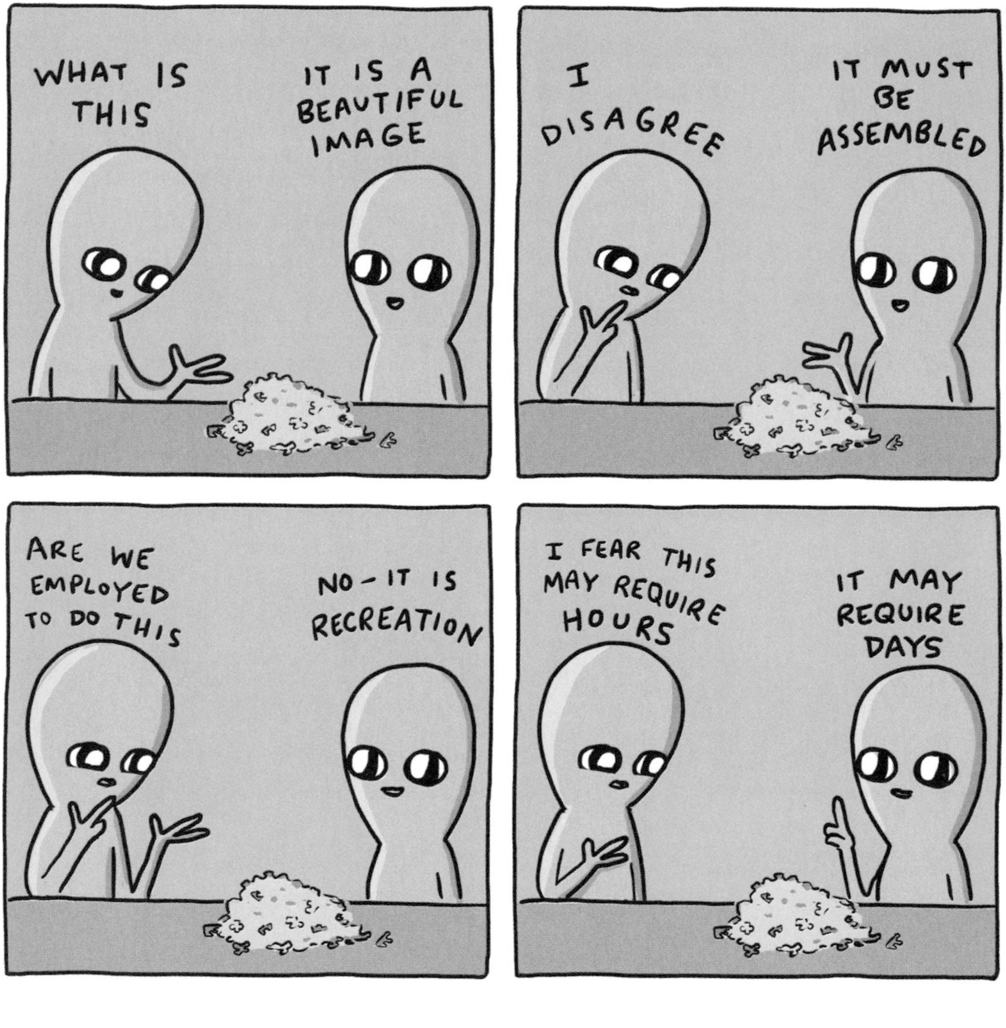
WHAT IS THIS
IT IS A BEAUTIFUL IMAGE
I DISAGREE
IT MUST BE ASSEMBLED
ARE WE EMPLOYED TO DO THIS
NO - IT IS RECREATION
I FEAR THIS MAY REQUIRE HOURS
IT MAY REQUIRE DAYS

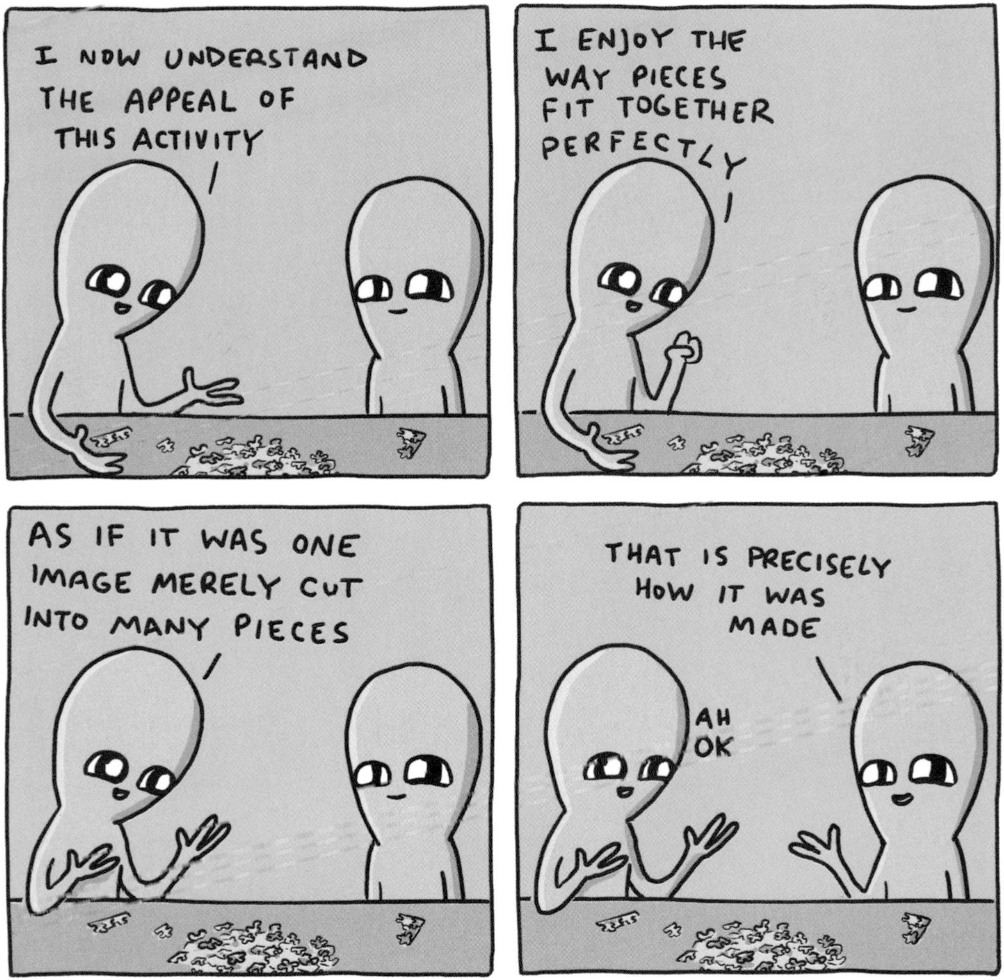
I NOW UNDERSTAND THE APPEAL OF THIS ACTIVITY
I ENJOY THE WAY PIECES FIT TOGETHER PERFECTLY
AS IF IT WAS ONE IMAGE MERELY CUT INTO MANY PIECES
THAT IS PRECISELY HOW IT WAS MADE
AH OK

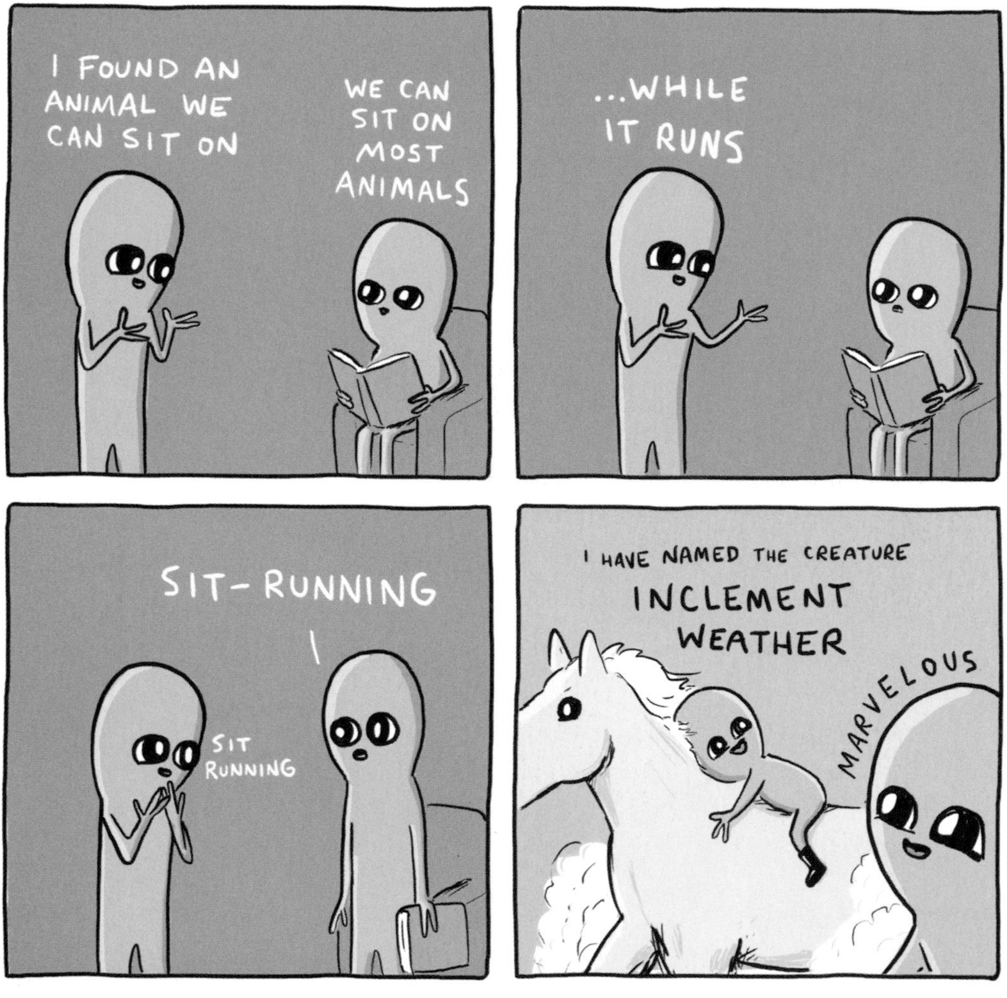
I FOUND AN ANIMAL WE CAN SIT ON
WE CAN SIT ON MOST ANIMALS
...WHILE IT RUNS
SIT-RUNNING
SIT RUNNING
I HAVE NAMED THE CREATURE
INCLEMENT WEATHER
MARVELOUS

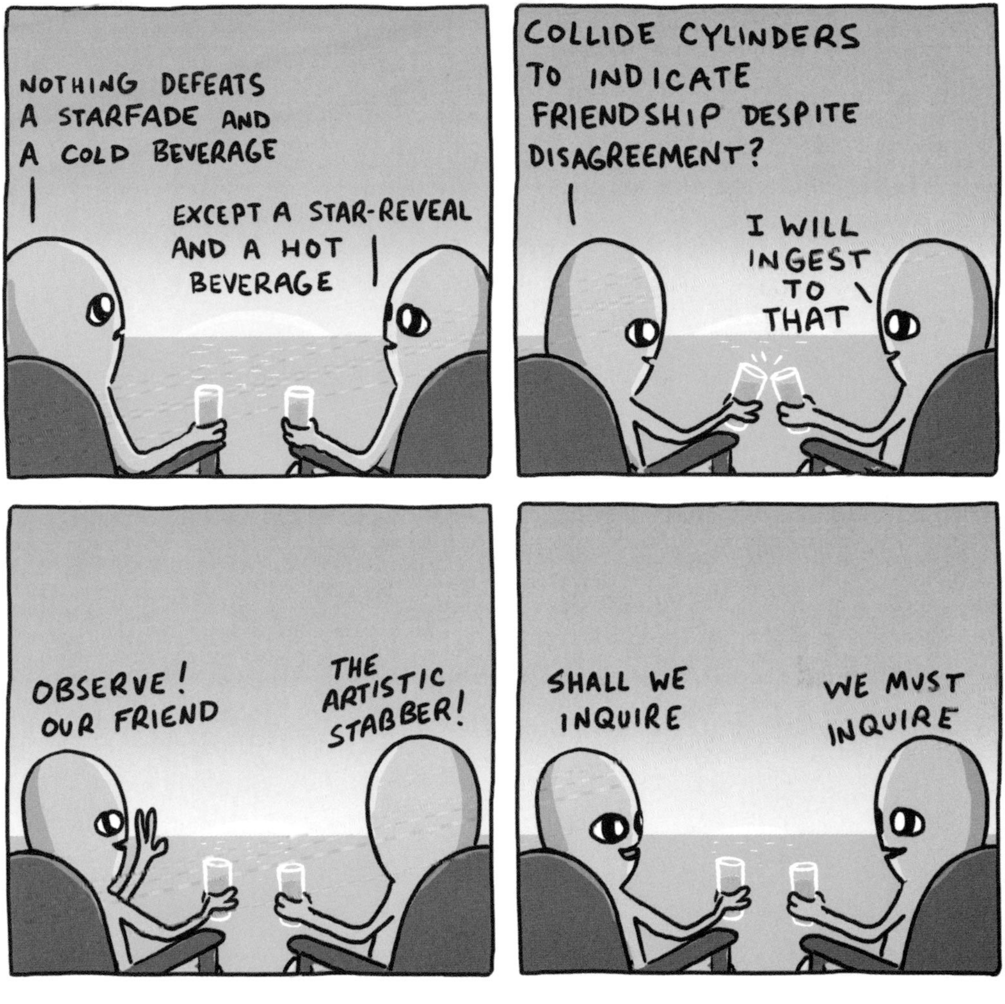
NOTHING DEFEATS A STARFADE AND A COLD BEVERAGE
EXCEPT A STAR-REVEAL AND A HOT BEVERAGE
COLLIDE CYLINDERS TO INDICATE FRIENDSHIP DESPITE DISAGREEMENT?
I WILL INGEST TO THAT
OBSERVE! OUR FRIEND
THE ARTISTIC STABBER!
SHALL WE INQUIRE
WE MUST INQUIRE

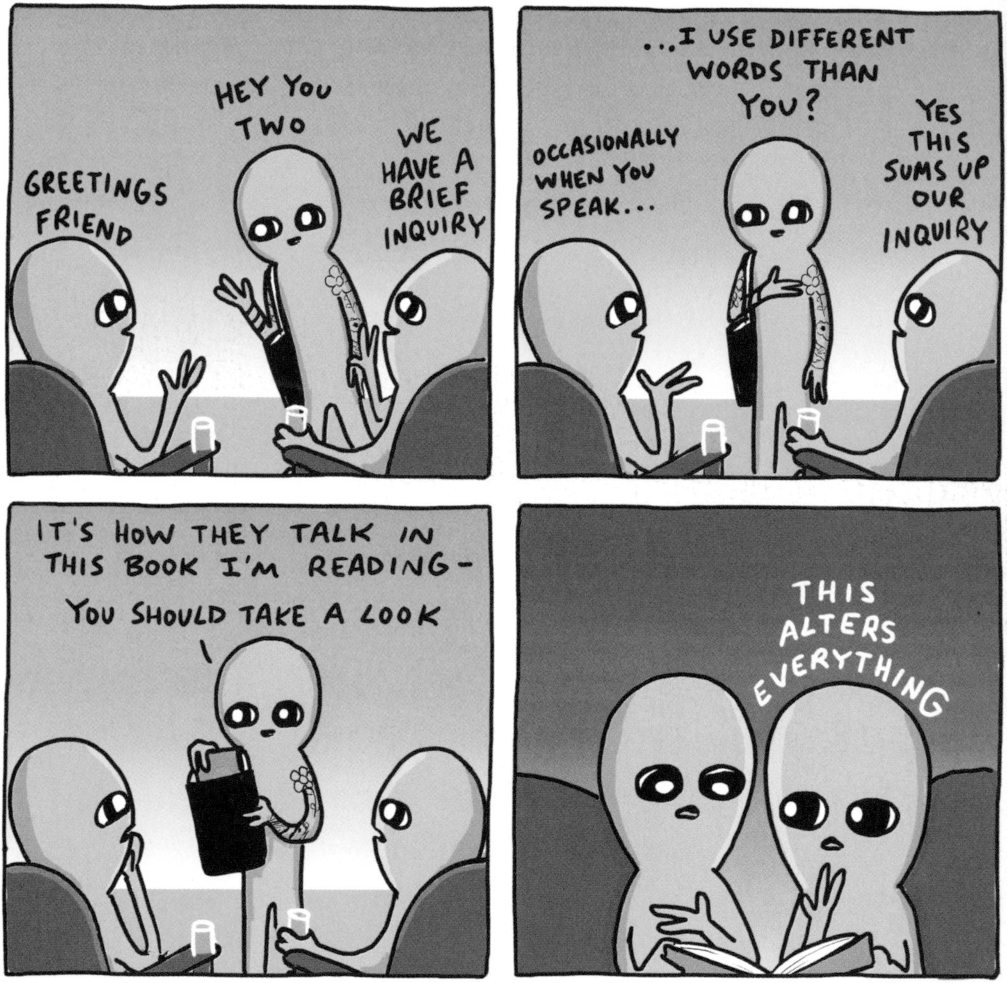
GREETINGS FRIEND
HEY YOU TWO
WE HAVE A BRIEF INQUIRY
OCCASIONALLY WHEN YOU SPEAK...
...I USE DIFFERENT WORDS THAN YOU?
YES THIS SUMS UP OUR INQUIRY
IT'S HOW THEY TALK IN THIS BOOK I'M READING-
YOU SHOULD TAKE A LOOK
THIS ALTERS EVERYTHING

COMMONLY OBSERVED OBJECTS

PERSONAL STAR DIMMERS

SERIOUSNESS CLOTH

ORB CATCHER HAT

FOOT RAMPS

FOOT FABRIC TUBES

STAND-UP RINSE OFF

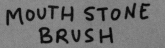

MOUTH STONE BRUSH

MOUTH STONE GOO

LEAF SMELL

FORCE STRING

COMMONLY OBSERVED OBJECTS

HYDRATION CYLINDER

EXCESS FUNGUS SLICES

VAST DOUGH CIRCLE

LEAFBUCKET

HOT LEAF LIQUID

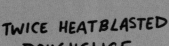

TWICE HEATBLASTED DOUGHSLICE

SWEET DISKS

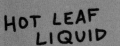

CRISS CROSS FLOP DISK

JITTER LIQUID

PLANT LIQUID PARTIALLY DIGESTED BY INSECTS AND THEN STOLEN

COMMONLY OBSERVED OBJECTS

ELASTIC BREATH
TRAPS

STAR DAMAGE
LIMITER

SPINBLASTER

ROLLSUCK

ROLLSUCK
SUPREME

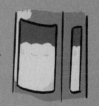

THE FILTH
WINDOW

TWO-WHEEL
FOOT PUSHER

GRAVITY-INDUCED
SUSTENANCE RELEASER

LOW-DETAIL
RENDERING

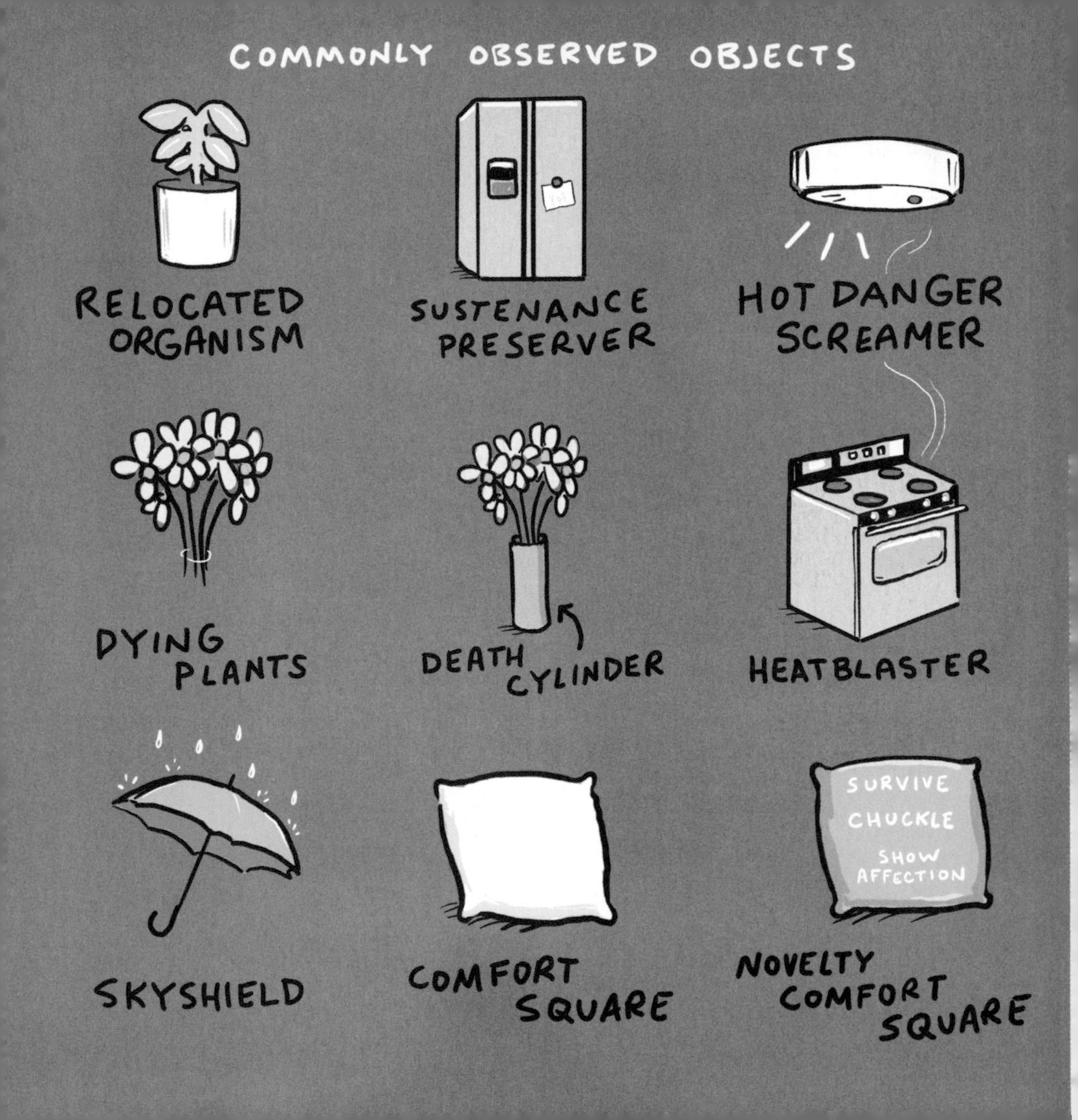
COMMONLY OBSERVED OBJECTS
RELOCATED ORGANISM
SUSTENANCE PRESERVER
HOT DANGER SCREAMER
DYING PLANTS
DEATH CYLINDER
HEATBLASTER
SKYSHIELD
COMFORT SQUARE
SURVIVE
CHUCKLE
SHOW AFFECTION
NOVELTY COMFORT SQUARE

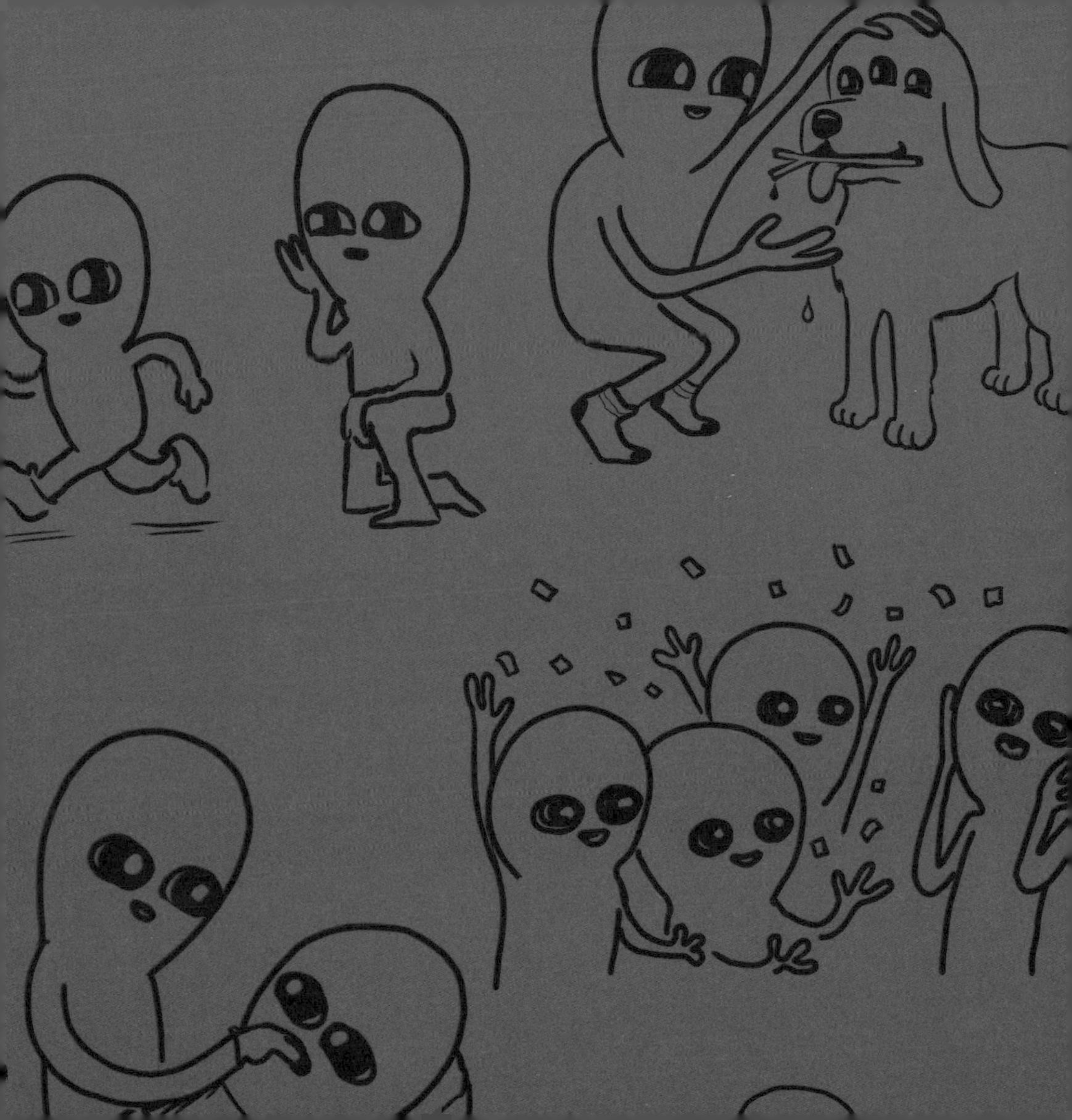

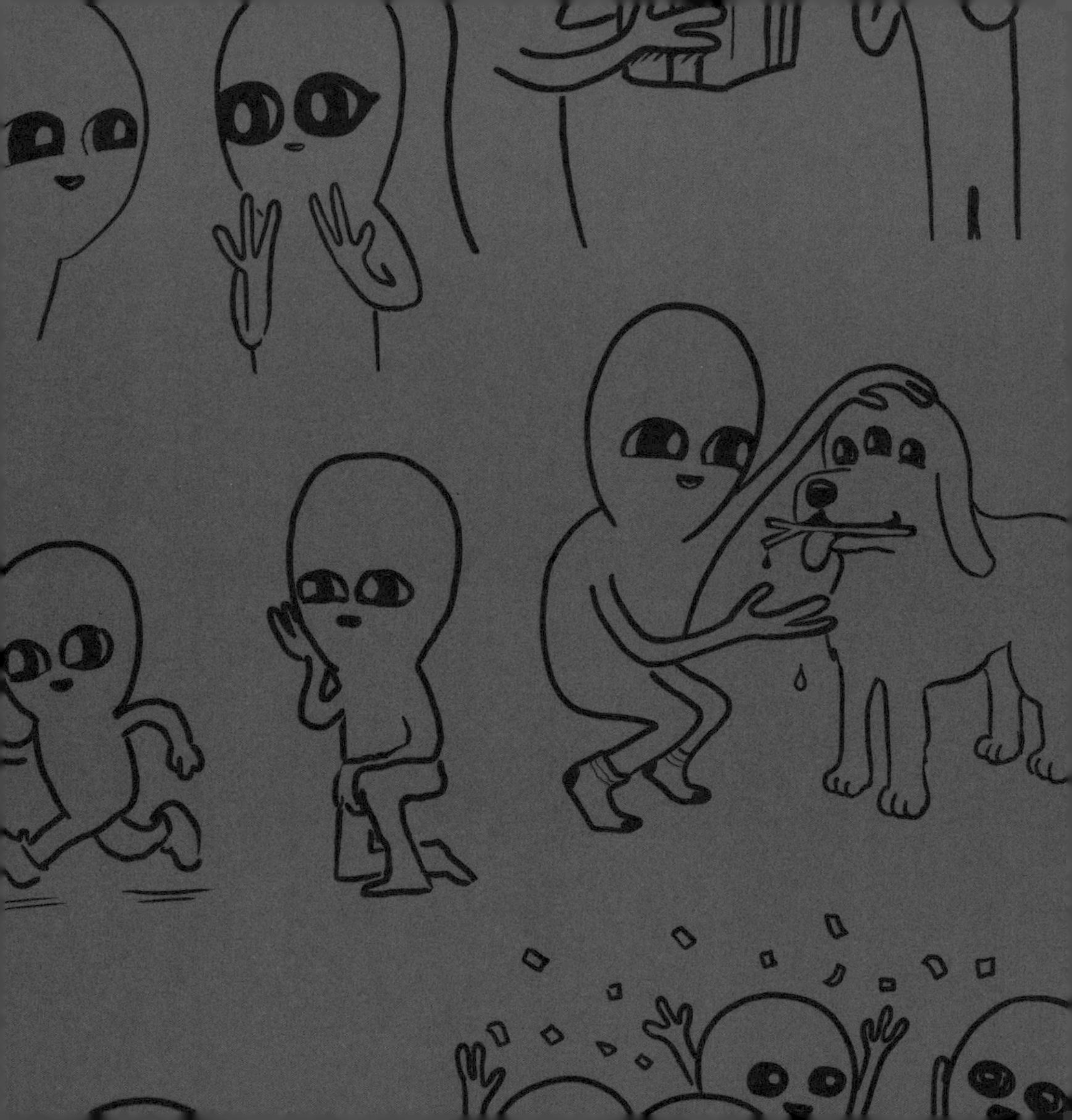